ADOPTION
MACHINE

For my favorite girl Molly and my little man Gavin,
my healers and the meaning of my life

For Siobhán, the love of my life

Dedicated to my parents
Jack and Anita Redmond

Paul Redmond was born in Castlepollard Mother and Baby Home in December 1964. Chairperson of the survivor umbrella group, the Coalition of Mother and Baby home Survivors (CMABS), Paul also produced the very first report highlighting the mortality rates and general cruelty in the Homes and calling for a public inquiry. After the Tuam 800 story broke, he was instrumental in working with the media to increase the public and political attention on the other Mother and Baby Homes and their mortality rates. He continues to advocate tirelessly on behalf of all survivors of Ireland's wider, forced adoption network.

The ADOPTION MACHINE

THE DARK HISTORY OF IRELAND'S MOTHER AND BABY HOMES AND THE INSIDE STORY OF HOW TUAM 800 BECAME A GLOBAL SCANDAL

PAUL JUDE REDMOND

MERRION
PRESS

First published in 2018 by
Merrion Press
An imprint of Irish Academic Press
10 George's Street
Newbridge
Co. Kildare
Ireland
www.merrionpress.ie

© Paul Jude Redmond, 2018

9781785371776 (Paper)
9781785371783 (Kindle)
9781785371790 (Epub)
9781785371806 (PDF)

British Library Cataloguing in Publication Data
An entry can be found on request

Library of Congress Cataloging in Publication Data
An entry can be found on request

Interior design by www.jminfotechindia.com
Typeset in Minion Pro 11.5/14.5 pt

Cover design by www.phoenix-graphicdesign.com
Cover/jacket front: A shrine in Tuam, Co. Galway, on 9 June 2014, erected in memory of up to 800 children who were allegedly buried at the site of the former home for unmarried mothers run by nuns. © Paul Faith/Getty Images.
Cover/jacket back: A homemade nail in the wall at Castlepollard Mother and Baby Home Angels' Plot. The workmen hammered these nails into the wall every time they buried a baby, as a memorial. ©Kim Haughton/*The Sunday Times*.

Contents

Acknowledgements

This book would not have been possible without so many people. Some do not wish to be named but they know they are in my thoughts and my heart.

Family: Susan, John, Martin and Alan Redmond. Barbara, Roger, Sharon, Judith. Ciara and Jamie; Jake, Jodie and Caleb; Mark, Amie and Laureen. And I nearly forgot Gemma and Shannon and Shane. All the Redmonds, Darcys, Finns, Sinnotts, Whittys, Curtises and Fortunes scattered around the world. For Dolly Costello, and all the family and remembering Willie Costello (RIP). Hi to all the Merciers and thanks to Paul and Mel for all the encourgagement and advice!

Friends: Peter 'Circut 3' Fitzpatrick and all the Fitzpatricks, Pat 'Pappie' Donovan, Neil Michael, Mary O'Donovan, Antonella Brusco, Ruairí O'Dwyer, and a special Hey! Hey! to Liam, Tatjana and Felix Bodenhamski!

The entire Castlepollard group – thanks to all of you for your love and support over the years brothers and sisters particularly: especially Geraldine Cronin, Ruth Noonan, Paul, Jenny from Wexford, Michelle from Wexford!, Chris Finnegan, Mary Creighton, Mary Borg, Kim Fleming and Mary W., Bernie McG, Mary 'Bookie' Kenny, Mike Byrne, Una O'Neill-D'Arcy, Ken and Marion Matthews, the heroic Ray Loftus and his brilliant crib mate Mal K. Gerry Russel, Rosie Rogers, playwright Jacqueline Nolan, Joseph Ennis, Michelle and Liam and Philip Burke, the very special Rita Kelty and the wonderful Christy, my special twinnie Ann Harrington and all the '64 babes. Geraldine McArdle, Mary O'Donovan, Ciaran Adams, Susan Flanagan, Marita Maher Ryan, Carmel Ziemann, Declan Kelly, Jackie Keegan, Stephen Quinn, Theresa Carroll, David Cretzan, Marie McGee, Noreen Briddigkeit Quinn, Mary Joyce, James Dowd, David Rogers, Ann F. Boukater, Margot McG, John Hegarty, Mary Mulligan, Mono Monaghan, Nancy Polka, Anne Larrigan, Irene McGuire, John Ginty, Jennifer Hayden, Mary Nasri,

Fiona Crosbie, Peter Shelton, Lily Bracken, Rosaleen Toher-Ginty and Mickey (RIP), Kateleen Tuite, Fidelma Mullen, Maeve Hackett, Jenny Leavy, Mary Butt, Maureen Nelson McGovern, Manon McGinty, Marion Hoban, Jimmy Malone, Michael Fitzpatrick, Kelley Blaylock, Bert Versey.

A special shout to the '67 party girls, Princess Miriam Barry, Edel Morrison, Laureen Murphy-Shaw. Our Banished brothers and sisters: Ann Biggs, Kevin Di Palma, Frank Uccelini, Patrick Wolfe, Mike and Mary Kay Daniel (best hugs ever!!), Mary Beth Cronin Ferrini and family, Patricia Zuclich-Ford, Winnie (RIP), Judi VanBuskirk, Michael Terence Murphy, Marge Skinner, Kathleen Kampmann Taché, Maureen Collins Giordano, Maureen Dillon-Bowers, Mary Murry-Alexander, Linda Boyd-McCullough, John R. Hoge, Erin McCormack-Staats, Tom Ferstle, and Jimmy and Charmaine Walsh (welcome home, guys!). And everyone else in the group.

The Coalition of Mother And Baby home Survivors (CMABS): the incredible Derek Leinster, the fabulous Clodagh Malone, the fighting Theresa Hiney Tinggal, and all our friends: the wonderful Rosemary Adazer and sticky bun Margeret McGuckin! Carol Linster, Nancy Saur, Colleen Anderson, Joyce McSharry, Victor Stephenson (RIP), Dr. Niall Meehan.

Wider community: the wonderful Therese Nolan, Finbarr O'Regan, Christopher Kirwan, Karl O'Kelly, Anthony Kelly, Ruth 'shoes and strong coffee now!, Mercy B. River, Linda Dublin and Maria Keating-Dumbell, Adrian McKenna and the fabulous Maria Teresa Mullen.

To Maureen Sullivan, hero of the Magdalene Laundries and a special shout out to Rose O'Brien Harrington and her Aunt Ester who spent 70 years in a Magdalene Laundry and all the Magdalene Ladies.

All the industrial school survivors and their supporters, Jack C., Robert Artane, Oliver Whelan, Séan A., Rob Nortall, John Deegan and Sean Boswell.

Supportive people and organisations: Michael Nugent, Ashling O'Brien, Jane Donnelly, Milana Milasaukaite-Kearns, Philip Garland and Audrey Muddiman. Best wishes to our northern brothers and sisters still fighting for justice. A very special thank you to everyone at the the Public Interest Law Alliance.

Media: Tanya Gold, Sharon Lawless and all at Flawless Films, Conall Ó Fátharta, Joe Little and crew, Claire Scott, Steven O'Gorman and Alison O'Reilly.

Political: A very very special shout to the totally awesome Clare Daly TD and brilliant Rhona McCord. Also Mary Lou McDonald TD, Robert Troy TD, Gerry Adams TD, Colm Keavney TD and Anne Rabbit TD and Billy Kelleher TD and everyone in all the offices.

The international crew: Martha Shideler, Warren Musselman, Gwen Berndt Soldelius, Princess Julia Freebourne, Clayton and Jes, and all the Adoption Voices crew especially Caroline D'Agostino, Kate Mitchell, and the ever generous Jacqui Haycroft, June Hamilton, Lisa Floyd (x), Maggie Watanabe, Cat Henderson, Lesley Pearse, Maggie Smith, Julie Kelly from Anti Adoption; Mary Macaskill Cannon, and Lizzy Howard and btw, you're all mad bastards, just like me lol. A very special thanks to Georgiana 'perfect timing' Macavie and Valerie Andrews and all the international Origins crew. Huge shout out for the Vance Twins, Jenette and Janine, you rock!! Arun Doyle (Against Child Trafficking), Rolie Post and all the hardcore activists around the world.

A massive thanks to my literary agent, Jonathan Williams and all at Merrion Press: Conor Graham, Fiona Dunne, Myles McCionnaith, Dermott Barrett, Eileen O'Neill, and Peter O'Connell of Peter O'Connell Media.

Sincere apologies if I missed anyone. There are just so many decent and wonderful people in my life.

10% of all author royalties will be donated to good causes.

Foreword

As Ireland gears up for yet another national debate about women's reproductive rights with the 8th Amendment referendum, Paul Redmond's *The Adoption Machine* is a timely reminder of how women and girls who 'got into trouble' were dealt with in the early years of the new state, up to the end of the last century.

This book is a personal story and a crusade, one of the first and clearest accounts of conditions in the misnamed Mother and Baby Homes, a cruel mix of Victorian and Catholic morality, institutions which he describes 'were generally a cross between a maternity hospital with no doctors or nurses and a low-to-medium prison'.

This was the worst manifestation of the repression of women, the collusion of Church and State to restrict reproductive rights. Fear of women's sexuality created an entrenchment and an over-reaction that led to intrusive levels of supervision on a parish basis into the lives of young women and men.

Irish women, especially those from the working classes and rural poor, who became pregnant outside of marriage during the greater part of the twentieth century, were considered a great shame; they were castigated as sinners, shunned, tainted and ultimately cornered. Removed from their families and communities and hidden behind the grey walls of 'Mother and Baby Homes' to give birth in secret. They were completely isolated and helpless when their children were taken from them. This book documents how initially the children were neglected and starved and often died in alarming numbers while nobody noticed or cared. Later the potential for the religious orders to earn enormous sums of money from adopting out the children, often illegally, became a thriving industry with babies delivered to Catholic couples from Ireland, Britain and the United States.

The relentless journeys of natural mothers and their children to deal with the scars of that separation are brutally and yet sensitively told in this contemporary account. This is a lived and living history, of lives still unfolding and quests still incomplete – all the more powerful because you know that this is now.

This is the biggest scandal of Independent Ireland, the biggest cover-up, the bitter result of Church and State collusion, and yet there is very little said about it in the national narrative. Often confused with the Magdalene Laundries, which specifically didn't take pregnant girls, the Mother and Baby Homes never made the headlines until Catherine Corless made her claims of 800 dead babies in Tuam, ultimately forcing a commission of investigation which is presently ongoing.

Paul Redmond was instrumental in the campaign to secure that investigation. Born in Castlepollard Mother and Baby Home in the 1960s, Paul's personal story is interwoven with the history of Castlepollard and all the Homes. His personal journey was one made all the more poignant because he makes it with and for his crib mates and particularly on behalf of the fallen ones, the ones that didn't make it. He tells of himself and another man, along with five women all survivors who made the trip to Castlepollard in August 2011. 'It was an odd situation. We shared so much and yet we were strangers walking into the unknown together ... I left the cemetery a fundamentally different person, a man with a mission, hellbent to do something. I hadn't a clue what to do or how to do it but I knew something had to be done.' And he did!

In fact, Paul continues to do so much. He is the author of the first serious research into mortality rates and conditions in Mother and Baby Homes, an advocate for the rights of adopted persons and their natural mothers, a serious campaigner who worked with many of the groups and key individuals who organised around these issues, Paul is a big man with a big heart, tireless energy and unrelenting patience and humanity.

Paul touches on a story of a woman who got in touch with my Dáil office after spending years going through official channels to locate her daughter, who had been taken from her, without her consent, in Castlepollard on St Patrick's Day in 1966. Wanting her daughter to have her medical history and worried that she was running out of time, she wrote of being led up the garden path so many times by those from whom she sought help to trace her. She had spent a lifetime searching and finding nothing. In three days Paul found her and within the week successful phone contact was made. The endings are rarely so happy but there is no pain worse than that of not knowing. The struggle for your own identity is one everyone makes, but it can be a longer road with substantial barriers placed in the way when you are adopted.

This book is necessary; it's about the history of Irish adoptions, particularly the heart-breaking illegal adoptions. It is about the struggle that Paul Redmond took up, on behalf of his crib mates. It tells of his growth as an advocate and campaigner. No doubt the experience has been a learning curve for him, but throughout it all he remains calm, reasonable and determined. It is a subject that would make any person seethe with anger. When I first met Paul in 2012, he stood out as someone who had taken control and directed his energy into a fight for justice. For those who had their identities stolen, who had subsequently been grossly mislead and ignored, they may never find closure but they have a true advocate in Paul Redmond.

Clare Daly TD
March 2018

Prologue

In August 2011, I visited my birthplace, Castlepollard Mother and Baby Home, in the company of six other people adopted from there. We had met on Facebook and another lady and I had organised the visit. Years later we realised that we were the first known group of adoptees to return to their old home as a group.

My childhood fantasy was of an old Georgian house with my young mother in an oversized chair that was covered with warm, colourful throws, by a window where golden sunshine streamed in as I lay swaddled in her arms. Gentle nuns fluttered around, cooing and happy.

The reality in 2011 was a cold, grey, ugly institution. Empty rooms and peeling paint. Our group visited the Angels' Plot and stood on the narrow strip where unknown hundreds of babies and children had been buried just a few feet below where we walked around. We planted a tree in their memory.

That forgotten plot affected me deeply. It was life-changing. I left as a survivor determined to do 'something'. In the days and finally years that followed, I hunted down every scrap of information I could find about Castlepollard and particularly the Angels' Plot, and then I broadened my attention to the other Mother and Baby Homes in Ireland. More Angels' Plots. More horrors. I became an activist by default. The 'something' I wanted to do, I realised afterwards, included never letting people forget. I wanted to ram hard facts and figures down Ireland's throat.

I published all my research, nearly 100,000 words, across the various adoption groups. I did a little unpaid citizen journalism about the Homes and our campaign for truth and justice. Over the years, my family, friends and fellow activists increasingly nagged me to write a book and tell the story properly, and I finally cracked and agreed to do it in early 2017. I took four months off work over the summer and simply sat down and wrote. And I couldn't stop. The book grew to twice its intended size before I was finished, and I still feel it is not enough.

Approximately 100,000 girls and women lost their babies to forced separation since independence in 1922. Church and State considered the illegitimate babies as barely human. At least 6,000 babies died in the nine Mother and Baby Homes where some 35,000 girls as young as 12, and women as old as 44, spent years of their lives, and almost no one cared. Even now, mothers and babies still cry out for remembrance and justice. Their cries from beyond the grave are ignored by Irish society, just as the cries of their short poignant lives were ignored in the Homes.

The Adoption Machine is not just a book. It is also an activist tactic and part of our ongoing campaign to ensure that the last, dirty secret of Holy Catholic Ireland is finally dragged into the light. It is a rage against the machine. A voice in the wilderness. A memorial to my fallen crib mates.

And, as I write from the deepest part of my heart, I still hear the voices of the angels crying for justice. And remembrance. And love.

There are many villains in this story. There are a handful of heroes too. These heroes are all too human; flawed, stubborn products of their time. Yet they all share one feature: they had good hearts. Whether they succeeded or failed is not important, they tried their best. They too should be remembered: Aneenee FitzGerald-Kenney, Alice Litster, Dr James Deeny, June Goulding, among others.

This story begins with such a hero, Captain Thomas Coram ...

PART 1

BACKGROUND AND FOUNDATIONS, 1739–1944

CHAPTER ONE

The Age of the Institutions

Captain Thomas Coram challenged eighteenth-century perceptions that babies of poor families were worthless, and believed that all babies had equal human rights. Before his Foundling Hospital opened in London in 1739, childcare for most babies from deprived backgrounds was virtually unknown in Britain and Ireland, except for charitable initiatives undertaken by people associated with local churches. Babies and young children were often considered a mixed blessing, as they placed a burden on poor families and contributed no income for the first several years of their lives. Orphans and 'bastards' had no value in society. It was only when children started to become useful, at around seven or eight years of age, that they became valued by society. Parents were forced through necessity and grinding poverty to be extremely practical in very hard times.

Unwanted babies were dumped in public places and on church doorsteps and generally ended up in the local workhouse. If the parish did not have its own workhouse, they were sent to the nearest available one for an agreed weekly or monthly fee. The only alternative was to employ local wet nurses for a few years and then send the children, by then aged three or four, to the workhouse. On rare occasions, the lucky ones were informally adopted by their nurse or a local family. The care available to abandoned babies was unregulated and varied hugely from parish to parish, and mortality rates were appallingly high. Not long before Captain Coram stepped in, one English workhouse received 2,000 children over a period of twenty-eight years and none survived.[1]

Coram decided to change the babies' names upon entering his hospital, and the result was a loss of identity with no names to connect those children to their history or heritage. The first boy and girl to arrive in the hospital were baptised and renamed after the Captain and his wife, Thomas and Eunice Coram.[2] Tens of millions of people lost their names and identities due to this practice.

Captain Coram started a revolution in childcare and, although social change was slow, the changes he initiated took hold. Two of the governors of the Foundling Hospital were instrumental in founding another new type of institution in Whitechapel in 1758 – London's Magdalene Laundry.[3] It was far smaller in size and scale than the hospital and had a completely different function. It was for so-called 'fallen women', a catch-all term for prostitutes and unmarried mothers who found themselves pregnant and with no hope for themselves or their babies.

Ireland in the Eighteenth Century

A law providing for a House of Industry in Dublin was enacted in 1703. This was essentially a workhouse by any other name and was erected in Dublin's south inner-city on what is now the site of St. James's Hospital. Several more buildings were added to the original workhouse and the site eventually covered fifty acres and evolved into St. James's Hospital. Abandoned babies and children, who ended up in the House of Industry, were sent outside to be nursed until around age five and were then returned to the workhouse from where they could be apprenticed out from the age of twelve. In 1730, the authorities renovated and divided up the workhouse with a large section set aside for babies and children, which was named the 'Foundling Hospital'. They adopted the European custom of installing a 'baby wheel' (a revolving device on which babies were placed in order to gain entry to a building) and a bell to alert the doorman to a new baby's arrival. Like Coram's Foundling Hospital there were no questions asked, but the similarities end there. Dublin's Foundling Hospital was swarming with vermin, highly unsanitary and no better than the workhouses. Around 57,000 children were resident in Dublin's Foundling Hospital up to 1818. Of the 51,000 children who entered the hospital between 1796 and 1826, over 41,000 died. Between

1790 and 1796, a further investigation by the British Parliament discovered that 12,768 children had been admitted to the Dublin Foundling Hospital and 9,786 had died. Another 2,847 had simply vanished from the system entirely, and there was no record of them. It is believed that only 135 survived. If the vanished are presumed to have died, and they almost certainly did, then the inclusive mortality rate of those seven years was 99%.

Seven years after the first Magdalene Laundry opened in London in 1758, a similar project was launched in Ireland. Dublin's laundry was founded in 1765 and it took two years to prepare the building and finances for its official opening. Lady Denny's Magdalene Laundry opened in June 1767 at 8 Lower Leeson Street, a converted Georgian house of four storeys over basement in Dublin's city centre. Protestant women and girls under the age of twenty and pregnant were admitted to the new residential laundry.[4] The daily routine of drudgery and poor food included regular daily prayers and preaching by clergy and lay Protestants. Several customs that developed in Britain's Magdalene Laundries were adopted in Dublin during the early years; for example, the new arrivals had their heads shaved. This was originally intended to remedy the common problem of lice. Staff quickly realised, however, that bald-headed girls were less likely to leave the laundry owing to public stigma. Later, as attitudes hardened, shaving the girls' heads became an integral part of their punishment for 'sins'. The Good Shepherd nuns in Britain introduced another tradition that became part of the punishment aspect of future institutional 'care'. They issued new residents with 'house names'. This custom originally had good intentions of 'protecting' the girls and saving them from their perceived shame. However, the practice ultimately warped into another instrument of punishment. Erasing identities and self-esteem became a process that would humiliate and stigmatise hundreds of thousands of girls and women across the world for centuries to come.

Victorian Britain

From the 1830s to 1900, Victorian Britain was infected with a drive to build new institutions, now considered a magical answer to society's problems. Dozens of social laws were passed and institutions were converted or built by the hundred, by both the public and private sectors. Industrial schools, reformatories and Magdalene Laundries sprang up across Ireland and Britain. New orphanages from the late 1800s were imbued with not just a specific religious ethos but with a well-defined class role. There are many descriptions of these orphanages by the religious or lay Catholics who ran them in Britain and Ireland, and the terms used include 'from respectable families', 'of the upper class', and 'middle-class families'.

Queen Victoria's coronation in 1837 was the same year that saw the introduction of important new social legislation. It became compulsory to register all births, deaths and marriages with the government, a public service that was previously the domain of the various Churches.

The institution of marriage and producing legitimate children were key components of the new social order. In the first thirty or forty years of Queen Victoria's reign, single mothers and their babies and children were increasingly demonised by the newly 'respectable' society. They were hidden away from genteel, respectable people in the booming network of Victorian workhouses and Magdalene Laundries where they were transformed from half-pitied, half-despised sinners into 'inmates' and given uniforms to wear like prisoners. In some of the British workhouses, single mothers and prostitutes were for a time forced to wear distinctive clothing; prostitutes were assigned yellow dresses, while pregnant single women were issued with red or scarlet dresses. They were separated from the 'respectable poor', who were encouraged to regard themselves as a distinct class above single mothers and their illegitimate children. Ironically, forcing single mothers and their children out of society and into the workhouses reinforced the prejudices towards them: they were now a burden on the taxpayer and the public purse. It was a vicious circle of stigmatisation and shame.

Church Disorganisation in Ireland after Catholic Emancipation

When Ireland's Penal Laws that discriminated against Catholics were revoked in 1829, what was left of the Irish Catholic Church was almost penniless and disorganised, and sought international help from its nearest Catholic neighbours in France. The orders of French nuns who arrived soon dominated the various religious institutions being established around Ireland. These included the Bon Secours (France), the Good Shepherds (France), the Daughters of Charity of St. Vincent de Paul (France), and later the Sisters of the Sacred Hearts of Jesus and Mary (originally French from 1866 and then British from 1905). From the 1840s, the French orders of nuns expeditiously established or took control of the industrial and reformatory schools, while Magdalene Laundries were set up in all the major cities where there was enough business for a commercial laundry to survive. The Irish Sisters of Mercy were founded just two years after emancipation and played an important role in the country's new institutions.

One point that continues to confuse people even today is the difference between Magdalene Laundries and Mother and Baby Homes. Most of the confusion is because the Catholic version of a Magdalene Laundry was completely different to the Protestant model in one key respect: Catholic laundries did not admit pregnant women and girls or their babies. The Catholic nuns thereby redefined what was meant by a Magdalene Laundry. From the 1840s onwards, pregnant girls were sent to the nearest public workhouse. Single mothers who turned up at the Catholic laundries, or arrived in the custody of a priest or local official, were admitted, but the child or children were placed in a nearby workhouse or industrial school also run by a Catholic order. Sometimes the different institutions were on the same land and even run by the same order of nuns, but were separated by high walls. Mothers and children were separated and never allowed to have contact again, despite living only yards apart.

Women and girls in the Catholic laundries were essentially prisoners, and conditions grew steadily worse with time. What were originally intended as refuges became de facto prisons. 'Fallen women' had no rights. They were sometimes worked up to 100 hours over a six-day week. Constant hunger, exhaustion and despair were the lot of these women. Many were incarcerated for life and when they died they were buried on-site in mass graves, with no names or markers, let alone proper headstones.

The difference between the Catholic and Protestant laundries are still widely misunderstood by the public and some academics and survivor activists. There is a similar difference between early Catholic and Protestant models of Mother and Baby Homes to which we shall return shortly.

Hardening Attitudes to Single Pregnant Women

By the early twentieth century, single mothers were regarded as sinners, fallen women, strumpets, prostitutes, brazen hussies, Jezebels riddled with venereal diseases, tramps and sluts, while illegitimate babies were simiarly vilified as bastards, weaklings, runts of the litter and the spawn of Satan.

By 1900, public policy was to dispatch single pregnant girls to public workhouses where they were separated from the 'respectable poor' and treated appallingly. It is imperative to understand the attitude that developed over the years of Queen Victoria's reign in both Britain and Ireland. The stigmatisation of single mothers by Irish society had a detrimental effect on their physical, mental and emotional well-being, and consequently a harmful effect on their babies. This may partly explain the high mortality rates among illegitimate babies. Treat a pregnant woman badly and her baby will be equally affected. Canon Law bars illegitimate adults from joining the Catholic priesthood and that injunction remains in place today, unless one receives 'special dispensation' from the Pope. The traditional prejudice of the Catholic Church towards illegitimacy contributed to poisoning Irish society's attitudes and was reinforced by the new Victorian morality, which was becoming ever more prevalent in civil society across Britain and Ireland.

From 1890 onwards, however, there was a small backlash in Britain against the treatment of single mothers. Several groups were founded to support them and absolve their illegitimate babies of their sinful stain. The Protestant Salvation Army was the first group to open a dedicated home for single mothers and their babies in Hackney in 1887. This home supported new mothers in their decisions, whether their choice was to hand their babies over to the 'system' to be initially placed with families and later end up in the industrial schools, or to keep their babies and raise them alone. This small resistance movement in Britain had a long way to go in its battle against what were now mainstream attitudes.

In 1890, relatively rapid social and economic changes created yet another new type of Catholic institution that exhibited all the arrogance and harsh discipline associated with an increasingly confident Catholic Church. St. Pelagia's Home, the first 'Mother and Baby Home' as we understand the designation today, was founded in 1890 when the Diocese of Westminster in London purchased two adjoining houses at 27 Bickerton Road, Highgate.[5]

St. Pelagia's also firmly believed that the permanent separation of single mothers and their babies was a vital punishment for being single but it is again important to note the fundamental difference between the Catholic and Protestant versions of Mother and Baby Homes. Although, in time, most of the Protestant homes would regress to systematically separating single mothers and their babies, the Catholic homes were founded on the principles of punishment and attempted to 'reform' or 'save' the residents, and this included severely limiting the time they spent with their babies and then forcibly separating them for life. In London, a Miss Gee ran the new Catholic Mother and Baby Home when it opened but, within a year, the Westminster Diocese had invited a small French order with a presence in Britain to take over.

The Rise of the Sacred Heart Nuns

Of all the religious orders that ran Mother and Baby Homes in Ireland, the Sacred Hearts are by far the most important. Their three homes were the second-, third- and fourth-largest of the nine that existed. Around half the women and girls who went to a Mother and Baby Home in Ireland went to a Sacred Heart home.

The order that became the Congregation of the Sisters of the Sacred Hearts of Jesus and Mary was founded in 1866 by a French priest, Father Peter Victor Braun, while he was on assignment to Paris, and the original order was named the 'Servants of the Sacred Heart'. They spread rapidly across Europe, being part of the reaction by the Catholic

Church to the revisionism of the reformed Protestant Churches sweeping the continent and Britain in the second part of the nineteenth century. The English Province of the order was founded accidentally when the nuns fled France after the outbreak of the Franco-Prussian war in 1870, initiating their later breaking away from their original Mother House. The order rapidly grew in size, power and influence and by the 1890s Irish nuns dominated the English branch, notably Sisters Winefride (originally Bridget) Tyrrell from Monasterevin, Co. Kildare, and Sylvester Halpin (originally Mary Jane Halfpenny) from Lobinstown, Co. Meath. Another young Irish girl, Mary Daly from Skeyne, Co. Westmeath, joined the original order in France aged just 15. She was later transferred to England and rose to become head of the new order in 1927.

The Servants of the Sacred Heart accepted the invitation of the Diocese of Westminster to take over their new Mother and Baby Home, and they re-named it St. Pelagia's. It is interesting to note that, although there is some confusion historically, there were essentially two Pelagias; one was a young maiden (virgin) who committed suicide rather than agree to a forced marriage, and the other was a reformed prostitute and actress who converted to Christianity.

The single mothers in the new home remained there for a year after their babies were born and were taught domestic skills such as dressmaking and cooking until they were discharged. 'Domestic skills' was a euphemism for hard work around the home or some enterprise such as making religious regalia for commercial sale. Aged one year old, when their mothers were discharged, the children were sent to a Sacred Hearts' nursery in Chadwell in east London. The children were then placed with local Catholic families for periods of anything from several weeks to several years. These families were paid for their care. From there the children were sent to so-called orphanages, which usually meant a Catholic industrial school or similar institution. The mothers who had been discharged were expected to pay for their baby's nursing out. This payment came to be known as 'parental monies'.

In 1897, the Sacred Hearts opened a second Mother and Baby Home in Kelton, Liverpool, when Monsignor James Nugent invited them to run a large manor house he had rented for the purpose. Following the example of the Magdalene Laundries dotted around Britain, this home took in commercial laundry from the ships in Liverpool's busy port to be hand-washed by the residents, thus ensuring the nuns a steady income from an unpaid and captive workforce of pregnant girls and single mothers.

Because of their rapid growth and success during the 1890s, the English Sacred Hearts were restless and eager to be freed from their Mother House in France and they finally broke away in 1902. Three years later, on 5 March 1905, the new order was formally recognised by the Holy See in Rome as 'The Congregation of the Sisters of the Sacred Hearts of Jesus and Mary.' It is important to note that a 'congregation' is a second-class designation and considered inferior to an 'order'. Winifride Tyrrell became the first Mother Superior General and was succeeded by Sylvester Halpin in 1908. The Sacred Heart nuns later opened two other Mother and Baby Homes in Britain, one in Scotland and their last in 1944 in Brettargholt, Kendal, in the Lake District. They arrived in Ireland in 1922.

There is one last piece of important legislation to consider before the previous century ended – the 1899 Poor Law Act. Although it is widely believed in the adoption community that the Adoption Act 1952 was the first piece of adoption legislation in Ireland, it was, in fact, the first piece of standalone adoption legislation. A section of the 1899 Poor Law Act legalised adoption by resolution. Generally, it was used in two ways; firstly, to adopt newborn babies and very young children and secondly, to adopt former foster children into the family once they had turned 16 years old. Weekly payments for fostering a child ceased on that date.

By 1900, industrial and reformatory schools had developed a negative reputation because the former inmates had none of the social skills necessary to function in civil society. Their health was destroyed by their regimented existence and poor diet. Britain reluctantly accepted that caring for children in large institutions was a failed social experiment and began to phase out the institutions that had shattered tens of thousands of lives.

In the early twentieth century, the rest of the English-speaking world, particularly in the United States, followed the British lead and began to phase out large-scale institutional care. Ireland was the exception. The Irish Catholic Church had fought long and hard to own and/or control all the different types of institutions spreading across the country and were not about to give them up. The Church fiercely resisted the new British policy, and following independence in 1922, moved swiftly to consolidate its control and ownership of the institutions.

Local Government Reports

In 1922, practically all welfare and public health matters were the sole responsibility of local authorities and, from the time that these forerunners of local county councils came into existence in 1872, a new government department headed by a cabinet minister issued an annual report. These Local Government Reports (*LGRs*) are a primary source for researchers into the Mother and Baby Homes up to 1945.

Section IV of the *LGRs* was entitled 'Public Assistance' and dealt with what would now be considered social welfare and some health-related matters. That section contained an annual report on 'Unmarried Mothers' and related issues, which varied from year to year, such as infant mortality rates and explanations and interpretations of new legislation. Some years contained facts and figures, others did not. By the mid-1930s, the sections dealing with 'Unmarried Mothers' began to shrink and, by the final year in 1945, amounted to just a couple of brief paragraphs with no useful or illuminating information.

Although the main-section narratives of the *LGRs* were written by anonymous civil servants, at least one and often two special reports were written every year by the 'National Inspectors of Boarded-Out Children': Aneenee Fitzgerald-Kenney and Alice Litster. Having served under the Senior Inspector, Fitzgerald-Kenney was the more senior; Marie Dickie had served since her appointment in 1903 and as a National Inspector from at least 1910. Litster was later also appointed National Inspector. Products of the sensitive and enlightened approach to childcare originating in Britain, their reports were mainly narrative, and significant parts were printed verbatim in the 1927/1928 *LGR* in the main section. The following year, their reports were relegated to the Appendices section and in smaller print than the main section.

Fitzgerald-Kenney's and Litster's Protestant backgrounds are vital to a full understanding of the ideological and religious battle waged in the sub text of the reports year on year. Anyone interested in the treatment of single mothers in Ireland during the 1920s and 1930s should read these reports, including Fitzgerald-Kenney's and Litster's individual reports in the Appendices from 1928. The complete narrative offers a fascinating insight into the Inspectors' philosophy about single mothers and their babies. Their views on the care of children are clear and progressive, unlike the woefully out-of-date ramblings of the Catholic Irish civil servants.

While the language in the reports is very dated and would be considered offensive by today's standards, the fundamental compassion shown by Fitzgerald-Kenney and Litster is clearly evident. They followed international best practice throughout the 1920s, 1930s and 1940s, and regularly cited League of Nations research and recommendations. They firmly believed that a child's best interests were served by being fostered out to certified and loving families who should be fairly compensated, followed up with regular inspections and proper record-keeping. Fitzgerald-Kenney and Litster fought a losing battle from the start. While they occasionally displayed prejudices (Litster was unsympathetic towards 'repeat offenders'), they were in many ways decades ahead of their time in insular Catholic Ireland, which had reverted after 1922 to a system of incarceration for pregnant single women.

There is a distinct difference in the attitudes of the Inspectors compared to those of the Catholic civil servants who compiled the main report. The Inspectors consistently demonstrated compassion and understanding of the children's situations, as far back as 1915 in FitzGerald-Kenney's case: '[Boarding-out is] infinitely superior to the unfortunate system which condemns young and innocent children to the Workhouse as their home ... The system of hiring-out is still an unsatisfactory one, and very low wages continue to be paid.'[6]

The transition to Irish independence must have been a profoundly disturbing time for the Inspectors, with an uneasy standoff between the old guard of senior civil servants and the new nationalist regime that assumed power after the Anglo-Irish Treaty was signed in 1921. This tension is discernible in the *LGRs* from 1922 to 1945.

In 1924 the new Department of Education noted that there were more children in industrial schools in the Irish Free State than in all the United Kingdom. Catholic Ireland continued to judge and punish single mothers and their babies, with Local Authorities, County Councils, the National Society for the Prevention of Cruelty to Children's Inspectors, the new police force, An Garda Síochána, and the courts committing an average of 1,000 children a year to the industrial schools, while women were poured into the Magdalene Laundries via the courts or other unofficial means.

It is clear from the *LGRs* that it was considerably more expensive to keep children in institutions than it was to place them in properly inspected foster homes, but the State continued to push women and children into institutions. The Children's Act of 1929 clearly demonstrates a decisive choice the Irish State made only seven years after independence, significantly expanding the reasons children could be sent to industrial schools and streamlining the process of committing them. Britain closed its last industrial school in 1933 while Irish industrial schools and Magdalene Laundries flourished, and new Mother and Baby Homes continued to open.

There has been considerable confusion and misunderstanding about the statistics used in the *LGRs*. For example, the old workhouses were rebranded as 'County Homes'. Commentators and academics have understood the references to 'Poor Law Institutions' to always mean 'County Homes'. In fact, the figures given for 'Poor Law Institutions' *always* included the public Mother and Baby Homes (Pelletstown, Kilrush and Tuam) and *sometimes* included private Mother and Baby Homes known as 'extern institutions', which were subcontracted by the government (Bessboro, Sean Ross Abbey and Castlepollard). The *LGRs* are simply unclear at times and the figures used also changed in definition. The civil servants who compiled the reports either presumed people would understand, or they were deliberately obscuring the truth. Some basic errors in the reports also lead to the conclusion that many civil servants were lazy or incompetent, or both.

As a general guide, approximately 900–1,100 single mothers were in the various institutions at any one time during the 1920s and 1930s. These include the Workhouses/County Homes, a small number in the

County Hospitals during their confinement, and the public and private Mother and Baby Homes. Overall there were approximately 1,500 illegitimate babies born in 1922, rising to over 2,000 by the early 1930s before decreasing to 1,700 at the start of the Second World War. During the war, that figure increased to over 2,600 in 1945, and we will examine the reasons in later chapters. The Protestant Bethany Mother and Baby Home is absent from all the *LGRs*, reflecting the State's attitude that Bethany simply didn't exist.

It must also be remembered that the facts stated in the *LGRs* reveal only a snapshot of a particular moment in time. Taking the figures on 31 March 1940 for Pelletstown, there were 135 mothers in the home on that date. However, 243 had been admitted during the previous year while 273 were discharged.

CHAPTER TWO

Building High Walls: The First Mother and Baby Home and Other Institutions

Rather than survey each individual home and adoption society over their lifetimes, this book explains their foundations and returns to examine their daily conditions, funding and notable incidents in particular homes. The early years of Pelletstown are examined in greater detail as it was the first of the Mother and Baby Homes and set the template for many of the homes that followed.

Rotunda Girls Aid Society

Dr Sir Arthur Macan was Master of the Rotunda Maternity Hospital in Dublin from 1882 to 1889 and is chiefly remembered for performing the hospital's first caesarean section.[1] His wife Mary Macan (née Wanklyn) from Surrey in England was an active reformer and philanthropist like her husband, and she founded the 'Rotunda Girls Aid Society' (RGAS) in the Catholic parish of St. Mary's Pro Cathedral in Dublin in 1881.

The RGAS was one of hundreds of 'rescue societies' set up during the nineteenth century and survived because no other group could provide its specific services. In its annual report for 1887/88, the society noted the death of its founder by remarking that Mrs Macan had 'saved many from shame, sin and sorrow'.[2] RGAS was based in 82 Marlborough Street, which is the presbytery beside the Pro Cathedral in Dublin, and in other offices in the same area over its lifetime. It quickly evolved into an organisation run by Catholic laywomen almost exclusively for Catholics, although these women provided their services regardless of religion. While they offered practical help and advice to girls to rebuild their lives, this was only after the girls had given up their children. The primary mission of RGAS was to help find respectable homes for children and then inspect the homes to safeguard the welfare of the babies and children in their care. RGAS helped reunite women with their children if their circumstances had changed enough to ensure they could care for their own children without assistance. Usually the women had married and their new husbands were willing to 'take on' their children. The Poor Law of 1899 legislated for adoption by resolution and the RGAS used it when sourcing families who sought to adopt children rather than take cash for boarding them out.

The early decades of RGAS reflected a contradiction of contemporary Victorian and Catholic judgement and yet also contained elements of the emerging Women's Liberation movement and some genuine Christian sentiment. Like many of the rescue societies, their hearts were essentially in the right place, but the climate of the times also influenced their personal attitudes and behaviour. The girls RGAS aided were reminded of their shame on a regular basis but men were equally castigated for their failure to accept responsibility. In later years RGAS became more judgemental and secretive. From its outset, and despite its name, the society had a large catchment area not confined to the Rotunda Hospital. Up to the 1950s, RGAS placed babies in dozens of small nursing homes in north-inner-city Dublin, and with residents of the surrounding genteel suburbs of Drumcondra. After the 1952 Adoption Act, RGAS found and matched married couples who wanted to adopt babies.

RGAS was sued in the late 1990s by two informally adopted women who demanded their personal files and details. RGAS refused, as it was legally required to do, and the case went all the way to the Supreme Court. Towards the end of its existence, RGAS stopped facilitating adoptions and concentrated solely on tracing and reuniting natural mothers and their adult children, although the adoption community's memories of dealing with RGAS are decidedly mixed. The society closed quietly and handed over its records and files to the Health Service Executive (HSE) in 2009 after protracted negotiations to protect itself from potential legal actions.

Pelletstown Mother and Baby Home (aka St. Patrick's)

The first and biggest of Ireland's Mother and Baby Homes was Pelletstown (also known as St. Patrick's) auxiliary workhouse, situated on the north-west outskirts of Dublin at 381 Navan Road. It was an 'auxiliary' unit of the South Dublin Union's workhouse complex based in James' Street and operated by the Dublin Board of Guardians. The network of workhouses and Boards of Guardians around Ireland sent the children in their care to local schools, but separated them within the classroom from the local 'respectable' children. There were four specific workhouse schools around Ireland, two of them in Dublin, run respectively by the North and South Dublin Unions. Pelletstown was the South Dublin Union School and held about 350 children at full capacity. It eventually became 'St. Patrick's Mother and Baby Home' but there are currently no records available to record when and how this happened: it is likely that it evolved slowly over a period of years.

The single biggest problem with researching Mother and Baby Homes, and indeed the whole subject of adoption, is the secrecy built into the system from the very beginning when babies arriving at Coram's Foundling Hospital were renamed and had their original identities sealed. Both the Catholic and Protestant Churches were fanatical about secrecy when it came to single mothers. Because of the nature of the system, there are no memories or memoirs from this period, and it is not until the 1940s that we begin to gain serious insights into the homes from those sources. Memoirs describing events and experiences from the 1940s were written only from the 1990s onwards, rather than contemporaneously.

Even in 2017, adoption records in Ireland are sealed for life and the Adoption Authority is exempt from the various Freedom of Information Acts and the Data Protection Act. Trying to get information about Mother and Baby Homes and adoption is frustratingly difficult, and any information received is painfully scant. I fought for nearly thirty years for the results of a medical examination I underwent when I was 15 days old in Pelletstown/St. Patrick's in 1964. When I finally managed to get the information, I was given two photocopies of the front and back of a card about three inches by two. One side had originally contained nothing but my original name and was blanked out. The other side had four words – 'normal healthy male infant'. I finally obtained the information in 2015, having sought it since the mid-1980s. The further back one researches, the sparser the record-keeping and the scarcer the details.

Paul Michael Garrett from NUI Galway's School of Political Science and Sociology identifies the date for the beginning of Pelletstown/St. Patrick's as the 'late nineteenth century'.[3] He cites the Interdepartmental Report about Mother and Baby Homes from 2014 as his source. However, all that report says is that a team of civil servants working for a couple of months with full access to all government records could only stipulate that the founding of Pelletstown 'predated the foundation of the state'. This author claims 1904 because it was the year George Patrick Sheridan began his extensive works (see below). But 1906 and 1911 have also been cited. Mary Raftery in her book *Suffer the Little Children* uses the year 1918 but provides no references. To date, the best evidence comes from Eileen Conway, who worked in Dublin for the Health Service Executive in a senior capacity on an adoption 'information and tracing' team. She did a PhD on adoption policy practice in Ireland in the 1980s. In December 2009, Conway told the Oireachtas Joint Committee on Health and Children that: 'We hold the records for St. Patrick's Mother and Baby Home, so we have thousands of records of mothers who gave birth, from approximately 1900.'

Conway's evidence dovetails with another clue: the architect George Patrick Sheridan was commissioned to undertake extensive additions and alterations to Pelletstown between 1904 and 1906 at a cost of £10,970, although *The Dictionary of Dublin Architects* is ambiguous about the work done. Does Conway's testimony about records from 1900 mean that Sheridan's work was to facilitate or customise part of Pelletstown as a Mother and Baby Home to sit alongside the workhouse school? The *LGRs* give annual figures for the total numbers of children housed in both Pelletstown and Cabra workhouse schools at 635 in 1915 and 639 in 1918 so there is no question that Pelletstown was still being used as a residential workhouse school until at least 1918. The North and South Dublin Unions were merged in 1918 and Pelletstown may have been officially designated a Mother and Baby Home, or a 'special institution' as they were called at the time. Once again, however, there is no available record of such designation.

Other records from this time are scant because social and civil unrest consumed public and political attention in Ireland, compounded by a severe shortage of paper during the First World War. Single pregnant women were already hidden away from 'respectable' society and there was little interest in keeping detailed records about them.

Most institutions recorded only the barest and most basic details. As a rule, they used a single or double line across the page, or two pages at a time, to record essential facts such as names and addresses, dates of birth, the dates when a person entered and left, and their destination upon leaving. There was also information such as the name and date of birth of any baby born, whether born dead or alive, and where they were placed. Many of these records are lost or incomplete, although most that have survived are in excellent condition because of the top-quality leatherbound ledgers that were used. Record-keeping also tended to be inaccurate in many of the homes, whether by accident, design or plain laziness.

The most likely explanation for the confusion about Pelletstown is that the South Dublin Union decided to unofficially assign it a dual purpose. It is likely that single, pregnant women were quietly transferred over many years from the main workhouse in James' Street to a segregated part of Pelletstown to separate them from the 'respectable' poor. Ireland's first Mother and Baby Home was co-located with the Dublin auxiliary workhouse school. It may also

have been that many of the children in the workhouse school were the children of single mothers residing in the same building but kept apart from one other.

The Pelletstown school needed women and girls to do the laundry and domestic work, and a perfect solution for the South Dublin union could have been to transfer the unmarried mothers from the main workhouse in Dublin city centre to a segregated section of Pelletstown. What we can definitively say is that sometime after 1918 and before 1922, the older school-aged children were moved out and Pelletstown was designated a 'special institution' *exclusively* for single mothers.

It was administered by yet another French order of nuns, the Sisters of the Daughters of St. Vincent de Paul (later called the Daughters of Charity), founded in 1633 and not in any way related to the Society of St. Vincent de Paul. The order had extensive experience in Britain, where they ran dozens of institutions for children and babies. They continued to run the home on the Navan Road until it finally closed in 1985 and they downsized to a period house in Donnybrook, Dublin 4, where they reinvented the institution as 'supervised flatlets'.

From the time Pelletstown became a Mother and Baby Home, the everyday routine of the workhouse regime continued. Women stayed for up to two years and then left their children in the home and went to find accommodation and work outside. The nuns often arranged work placements, ensuring that they could check on the former occupants via their new employers. The women were expected to pay for their children's upkeep and contribute substantial sums from their meagre wages for many years, even if their child was with a family. These 'parental monies' were collected by the local Gardaí. The Department of Education administered the scheme, although there are few or no records left to explain its precise workings.

The nuns always referred to the women and girls in Pelletstown as 'girls', a psychological ploy used in all the Mother and Baby Homes where women in their twenties, thirties and forties were treated as naughty children rather than as adults. Older women were told that their parents would be contacted if they did not behave themselves. Another method of controlling the residents was to intimidate them with threatened removals to another institution with a harsher reputation. This was common across the system of institutional care. Children in orphanages were threatened with being sent to the industrial schools; women in the Mother and Baby Homes were threatened with Magdalene Laundries or, the most feared of all the institutions, mental asylums.

Pelletstown, in common with many of the major Mother and Baby Homes, was the recipient of generous Irish Hospitals' Sweepstake grants during the early 1930s, and maternity units were established so that the pregnant women and girls would not have to be sent to the workhouse hospital in Dublin. In 1933, Pelletstown received over £8,000 (nearly €650,000 in 2016 values) for a maternity unit. Pelletstown Auxiliary Hospital, as it was officially known, was granted over £43,000 (over €3.5 million at 2016 values) in Sweepstakes funds.

The homes' emphasis was on the punishment and rehabilitation of 'first-time offenders'. Second-time or 'repeat offenders', as they were known, were treated brutally from the moment they arrived. They often remained in the homes for years, working as virtual slaves, constantly reminded by the nuns of their inferior status. In Pelletstown there was a segregated secure unit for repeat offenders from at least the late 1950s onwards. The secrecy surrounding the Mother and Baby Homes means that there are no records available about this unit. Its existence would be unknown if it were not for the personal testimonies of former residents. The secure unit may have existed from the beginning in some form or other. The other Mother and Baby Homes, particularly the private ones, usually refused repeat offenders and sent them to Pelletstown/St. Patrick's.

Pelletstown was later certified for 149 mothers and 560 cots. It was common in all the homes to have more cots than beds for mothers so that the homes could accept unaccompanied illegitimate babies from all other sources, such as home births or women presenting in labour to public hospitals. Pelletstown was very large compared to the later homes and its boarding-out system struggled to find enough foster parents willing to take the babies and children. Conveniently, the sisters already had an orphanage and school in Dublin's North William Street since the 1860s. They opened St. Philomena's in Stillorgan, Co.

Dublin, in 1933 (in the grounds of the present St. Raphaela's School) for the sole purpose of keeping children between the ages of 3 and 4, and up to 8 years of age. According to the *LGR*, it was 'certified in pursuance of the Pauper Children (Ireland) Act 1889, for the reception of boys and girls who may be eligible to be sent to certified schools'. In this case 'certified school' means industrial school. St. Philomena's was exclusively for children too old for the nursery wards in Pelletstown but too young for the industrial schools. Philomena's was later split when the boys were transferred to another auxiliary orphanage the nuns founded, St. Theresa's, in nearby Blackrock. The strict division of the genders varied back and forth over the years as numbers and needs dictated. St. Theresa's and St. Philomena's were also used occasionally to hold 'the better class' of children between foster placements. When the children reached the age of 7 or 8, girls were normally transferred to Lakelands industrial school at Gilford Road, Sandymount, Dublin 4, while the boys were sent to the Artane industrial school on Dublin's northside. There are also records of children going to other institutions around the country, such as Tralee industrial school in Kerry.

There is strong anecdotal evidence to suggest that, at some point, mixed-race babies from around the country were routinely transferred to Pelletstown and possibly kept in a segregated ward. The 'coloured' babies, as they were called, were held until they were old enough to be transferred to St. Philomena's or St. Theresa's and it was extremely rare for them to be adopted. Casual racism and sectarianism were commonplace in the homes; mixed-race babies and children were subjected to additional beatings, racist verbal abuse and shaming throughout their time in State 'care'. They almost universally ended up in the industrial schools, whose survivors still bear the scars of their shameful treatment. Most of these survivors left Ireland as soon as they were freed from the system and, over the last few years, have organised themselves into the 'Association of Mixed Race Irish' founded by activist Rosemary Adaser. They have become a powerful campaigning group with several members bravely speaking out about their personal stories. Pelletstown features in practically every story.

By far the best evidence relating to conditions in the homes from the 1920s and 1930s are the records of 'infant mortality rates'. Before looking in detail at the available records from Pelletstown, it is important to understand exactly how 'infant mortality rates' (IMR) work and how to interpret them. Sadly, it is necessary to go into detail about this tragic, and often taboo, subject.

Mortality Rates

The term 'infant mortality rate' is used by countless commentators who may have different understandings of its proper definition and usage. The IMR is correctly defined as the percentage figure of the number of babies who were born alive but did not survive until their first birthday. The number of babies who survived their first year is compared to those who did not survive in any given area or institution. It is expressed in two ways: as a percentage figure or as a total number of deaths out of 1,000. The percentage version will be used in this book.

It is imperative to have a basic grasp of the overall IMR in Ireland since 1922 to fully understand the figures given for infant deaths throughout the rest of this book. In 1900, the IMR in Ireland was 9.9%. In other words, one in every ten babies born alive did not live to see his or her first birthday. This figure includes both legitimate and illegitimate babies. The IMR has dropped steadily around the world due to the availability of modern medicine.

Throughout the 1920s, the national IMR was roughly around 6% and 7%, year on year, and the figures include all babies, whether born to married or single mothers. The IMR in Ireland improved with every passing decade. By 1950 the rate was down to 4.7%, and medical science and upgraded hospitals have slowly brought the rate down to its present 0.033%, making Ireland one of the safest countries in which to give birth today. This is the baseline set of figures since 1922, against which all infant mortality rates from Mother and Baby Home must be compared.

However, when we look more closely at the 1920s and separate the legitimate and illegitimate mortality rates, a completely different picture emerges. Here are some of the national figures for Ireland – after 1922 – which speak for themselves:

Year	Infant mortality rate*	Illegitimate infant mortality rate
1923	6.6%	34.4%
1924	7.2%	31.5%
1925	6.8%	28.7%
1926	7.4%	32.3%
1927	7.1%	28.8%
1928	6.8%	30.7%
1929	7.0%	29.5%
1930	6.8%	25.1%

* The national IMR includes legitimate and illegitimate babies and would be lower if the births and deaths of illegitimate babies were removed.

The national statistics show that in Ireland after 1922, illegitimate babies were dying at four and five times the rate of legitimate babies throughout the 1920s. Many of the illegitimate babies were born and died in the five Mother and Baby Homes, including Pelletstown/St. Patrick's (1900), Bethany (1921), Kilrush (1922), Bessboro (1924) and Tuam (1926). (Opening years in brackets).

Below is an extract taken from the *LGR* of 1930/31. This report, documenting the discrepancy between mortality rates of legitimate and illegitimate babies in Ireland, was available to the public and media of the time.

Mortality of Illegitimate Children

The decline noted in the year 1930 in the death rate of infants generally was reflected to an enhanced degree in the corresponding rate for children born out of wedlock, the figure being 251 per 1,000 births in comparison with 295 for 1929, a decrease of 15%, and the lowest rate recorded by the Registrar-General since such mortality was classified separately in 1923. The margin for improvement regarding the mortality incidence in this class is, however, greater than in the case of legitimate children, seeing that even with this more favourable record one out of every four illegitimate infants died during 1930 in the first year of life, or in other terms, their mortality rate was more than four times greater than that of the children of married parents. The death-rate of illegitimate children in the Saorstát [Independent Ireland] is markedly more than the corresponding rates of the same year in Northern Ireland (140 per 1,000 births) and in England and Wales (105 per 1,000 births). There was an increase of ten in the number of illegitimate births in this country in 1930 as compared with the preceding year and a reduction of 79 in the number of deaths of such infants.

The comparison with Britain's figures for the same time is illuminating. In 1930, Ireland's illegitimate babies were dying at the rate of 25.1%, while just across the border in Northern Ireland the rate was 14%. In England and Wales, it was down to 10.5% and falling. The civil servants and religious who were actively involved with single mothers and their babies were also undoubtedly aware that Britain was closing its large institutions in favour of smaller, more compassionate orphanages and foster homes. This had already resulted in lower mortality rates and an increase in social skills and training for the young adults leaving the homes. The mortality rates in Ireland's Mother and Baby Homes were higher than the national mortality rate for illegitimate babies and remained very high until the late 1940s. Despite the good intentions and best efforts of certain civil servants, Catholic and Protestant, and some caring politicians, the system in Ireland carried on regardless of the indisputable proof that babies were dying in their thousands in the Mother and Baby Homes and workhouses/county homes.

Armed with this information, a closer inspection of exact mortality rates in Pelletstown in the 1920s is revealing. The precise figures for the number of children in institutions, and the number of deaths for Ireland's first Mother and Baby Home, were reproduced in the *LGR* for 1929/30. However, the 'mortality rate' (rounded to the nearest full

Year	Children in the Institution	Number of Deaths	Mortality Rate
1924	259	96	37%
1925	240	119*	50%
1926	271	94	35%
1927	263	111	42%
1928	294	95	32%
1929	330	81	25%
1930	336	66	20%

*Measles epidemic

number), as added below, did not appear in the original *LRG* and does not represent the precise infant mortality rate as defined above. Some of the deaths were of children aged over one year and most of the children and babies who died were in the large wards for unaccompanied babies in Pelletstown/St. Patrick's, including many whose mothers were never in Pelletstown. Even with these caveats, the mortality rates were excessive by any civilised standard. The total numbers given for the deaths in Pelletstown are 622 children out of 1,993, over seven years: an average IMR of over 31% for the seven years, peaking at 50% in 1925. Babies and children in Pelletstown were dying at the rate of almost two per week over those seven years. The *LGR* for 1925/27 at Pelletstown produced a rare negative reaction from the office of Local Government, as shown below.

Deaths of Illegitimate Infants

The Annual Reports of the Registrar-General for the years 1925 and 1926 disclose that the mortality rate amongst infants born out of wedlock was about five times greater than that of legitimate infants, and that one out of every three of the first-mentioned class died before the completion of the first year of life.

It is recognised that illegitimate infants are handicapped by constitutional and environmental disadvantages which tend to a heavy incidence of infant mortality, but even when allowance has been made for these adverse factors, the death-rate of such infants is still disproportionately high in view of the experience of other countries.

From an analysis of the statistics it is evident that this excessive mortality is accentuated at the age period from fourteen days up to three months and in point of causation is associated with Diarrhoea and Enteritis. It may, therefore, be inferred that the unfavourable results are traceable to the early separation of mother and infant and to the influence of unsuitable artificial feeding.

The supervision of the illegitimate child is partly a matter of Poor Law (e.g., maintenance and liability), of Police (inquests and proceedings for neglect) and of Child Welfare (general protective arrangements).

The deplorable loss of life amongst these children shows the necessity for more efficient administration by local authorities of the powers conferred by the Children Act, 1908, the Notification of Birth Acts, 1907 and 1915, and the Midwives Act, 1918.

For those children who were placed with families, the future was little better, as this *LGR* excerpt shows:

Nurse children: The provisions of part I of the Children Act, 1908, relating to undertaking the care of infants for gain was actively administered during the year in the Dublin union, the area where the need for supervision of nurse children is greatest. There has been a steady increase in recent years in the number of registrations, while the death rate though higher than in 1927–28, compares favourably with earlier years. The number of nurse children within the cognisance of the Dublin union authorities on the 1 March 1929 was 1,261. The following are comparative figures for five years for Dublin union:

	1924–5	1925–6	1926–7	1927–8	1928–9
Children registered	523	527	591	489	620
Deaths of infants	83	85	111	49	66
Homes condemned	46	87	138	162	161
Prosecutions	11	15	26	25	26

Mortality rates among boarded-out children ranged from 10% to 20% after 1922 until well into the 1930s. There is very little evidence as to where exactly those children came from but many, if not the majority, were sent from Mother and Baby Homes around the country.

One key point to note is that the nuns who ran the homes also brought the lists of births and deaths to the local registry offices to be officially recorded. As it is the nuns themselves who are the direct source of the infant mortality rates, they are not in a position to dismiss the inhumanity and brutality of the figures or to distance themselves in any way from the evidence.

Of the nine Mother and Baby Homes, six were horrific and Pelletstown/St. Patrick's was, in terms of the vast numbers of deaths, by far the worst. The current Inquiry into Mother and Baby Homes is restricted to investigating from the year 1922 and therefore Pelletstown will never be formally investigated before that date. The Interdepartmental Report from 2014 states that 6,596 births were registered in Pelletstown but only seven of those births were registered up to 1934 because the home had no maternity wards of its own for the first thirty-four years of its 85-year operation. The final figure for Pelletstown will never be known, but it likely to be above 10,000 single mothers and therefore approximately 10,000 babies. In time, it will be known as the biggest residential institution, in terms of numbers, in Ireland. The figure may be as high as 25,000 mothers and babies and that is without counting the thousands of unaccompanied babies and children transferred to Pelletstown's wards from various outside sources.

There were 622 children listed as dying in the *LGR* noted above. If the rate of deaths in Pelletstown from the 1920s – nearly two children per week – was replicated before 1922 and up to 1940, the final figure from 1900 to 1940 would be more than 3,000 children. At present, there is also a confirmed minimum figure for the number of babies who died between 1940 and 1965: 474, a number recently confirmed in the Dáil by the Minister for Children and Youth Affairs, Katherine Zappone. The two confirmed figures alone (622 + 474) add up to 1,096 and that is only what we can presently confirm with the earlier and undoubtedly worst decades missing. The total number that died will be shocking but will still be only part of the full picture of institutional neglect in Ireland since 1900.

During the 1916 Easter Rising, 500 men, women and children died. Yet at the very least, over four times that number of Irish citizens – mothers, infants and children – died in Pelletstown. There is no commemoration for this tragic institution in our history. There are no plaques or annual marches down O'Connell Street with planes flying overhead. There is only a black hole in our collective folk memory and history books.

St. Patrick's Guild and St. Patrick's Infant Hospital

Of all the sources of confusion in the adoption and survivor communities, the worst is unquestionably St. Patrick's. There were three major St. Patrick's institutions, each with a different function. Many adoptees and survivors are unaware of this until they start looking for information.

St. Patrick's Guild (SPG) spent decades organising boarding out for illegitimate babies and some post-separation support for single mothers. After 1952, it grew into one of the biggest adoption agencies in Ireland and arranged nearly a quarter of all legal adoptions. The Catholic Protection and Rescue Society was of a comparable size. SPG also owned a 'holding centre' named 'St. Patrick's Infant Hospital' in Blackrock, Co. Dublin. It is customarily called 'Temple Hill' to distinguish it from the other two St. Patrick's. Both the SPG adoption agency and the holding centre share a name with St. Patrick's – the Mother and Baby Home also known as Pelletstown on the Navan Road in Dublin. To make matters even more complicated, all three St. Patrick's were based in Dublin and regularly worked closely together. There are many instances of babies born in St. Patrick's Mother and Baby Home, then transferred to St. Patrick's Infant Hospital and later adopted through the St. Patrick's Guild adoption agency.

St. Patrick's Guild was founded by Mary Josephine Cruice in 1910 to counteract the influence of the Protestant rescue societies. Those rescue societies were involved in arranging boarding out and it was feared that they would 'snatch' Catholic children for baptism in one of the Protestant Churches before their placement. SPG was for the 'better class' of Catholic single mothers and Cruice was motivated by money as much as by religious zeal.[4] SPG's motto was 'Save the child' and its original office was in 46 Middle Abbey Street in Dublin, before moving up a couple of doors to number 50 in 1915. While Cruice was in charge, SPG kept meticulous records.

Cruice had a mixed reputation. She was a very tough character, according to many accounts, and she was certainly ambitious, and driven, at least in part, by greed. Around 1918 SPG opened its own 'holding centre' in 19 Mountjoy Square, a formerly genteel Georgian square in north Dublin where most of the four-storey-over-basement, red-brick family homes were turned into flats and overcrowded tenements. The holding centre was a new type of support institution to provide an overflow and/or temporary residence for illegitimate babies born in private nursing homes or public maternity hospitals such as the nearby Rotunda or Holles Street. SPG's holding centre later also supported the mainstream Mother and Baby Homes.

By 1930 its city holding centre was overcrowded and in disrepair, so SPG leased a large period residence in Temple Hill in Blackrock, at the opposite end of the village from where Lady Arabella Denny had lived. Built in 1767 and known as Temple Hill House, it was originally called Neptune House and was the seaside residence of the First Earl of Clonmel, also known as Copper Face Jack, who resided at his better-known house in Harcourt Street, Dublin. The architect Thomas Joseph Cullen was commissioned to design and build a proper laundry for the new centre, 'St. Patrick's Infant Hospital'.

There were only two, possibly three, 'holding centres' and they should not be confused with orphanages where children stayed for years. However, to further complicate matters, there were some children in Temple Hill who had confirmed stays of one and two years in the 1960s, 1970s and 1980s and even a handful of cases where babies stayed for three years. It is likely that several thousand, if not over 10,000, babies passed through the doors of these two holding centres.

According to Damien Corless in his splendid book about the Irish Hospitals' Sweepstake, in 1922 St. Patrick's Infant Hospital tried to organise an early type of lottery known as a 'Sweep', based on betting large sums on a chosen horse race. SPG threatened to close its home if its 'Save the Child' sweep did not go ahead. When the money started to flow from the government-licensed Sweepstakes, SRG and Temple Hill were quick to become involved and received large sums of Sweepstake money over the years. Of all the groups and institutions related to single mothers, SPG benefitted second only to the Sacred Heart nuns, receiving a total of over £100,000 (nearly €8 million at 2016 values) for reconstruction, additions and maintenance, and capital grants for Temple Hill.

St. Patrick's Guild was eventually taken over by the Sisters of Charity and shortly afterwards in 1942 came under the control of the Archbishop of Dublin, John Charles McQuaid, and his successors.

Conditions in Temple Hill holding centre, in both its locations, were a mystery until the mid-1960s. A small number of women have spoken about their time working there, supposedly training to be staff nurses, although this 'job' was often a sham. It was a common deception that was used by the nuns in a slightly different way in Castlepollard and Bessboro and probably in other homes as well. The majority of the girls who 'trained' in Temple Hill were assigned there after they had lost their babies to adoption. Many of them were in shock and had no other options in their lives. The pay in Temple Hill was poor and the girls' lives were highly regimented for fear that they would become 'repeat offenders'. The mothers who had recently lost their babies did the actual work and treated the babies as well as they could, but the regime was strict and any sort of bonding or affection was strongly discouraged. The girls worked hard to take advantage of the training opportunity, but many ended up with no formal qualifications except a reference from the nuns when they departed. Natural mothers never stayed in the holding centres and visiting their babies was strongly discouraged, at least from the 1960s, although there are recorded exceptions over the years. Therefore, we have two sources of direct testimony about conditions in Temple Hill from the mid-1960s, even though they are extremely limited with practically no paperwork or documentation of any substance available. Stories about the sisters in charge paint them as strict, uncaring and businesslike.

Testimony about conditions in Temple Hill for the babies from around 1970 indicate that they were left in their cots and given very little attention. The girls who cared for them were kept busy and had little time for any individual baby. Many commentators have expressed horror about one common practice in which the ends of babies' sleeves were attached to their mattresses with large safety pins so they could not move about or turn on their sides. However, that custom was very much the norm in society at the time because it was believed that keeping a baby on its back would prevent cot death. The practice was relatively harmless in normal conditions where babies are picked up after naps or sleep and then moved around and cuddled. In Temple Hill, the pinning caused serious problems because the babies were left on their backs in their cots almost constantly and, as a result, bedsores were common as well as associated infections and pain stemming from raw, untreated bedsores. If the general rule that conditions get worse the further back one researches, it is likely that the babies in Mountjoy Square and Temple Hill were dumped in cots in overcrowded wards and left alone for hours at a time during most of the six to nine years that the holding centres operated.

Babies must have died in Mountjoy Square and Temple Hill as overcrowded wards and the absence of proper isolation units led to the spread of infections, viruses and bacteria. It is unknown where babies who died were interred, although it was most likely in Glasnevin Cemetery. Deansgrange Cemetery, just a couple of kilometres south of Temple Hill, is also a possibility. The mortality rates in the early days were almost certain to have been well above the national average. Temple Hill closed in 1987 and the nuns sold the building for £426,000, tax-free, because religious orders are exempt from all forms of taxation. The current Inquiry into Mother and Baby Homes is not investigating Temple Hill and it may be that we will never know the full truth of what happened there.

St. Patrick's Guild itself later moved to 82 Haddington Road in south Dublin and then further south again into the suburbs, in the direction of Temple Hill, to 203 Merrion Road, where they officially closed in 2013. Their standards declined rapidly after the Sisters of Charity took over and they developed a reputation for issues related to falsifying records. In 1997 Alan Shatter TD attacked the Guild in the Dáil for knowingly giving false information to people trying to trace nature mothers or adopted people. In 2013 the Adoption Authority notified the Department of Children that St. Patrick's Guild is aware of 'several hundred illegal registrations but are waiting for people to contact them: they are not seeking the people involved.'[5] The illegally adopted people with fake and potentially lethal medical histories were once again compromised by both SPG and the government since neither of them proactively sought out the victims. The General Registry Office was also informed.

The Guild is also known to have settled a number of legal actions before they reached the courts. Issues associated with SPG include knowingly and illegally sending the children of married parents for adoption, and forging signatures. In one case they were so sure they were above the law that they made no attempt to imitate a natural mother's handwriting, and spelled her name incorrectly. They finally handed their files over to Tusla, the newly named branch of Social Services dealing with various matters including adoption, in 2016 after three years of protracted legal bartering. Everyone who was adopted through SPG was left in effective limbo for those three years, as were elderly natural mothers. People undoubtedly died while waiting for an appointment to trace. There has been no audit of SPG files and no criminal investigation. Despite heavy lobbying from several survivor and adoption rights groups, SPG was not included in the current Inquiry into Mother and Baby Homes.

Cúnamh, Miscellaneous Adoption and Forced Repatriation Agencies

St. Patrick's Guild and its predecessor, the Rotunda Girls Aid Society, were only the beginnings of a minor industry of agencies, and some are still with us today. The Catholic Protection and Rescue Society (CPRS), for example, founded in 1913, is still operating and is equal to St. Patrick's Guild in terms of overall numbers, with around 15,000 adoptions on its books. It rebranded as 'Cúnamh' in 1992 and is based in 30 South Anne Street, Dublin 2.

Each agency changed its function and ethos over the years. The larger agencies began as boarding-out and fostering societies and became adoption agencies after the introduction of proper adoption legislation in 1952. Some were started by well-intentioned lay people and others by religious organisations. Father P.J. Regan began his own agency called the St. Clare's Adoption Society that specialised mostly in foreign adoptions to the United States, while other agencies handled Irish adoptions only.

The CPRS was founded to prevent Protestant proselytisers convincing desperate Catholic single mothers to have their babies raised as Protestants. While sectarian motives were common in the foundations of many Catholic organisations, the CPRS had a unique role as a self-appointed judge and jury to 'rescue' single pregnant women and girls from Britain. From 1922 many expectant mothers boarded the ferries to Britain to escape losing their babies to the workhouses, their worldly possessions often little more than a change of clothes. The British customs officers learned to spot them instantly and they became so common that they earned a semi-official nickname – PFIs – Pregnant from Ireland. However, the British authorities viewed them as a 'burden to the public purse' so did everything they could to return them. That is where the CPRS came in, as the agency that took custody of runaway Irish girls and escorted them back to the workhouses or homes in Ireland. A variety of semi-official contacts between British authorities and the CPRS formed an underground practice of semi-forced repatriation. The network continued until at least the 1970s when there are several documented cases of single girls being forcibly repatriated. Nevertheless, thousands and probably tens of thousands of Irish women beat the customs officers and police and somehow avoided the informal networks of priests and volunteers. The majority ended up in Britain's widespread network of over one hundred Mother and Baby Homes, some run by Catholics, the majority by Protestants.

The agency system is complex and worthy of a book in its own right. There are still a handful of nuns involved and many are hate figures among the adoption and survivor communities. Certain nuns, right up to a couple of years ago, would regularly ask for 'donations' to fund their tracing efforts, even though their agencies were State-funded and the nuns themselves were sometimes employed by the State as paid social workers (the Sacred Heart nuns had their own agency called the 'Sacred Heart Adoption Society'). Many adoptees and natural mothers have missed the chance to reunite because of stalling and misinformation from nuns. The vast majority of the religious-based agencies have been handed over to the government, and social workers now do the tracing and searching in almost every case.

What is most startling is the difference of opinion in the active adoption and survivor communities regarding the various agencies. Some swear at a particular agency while others swear by it. The wild disparity in experience is sometimes due to successful or failed traces but, beyond that, individual nuns and social workers can have good and bad days like anyone else, or unreasonably take a dislike to an adoptee or natural mother. Outcomes for searches among the agencies, well into the 1990s, were overwhelmingly negative and often based on the whim of a stone-faced nun demanding to know if your 'adoption was happy and, if it was, then why are you here.' Many of the agencies began as secretive societies back in the late nineteenth century, either to protect or punish single mothers and their babies. That mentality persists in some agencies even now. All the agencies were covered legally by the 1952 'sealed-for-life' Adoption Act. Another point is that the various Catholic agencies cooperated with one another and had members in common and this has led to some confusion.

From the late 1980s, a tiny handful of people in the adoption agency industry and some highly qualified social workers with a genuine interest in adoption-related matters became more vocal about new-fangled ideas such as post-adoption support and properly facilitated reunions. However, the religious orders were still in charge and the newcomers faced a war of attrition to change existing attitudes.

There have always been long waiting lists before a social worker can be appointed. Some have stretched to five years from first contact;

delays of one to two years before a first meeting with a social worker are now common. While social services in Ireland have always been chronically underfunded, many of the delays are due to the fact that adoption tracing was, and still is, seen by many as a waste of time and thus assigned a low priority. The adoption and survivor communities today are still dealing with a system that is starved of resources.

CHAPTER 3

Going Our Own Way: The Mother and Baby Homes Expansion

Part of the Catholic Church's agenda for newly independent Ireland was to isolate single mothers from the general workhouse populations and move them to separate 'special institutions', as Mother and Baby Homes were originally called.

While single motherhood was never a crime, it was effectively treated as such. 'Repeat offenders' were considered 'mentally deficient' and needed to be 'committed' to an institution, just as a convicted criminal is 'committed' to jail for society's protection.

In September 1922, the 'Federation of Dublin Charities', under the control of Archbishop of Dublin Edward Byrne, submitted a proposal to the government for the future management of single mothers. It was a historic moment because it aimed to remove single mothers from the workhouses. It clearly had the approval of the archbishop himself as it was submitted by an organisation he controlled. The proposal was accepted by the Department of Local Government and the die was cast. Single mothers would leave the workhouses and go to a new type of 'special institution', and these new residential homes would be officially run by the religious orders.

The original Irish Catholic Mother and Baby Homes were generally a cross between a maternity hospital with no doctors or nurses and a low-to-medium-security prison. The permanent separation of unmarried mothers from their illegitimate babies was taken for granted. A network of smaller institutions grew to support the new 'special institutions'. Seven of these were built between 1921 and 1935.

Single mothers and their babies after 1922 were pushed further out of Irish society, out of the workhouses, and isolated in Mother and Baby Homes. Meanwhile, the fathers of many of the babies, often rapists, liars, child abusers and married men who abandoned their victims and pregnant girlfriends to the brutality of the workhouses, escaped all responsibility for their actions.

While the options available to single mothers narrowed greatly, a number of tough and determined women, with strong family support, somehow managed to keep their babies. It was a common solution for a girl's parents to informally adopt their grandchild as their own, with the baby's mother becoming its elder sister. Some single mothers kept their children even after being disowned by their families but endured a constant struggle to find childcare and employment. Many in the cities resorted to begging and prostitution. The new State and the Church often intervened, snatching illegitimate children from their single mothers on the slightest pretext before dispatching them to the nearest industrial school.

The Bethany Home

The Bethany Mother and Baby Home was Protestant and remained the only such Protestant Home that ever operated in Ireland. Because Bethany was the only Protestant Home, it served a variety of purposes over the years such as occasional use by the courts as a remand centre for Protestant girls and women. Bethany even incarcerated women and girls sentenced by the courts for criminal offences, including some as serious as infanticide. Unlike Pelletstown, its only counterpart at the time it was founded, Bethany was entirely a private home. It was founded when a number of Protestant rescue societies and charities such as 'Prison Gate' and 'The Midnight Mission' came together in 1921 and opened in a nondescript and shabby house in Blackhall Place in north-inner-city Dublin.

From 1922 the new Free State Government and the Bethany Home ignored one other. This is never remarked upon in the *LGRs*. In fact, the only mention of anything Protestant-related from 1925 to 1945 is that Braemar House on the Blackrock Road in Cork was added to the list of approved 'extern institutions' for the reception of destitute Protestant children in 1933.[1] Otherwise the Protestant Bethany Home and the network of orphanages that grew over time to accept the children from Bethany, and in other circumstances once they had reached the appropriate age, was close to officially invisible.

Bethany was administered by a management committee of clergy from various Protestant groups, including the Irish Church Missions and lay Protestants. Unusually for the time, men and women sat on the committee, and many were evangelical and born-again Christians, keen to save souls and rescue sinners. Bethany admitted the occasional Catholic, with the covert hope of converting them. In a bizarre incident in 1926, the Catholic St. Patrick's Guild organisation offered what was almost a prisoner swap by proposing to accept Bethany's Catholics in exchange for the Guild's Protestants. Bethany refused and some of its recorded history documents its sectarian battles with groups like the Catholic Protection and Rescue Society.

The small house at Blackhall Place was constantly overcrowded and conditions were dire. In 1934 the committee purchased a sizable period house in Orwell Road in Rathgar on Dublin's southside from one of their own members. That committee member held the rest of them to ransom by demanding a price 50% above its independent valuation. Since the old house at Blackhall Place was literally falling down and subject to a compulsory purchase order, the Bethany management committee paid the requested price.

There is much information available about the Bethany Home, thanks to the research of survivor Derek Leinster, who was later joined in the undertaking by Dr. Niall Meehan. A disturbing insight into its early years is the number of babies and children who died in a comparatively small home from 1922 to 1949: at least 227 deaths. That figure also includes stillbirths, and this is unique to Bethany. The most common causes of death were officially recorded as convulsions (54), heart failure (41), marasmus (26) and stillborn (16). 'Marasmus' is a medical term that is often recorded as the cause of death for babies from the homes; it means death from malnutrition. The children and babies were buried

at Mount Jerome Cemetery in Dublin in various sections including the
Paupers' Plot along the back wall.

Bethany's IMR soared during 1935 and 1936 and forty children
died. That spike brought attention to the home. The Bethany committee
considered withdrawing its registration under the Registration of
Maternity Homes Act 1934 to free itself from government involvment.
The Deputy Chief Medical Adviser, Sterling Berry, inspected the home
a number of times in the late 1930s. Berry was a Protestant and took
an interest in the Bethany Home. While it would now be considered
extraordinary, the main focus of the State officials and the Catholic
Protection and Rescue Society was to ensure that Catholic babies were
excluded from Bethany rather than investigating the horrific conditions
and hundreds of dead babies. Catholic babies were formally excluded
in 1939. Part of the problem was that Bethany received effectively no
State assistance up to 1948 when its application for funding was finally
approved after many unsuccessful previous applications. There is also
no record of Bethany receiving a single penny from Irish Hospitals'
Sweepstake grants while the Catholic Mother and Baby Homes received
substantial funding.[2] The conditions and mortality rates there did
improve after 1948, although this could be a reflection of the general
improvements across all the homes that began in 1945.

Unlike the Catholic homes, Bethany sent many children to Britain
and Northern Ireland and some even ended up as part of the child-export
schemes that thrived during the twentieth century. Bethany children
were sent to Canada and Australia and other far-flung destinations on
the edges of the British Empire. Protestant adoption agencies did not
embrace foreign adoptions after 1945 and sent only twenty-four babies
oversees, while the Catholic homes and agencies sent thousands.

Bethany never embraced formal adoption, preferring boarding or
fostering out, particularly in south Dublin and north Wicklow. Part
of the reason for this was because the town of Greystones expanded
significantly in the late nineteenth and early twentieth centuries with
the opening of the new east-coast railway. It also had a predominantly
Protestant population already: Protestants tended to settle in north
County Wicklow and the south Dublin suburb of Dún Laoghaire after
1922. The majority of Protestant orphanages and children's homes were

in these two areas, such as Westbank in Greystones and Avoca House in Wicklow. Bethany's most famous resident, Derek Leinster, was sent to north Wicklow where he was treated appallingly. Derek had left school early and was functionally illiterate. He later emigrated to England where he rebuilt his life with the help of Carol, his wife. He pulled himself up through sheer grit and determination and finally wrote two books, focusing on Bethany and his childhood. They are a harrowing read. Leinster's reproduced medical records, when he was sent to hospital from Bethany, are a shocking indictment of the wanton and wilful neglect he suffered.

The records for Bethany and many other related Protestant orphanages are held by PACT, the Protestant Adoption Society, at Arabella House in Rathfarnham in south Dublin.

Kilrush Mother and Baby Homes (aka The Nurseries)

Just after the Bethany Home was founded, the newly formed 'County Board of Health' in Co. Clare separated single mothers from all other residents of the workhouse in Ennis. It designated the small public auxiliary workhouse in Kilrush as a 'County Nursery', another early name for a Mother and Baby Home. It was administered on behalf of the County Board of Health by the Sisters of Mercy, who also ran many of the country's industrial schools for girls and retain a reputation as one of the cruelest orders of nuns. References to the 'Nurseries' in official documents of the time mean Kilrush Mother and Baby Home.

A newspaper article in the *Clare People* by Joe O'Muircheartaigh a couple of weeks after the Tuam 800 story broke shed considerable light on the home.[3] There are also some minor mentions in the *LGRs*. Like Tuam Mother and Baby Home, which opened in 1926, Kilrush Mother and Baby Home was flexible about who it accepted as residents. They took older children and even the occasional destitute mother and her children if referred from the main county home in Ennis or by the County Board of Health. The Nurseries was also known as the 'County Orphanage', although this was a local understanding of its function as distinct from an official designation.

A newspaper report in 1927 states that 'The Home is in a very poor condition of repair. There is no water supply and no bathing or sanitary accommodation and the lighting is by lamps.'[4] In fact, Kilrush had only its own well on-site and no connection to any mains water supplies or sewage outlet. The journalist went on to report how difficult life was for the nuns and how it was 'not fair' to expect them to remain in such conditions. The conditions for mothers and babies did not warrant the same level of indignation.

The Sisters of Mercy detained mothers for at least two years and found plenty to keep them busy. They scrubbed already clean floors, did general domestic duties and were hired out whenever possible for any suitable position. After a child turned 2 years old, mothers could leave, but were expected to find employment and contribute a substantial sum towards the maintenance of their child. They were also expected to visit their child and stay in touch. The majority did for at least a number of years while others stayed on in the Nurseries a little longer. The nuns often arranged positions for the women as domestic servants or on local farms. There were several recorded escape attempts and 'scaling the walls' seems to have been the chosen method. The local Gardaí rounded up the escapees and returned them for punishment. The women and girls were humiliated through shaving or clipping off their hair, a certain way to prevent future escape attempts. This was followed by a 'number one diet' consisting of bread and water. The Sisters of Mercy were well known for removing their heavy leather belts from their habits and savagely beating children in the industrial schools. There is no evidence that they beat the women and children in Kilrush but it is likely. Those who repeatedly attempted to escape were sent to the local county home/workhouse as a severe punishment.

The babies who lived to 2 years of age were 'boarded out' until they were roughly 8 years old and this may be a clue as to why Pelletstown was also listed as a workhouse school until at least 1918. It is possible, although still speculation, that the children in Pelletstown were the sons and daughters of single mothers also resident in the same buildings but not mentioned in annual reports. The children went to local schools when they came of age although they were strictly segregated from the local children. At any one time in Kilrush, there were around 150 mothers and children in the home and it was grossly overcrowded during its ten years of existence. At the end of 1928, there were twenty-seven single mothers who had given birth to their first child, while a further six mothers had two or more children.[5]

The known infant mortality rates for the Nurseries spell out clearly the grim regime of the Sisters of Mercy. While national mortality rates were 6–7% year on year in the 1920s, the rates in Kilrush were 'extraordinarily high and at any one time the death rates were between 23 and 61%'.[6] From what limited information is available, it is estimated that 700–800 women and girls passed through Kilrush and around 40–50% of the babies died, suggesting that more than 300 babies died in the Nurseries. There is still considerable confusion about where the babies were buried because this subject was never mentioned at the time. Nobody cared about them while they lived, so their deaths and burials were unworthy of any attention whatsoever. There is a quiet corner of the grounds of the former County Hospital that has been identified as an Angels' Plot for stillborn babies, directly across the road from the site of the former home. The widely held local belief is that this plot was used for babies from the Kilrush Home.[7] It is possible that some may be buried there, as was the practice in Tuam, which had its own Angels' Plot.

Kilrush closed in early 1932 and Fitzgerald-Kenney noted its closure in her annual report in the 1933 *LGR,* where she states that all remaining children were transferred to 'Shan Ross Abbey' [*sic*].[8] The Kilrush Home was demolished in 1936.

Bessboro Mother and Baby Home

The Sacred Heart nuns who had taken over the world's first Catholic model of a Mother and Baby Home back in 1891 arrived in Cork in Ireland in 1922 to open a similar institution. Michael Sugrue, originally from County Kerry, had emigrated as a young man to London. A prosperous businessman, he wholeheartedly supported St. Pelagia's Home, run by the Sacred Hearts in London. Sugrue received a letter from his cousin Mrs Neville in Cork, who convinced him there was dire need of a Mother and Baby Home in Cork. Sugrue approached Cardinal Francis Bourne of the Westminster Diocese, which immediately purchased a Georgian estate house, farm buildings and 210 acres of land in Bessboro, Co. Cork, on the edge of the city. Owing to the semi-forced emigration of many Protestant and Quaker landowners before and during the War of Independence and the bitter civil war that followed, property prices in Ireland were low and Bessboro was purchased for the bargain-basement price of £800.[9] According to the Sacred Hearts' official biography, Bessboro was opened on 1 February 1922 and the nuns and the inmates 'laboured together in harmony' in the fields to feed themselves.[10] Strangely, according to the Sacred Hearts themselves, Bessboro accepted children from the local workhouse when it opened and did not become a Mother and Baby Home until 1924 when it was approved by the government as an 'extern institution'. That meant it could be subcontracted by Local Authorities and County Councils as a home for 'first offenders'. It was the second-biggest in terms of numbers of all the homes after Pelletstown/St. Patrick's, and was the last to officially de-list as a home in 1996, although it continued as the Bessboro 'Care Centre'. Although currently on the market, it remains open at the time of writing with a gentler image as a 'refuge', and two single mothers sat their Leaving Certificates in Bessboro as late as 2009.[11]

At the outset, Bessboro did not have a maternity unit and, in common with Pelletstown, all the pregnant girls were sent to a local maternity hospital – the District Hospital in Cork, now called St. Finbarr's – a couple of weeks before they were due to give birth. They returned with their babies to Bessboro soon after. However, in 1933, according to the *LGR* for that year, the nuns received an Irish Hospitals' Sweepstake grant of £13,600 to convert the old stables into a maternity wing where all future births would take place, without doctors or painkillers. At least 3 Bessboro residents who gave birth to babies in the 1920s stayed for at least 10 years and became known as the 'old girls'. Similar stories have emerged from other homes and it appears that many of them never left.

Strangely enough, the figure for the Sweepstakes grants in the *LRG* is incomplete according to the official Sweepstakes book. Their official figure is that Bessboro received £26,605 for 'capital grants'. There is surely an innocent explanation for the discrepancy of precisely £8,000 (€640,000 at 2016 values).[12] £1,500 of the total (€120,000 at 2016 values) was granted to equip the maternity unit. However, June Goulding, who was a midwife in Bessboro in 1951, was adamant that there was no medical equipment in the maternity room except a bed with stirrups and a small medical cabinet containing a needle and surgical thread. Multiple testimonies from later years confirm Goulding was correct. From 1934, all births took place in Bessboro. In emergency cases, an ambulance was called, but this was very rare.

In the beginning, the nuns hired a minimal number of farm labourers locally, but the whole idea of purchasing the farmland with the house was that the residents could be used as free labour. The girls did the bulk of the farm work and they also scrubbed and cleaned the home and convent. Bessboro had its own laundry where all the washing for the home and convent was done by hand, and also had its own bakery. It later opened a farm shop where the top-quality produce was sold at full commercial value while the residents were fed on the substandard leftovers. The hard labour and the second-rate food were part of the punishment. The *LRG* for 1928/29, page 113, records that:

> This Home was opened in 1922 and is intended primarily for young mothers who have fallen for the first time and who are likely to be influenced towards a useful and respectable life. In the Home, they are trained in domestic work, cookery, needlework, dairy work, poultry keeping and gardening and instructed in their religion. After a period of training each is provided with a suitable situation and put in the way of self-support and the children are boarded out with reliable foster mothers. The rate of maintenance is three shillings a day for mother and child, but if the child dies there is no charge.
>
> There were 75 mothers resident on the 1 January 1928. During the following year 24 were admitted and 34 discharged, leaving 65 in residence at the end of the year. The number of children in the Home on 31 December 1928, was 64. The boards of public assistance responsible for maintenance were: South Cork, 40: Kilkenny, 11: Waterford, 8: Tipperary, N.R., 5, and Kerry, 1.

When the Interdepartmental Report was released in 2014 as a 'scoping exercise' into the Mother and Baby Homes after the Tuam 800 story broke, many commentators were surprised at the apparently low figure of 5,912 for births in Bessboro. However, the figure was missing the many hundreds born in St. Finbarr's for at least ten years during the 1920s and early 1930s as well as hundreds, if not thousands, of stillbirths over its lifetime. And, in 1986, following official pressure in the mid-1980s, Bessboro agreed to stop facilitating births in the home and all subsequent births took place once again in St. Finbarr's. For many years, this author has maintained that the final number of girls and women who went through the doors of Bessboro was between 8,000 and 10,000 and nothing to date has undermined that figure.

The nuns designated a small, anonymous area near their new home as a place for burying babies without coffins, markers or distinct graves. Although they did at one stage maintain a death register, they never kept any specific book or account of exactly who was buried there. The 'Angels' Plot' was neglected by the nuns, but when international attention focused on Bessboro after the Tuam 800 story exploded in May 2014, the nuns paid to have the plot turned into a twee memorial garden. For many years, urban legends among the survivor community maintained that over 2,000 babies were buried there. It is difficult to estimate the number but it is certainly well over 1,000 and probably more than 1,500. When stillbirths are included, that figure may exceed 2,000. Bessboro's on-site Angels' Plot is the largest of any of the homes.

According to one of the *LGRs*, thirty babies died between the years 1933 and 1935 in Bessboro. More than half of that total was due to 'marasmus', emaciation due to malnutrition. In later years there are records of well over one hundred babies a year dying. We shall return to Bessboro to compare conditions there in the late 1930s with its sister home in Castlepollard.

Tuam Mother and Baby Home (aka The Home)

The Mother and Baby Home in Tuam, Co. Galway, opened in 1926. Tuam was a converted workhouse owned and financed by the Poor Law Guardians and the local authority, which invited the Bon Secours nuns to run and administer Tuam on their behalf. According to the Interdepartmental Report of 2014, there were 1,101 births included in the records of the General Registers Office during the home's lifetime. This figure is so low because, once again, it does not reflect the fact that Tuam did not have its own maternity unit in the early years. There were three 'old girls' who gave birth in Tuam and stayed there for the rest of their lives.[13]

A maternity hospital was approved for Tuam in 1934 at a cost of £1,745 to the public purse. Overall, Tuam received £3,830 (over €300,000 at 2016 values) in Sweepstakes grants. Tuam was also used as an overflow by the local county home, so occasionally women with their children were sent there and stayed for months and even years, much as they had lived in the old workhouses now rebranded as county homes.

The following year, in 1935, it was reported that Tuam held 31 mothers and 191 children at the end of March, reflecting its status as a holding centre as much as a Mother and Baby Home. It is interesting to note what happened during the year when 113 mothers were released. Sixty returned to their families, forty were sent to positions, which undoubtedly meant menial jobs as domestic servants or to farm work; three were married. Of the sixty-six children who were discharged, only seventeen left with their mothers, while almost twice that number, thirty-two, were boarded out. The rest went either to relatives or what were referred to as 'suitable institutions'. The missing numbers, which are not specified, are the children who died.

The *LGRs* mention Tuam year after year and provide useful statistics but the numbers of children who died are notably absent during the whole of the 1930s, with the exception of 1933/34. That year shows 120 admissions to Tuam and that forty-two babies died. Any mortality rate extracted from these figures would be only a rough guide to the real figure but that rate is believed to be 35%. The omission of the numbers of deaths in the homes during the 1930s is actually divided in two. Tuam and Pelletstown facts and figures omit deaths during the 1930s while the three Sacred Heart homes have their deaths published year after year. Clearly someone did not want the government to be embarrassed so details of the deaths in the public homes were surpressed, while revealing the private homes' mortality rates for all to see. Tuam was similar to Bethany in that the nuns did not embrace legal adoption after 1952. Before that time, many of the babies born in the home stayed until they were 7 or 8 when they were transferred to industrial schools. After 1952, many children were still boarded out or sent to industrial schools, despite the availability of waiting families who wanted to adopt children. An official report about Tuam and Bessboro from 2012 was suppressed but unearthed by Conall Ó Fátharta in the *Irish Examiner*. It revealed a suspicion that the nuns were faking deaths and illegally selling the babies abroad.

There have been several first-hand accounts from Tuam that surfaced after the Tuam 800 story in May 2014. Conditions were grim and the buildings were old and decrepit. Overall, Tuam easily qualifies as one of the worst Mother and Baby Homes. The home closed in 1961 and is included in the Inquiry into Mother and Baby Homes.

Fermoy Nurseries

The *LGRs* mention the 'Nurseries' in Fermoy, Co. Cork, in the late 1920s and early 1930s but practically nothing is known about exactly what type of institution it was or how it functioned. It is noteworthy that Kilrush Mother and Baby Home was also referred to as the 'Nurseries' but, other than mentions in the *LGRs,* nothing is known about the Fermoy Nurseries except that it was used to hold unaccompanied babies. It is unknown if it accommodated single mothers in another part of the building. Numbers are impossible to estimate.

The Regina Coeli Hostel

Frank Duff is one of the most interesting and in some ways the most radical individual in the story of Ireland's treatment of single mothers and their babies. In him, the most vulnerable in Irish society had a rare champion who saved thousands of mothers and children from disaster.

Duff was born into a middle-class family and attended Blackrock College, a private school on the southside of Dublin. He joined the civil service in 1908 where he served with distinction until he left in 1934. Duff was a devout Catholic and genuine Christian in the charitable sense of the word. He firmly believed it was his duty as a Christian to actively help his fellow human beings. He was never an 'armchair activist' but a man of energy and action who devoted his life to the betterment of others. He was not without his flaws and could be deeply stubborn. In later life, he lost his hearing and when arguing would state his position and then pointedly turn off his hearing-aid. Duff was a velvet radical at a time when very few people dared to oppose the official policies of the Catholic Church.

Duff founded the Legion of Mary in 1921 as a lay Catholic organisation, and membership involved meeting up and saying prayers before going out to visit the most marginalised and forgotten in society. His legionnaires visited people who were sick, lonely and desperate alongside providing support for juvenile offenders and former prisoners whom they assisted in rebuilding their lives. The Legion is currently the largest international organisation ever founded in Ireland and boasts an astounding four million active members and another ten million auxiliary members around the world.

As discussed earlier, the north and south Dublin Unions merged in 1918 and the northside workhouse was closed and abandoned for a while. It was situated in north-inner-city Dublin just south of what is now the Broadstone bus depot. During the War of Independence, the British government managed to find a single solution to two of its problems, just as they had rid themselves of countless tens of thousands of orphans and bastards to the frontiers of the Empire, to conveniently populate it with white Christian 'stock'. Now it found itself overrun with First World War veterans who were suffering from shellshock (an early term for post-traumatic stress disorder), and a strange assortment of warmongers who simply missed the violence and military life. Ragtag former soldiers were recruited into an ill-disciplined army force and shipped off to Ireland. They proceeded to drink heavily, run amuck and terrorise the countryside by taking pot-shots at men, women and children working in the fields. The 'Black and Tans' as they were known, because of their uniforms, which consisted of military surplus, took possession of the former northside workhouse and used it as their headquarters and barracks. After the Treaty, the Black and Tans withdrew and once again the old workhouse was left derelict.

Enter Frank Duff. He persuaded the authorities to give him part of the workhouse as accommodation for homeless men and it opened in 1927 as the 'Morning Star' hostel. The narrow road leading up to the entrance was renamed 'Morning Star Avenue' and Duff later moved his mother into a house beside the hostel which had been the residence of the workhouse doctors.

On 5 October 1930, a segregated section of the former workhouse was opened for women and named Regina Coeli. At this time, around 70% of institutionalised single mothers were still in workhouses around the country and the rest were in Mother and Baby Homes. Duff's hostel was opened as a counterpart to the adjoining Morning Star but while the first women who entered the hostel were homeless, word quickly spread that Regina would admit single pregnant girls and single mothers with children. While Britain saw several organisations founded in the twenty years from 1900 to 1920 to represent and assist single mothers, Ireland would have to wait another fifty years before 'Cherish' was founded by single mothers to lobby for official recognition and support. Yet in 1930, when practically no one would defend single mothers for fear of being labelled a supporter of sin, here was a devout Catholic, famously obedient to the Church, opening a hostel that admitted single mothers and supported them in keeping and rearing their babies. Regina very quickly became a hostel exclusively for single mothers. It remains a testament to the depth of Duff's compassion that it housed and supported single mothers and illegitimate children when the rest of society disowned them and imprisoned them in institutions.

The buildings of the old North Union Workhouse were dilapidated and damp when Duff took possession. The women and their children slept in the large dormitories without any privacy and an open turf fire burned for most of the day as the only source of heat and cooking facilities. It was at times overrun with vermin and lice; bed-bugs and illness were rampant. But, for all its failings, it was the only refuge in Ireland for single mothers and was a place where they were treated with respect and dignity by the volunteer staff. It was an oasis in a country that despised single mothers and their 'bastards' and Duff was a saviour and saint to the residents of Regina.

The hostel was chronically underfunded from the start and the buildings were in need of constant maintenance but they muddled through. It was run by 'indoor sisters', voluntary members of the Legion of Mary who opted to live in the hostel for room and board. They were called 'Sister' by the residents, although they were not nuns or qualified nurses. The residents had to pay a nominal sum to stay but Regina would accept bottles or jam jars if a deposit could be redeemed. Duff and the staff did their best to brighten up the gloomy dormitories with limited funds or success. Regina was associated with the Coombe Maternity Hospital and, to a lesser extent, the Rotunda Maternity Hospital. Because it was unique in being the only refuge for single mothers, the dormitories were soon overcrowded. At one point, it held 107 mothers and 150 children. Even the 'lowest-of-the-low' repeat offenders were welcomed at Regina and treated with respect.

Some of the mothers were known as 'care mothers' who remained in the hostel to mind the children during the day. The other women went out to work in local businesses. Duff formed a network of business people to employ the women, mainly as waitresses and domestic help. When they were old enough, the children went out to local schools and Duff insisted that they were properly dressed and had decent schoolbooks so they would not be targeted or humiliated by the other children. Mothers and children had to leave when the child reached 12 years of age.

Many senior Church and State figures visited Regina and were unanimously generous in their praise of the hostel and Duff. There were sporadic donations from Church and State funds from 1935 onwards. Regina also received Irish Hospitals' Sweepstake grants totalling £10,830 for 'improvements' but mainly depended on charity, raffles and other fundraising events to acquire desperately needed funds to supplement the meagre contributions of the mothers from their day jobs.

A sister hostel to Regina opened briefly in Athlone and there was a short-lived attempt to open branches in Waterford and Belfast but only the Dublin Regina lasted. It is still open today and provides shelter and dignity to many vulnerable women on the margins of society.

We shall return to Regina in the 1940s when its mortality rates among children were at times as high as the worst Mother and Baby Homes. Despite its good intentions, hundreds of children died in Regina.

Sean Ross Abbey

In 1927, Mother Laurence Daly from Skeyne, Co. Westmeath, was elected the new Mother Superior General of the Congregation of the Sacred Hearts. She was a dynamic character and a brilliant administrator and is remembered with great pride to this day for opening one institution per year over her fourteen-year term of office. Two of those were Mother and Baby Homes in Ireland but were radically different because one was in her native Westmeath and was the order's prestige home.

Her first purchase in 1930 was Convilla House in Roscrea, Co. Tipperary, where the owner, Count John O'Byrne, had confided to a local priest that he might be forced to sell. Word got back to Daly because it was known that she was searching Ireland for an estate house with land. The Sacred Hearts, always eager for a good deal, purchased the Georgian manor with four cottages and 600 acres of pasture and forestry land with a river running through it.[14] The nuns renamed it 'Sean Ross Abbey' and it was approved as an 'extern institution' by the Minister for Local Government and certified for 152 mothers and 200 babies and children. Daly decided, unlike in Bessboro, to rent out the 600 acres and created workshops where various types of religious paraphernalia were produced for commercial sale. Some acres around the home were retained for basic food crops. There is some unconfirmed anecdotal evidence that at one point they produced children's coffins, for commercial sale rather than for the babies who died in Sean Ross. The nuns installed a commercial laundry that took in outside work for payment just as the Magdalene Laundries did. Unfortunately, this common feature has led to Sean Ross being designated a Magdalene Laundry by many commentators, but it was not. It was exclusively for single pregnant women and mothers.

Over the years, Sean Ross repeatedly applied for Sweepstakes grants and received a total of £44,063 (over €3.5 million at 2016 values).[15] The nuns hired the Dublin architect and builder T.J. Cullen to erect a chapel.

From the very start Sean Ross was one of the worst of the nine homes. The irrefutable evidence is in the infant mortality rate for its first year. There were 120 babies born and 60 who died. The mortality rates were available for several years in the *LGRs* of the 1930s and remained very high for a further twenty years before showing any signs of improvement. They deserve to be known far and wide, especially in Chigwell in Essex where the Sacred Hearts have been headquartered in a lavish period house they purchased in 1895 for £5,000. We shall return to Sean Ross in the late 1930s to compare conditions with their new sister home in Castlepollard.

Like their other home in Bessboro, Sean Ross had its own Angels' Plot. Private research carried out by members of Adoption Rights Now, and published in a report into adoption that focused on the three Sacred Heart homes, identified 800 registered deaths between 1930 and 1950. The final figure for the Angels' Plot is almost certainly around 1,000 as it operated for another twenty years albeit with far lower mortality rates due to changes in conditions after 1950. The stillbirths push the figure considerably higher. We shall return to this home and examine conditions and funding throughout its lifetime until it closed in 1969.

CHAPTER 4

Holy Catholic Ireland: A New Model

After Sean Ross Abbey, another three homes opened but they were all very different from their predecessors, as the rapid expansion of the network of private and lucrative nursing homes led to the last three homes responding to a perceived need by the upper and middle classes for a better quality of care for their pregnant daughters. Two of these homes, St. Gerard's and Dunboyne, were effectively private fee-paying homes, while Castlepollard was a mix of public and private patients.

Private Nursing Homes and Illegal Adoptions

About 300 maternity homes were registered under the 1934 Registration of Maternity Homes Act during its legal lifetime. Most of them were small nursing homes, usually in semi-converted Victorian and Edwardian red-brick houses of two and three storeys over basements. Some of them – but not all – accepted single pregnant women among their clients while a minority specialised in single mothers only. They were usually run by midwives or nurses.

The private nursing homes were the ultra-secret preserve of the wealthy and upper classes of the day who discreetly sent their daughters away to make their problems disappear. Many of the nursing homes played hard and fast with the birth registration rules; hundreds and probably thousands of babies were falsely registered as the natural children of married couples who adopted children in a financial transaction. There was an underground 'grey' market in child trafficking among the wealthy who could afford to use the private nursing homes either to hide their daughters' 'shame' or illicitly obtain babies for illegal adoption. Some of them were semi-integrated into the system. There are many records of unwanted babies whom they could not place being transferred to institutions such as Temple Hill, which was always happy to accept babies from any source.

Some nursing homes, such as St. Rita's in Sandford Road, Ranelagh, Dublin 6, owned by the notorious Mary Keating, were well-known for the political and criminal intrigue attached to them. One former Lord Mayor of Dublin and later a TD was closely associated with St. Rita's. The second edition of *Banished Babies* named a 'senior Fianna Fáil politician' from the first edition as former Taoiseach Charles Haughey.[1] A priest was jokingly told by Haughey that 'sure half the children born at St. Rita's were fathered by members of the Dáil'. The stories among the survivors' communities regularly mention senior politicians, and in some cases their wives, who were involved in the adoption agencies. A number of adoptees claim that they are the sons and daughters of senior politicians, including at least one former Taoiseach. Huge sums of money were paid for babies across Dublin where there was a thriving black market from the 1940s into the late 1960s. The nursing homes involved in black-market trafficking did not keep records or, if they did, they were falsified. Although there were criminal investigations, and senior politicians were alerted to the practice in the 1960s, nothing was done and the body politic and An Garda Síochána ignored matters for fear of opening an almighty can of worms that would certainly have attracted the interest of the international media.

Other nursing homes are unknown in the active survivor community let alone to the general public, even though they were bigger and in some cases custom-designed or remodelled as miniature Mother and Baby Homes. In 1938, for example, 'Lowville' at 11 Herbert Avenue, Dublin 4, was rebuilt and redesigned as a Mother and Baby Home by the same architect/builder who had built Sean Ross Abbey's maternity wing and new chapel (1933/35) and Castlepollard Mother and Baby Home and chapel (1937/41).

Theresa Hiney Tinggal, a fierce and effective campaigner for illegal adoptees, has carried out research that showed the reaction of the private nursing homes in the aftermath of a new Health Act, which promised tighter controls over nursing homes, in the early 1970s. Dozens of them closed down overnight, knowing that government inspections would have revealed their former malpractices and led to widespread prosecutions.

From the 1970s onwards, supervised 'flatlets' were opened in the same type of period houses, mostly in south Dublin around Donnybrook. St. Gerard's Mother and Baby Home could just as easily be classed as a large, private nursing home instead of a tiny Mother and Baby Home. The supervised flatlets survived well into the 1990s.

Frances Fitzgerald TD was a former social worker who went into politics. For many years while in opposition, she championed the cause of open adoption records and made passionate speeches in the Dáil about the rights of adoptees. Then Minister Fitzgerald was elected to government and did a U-turn on everything she had ever said. During her term as Minister for Children, illegal adoptions were reclassified as 'falsified birth registrations' and that repulsive and deeply dishonest phrase remains the official line today, in an effort to divert public attention away from the fact that what occurred was in fact human trafficking and slavery. There is no help of any description for the victims and survivors. The policy of the current government is a continuation of a long-standing effort to ignore illegal adoptees and pretend that they do not exist.

Most illegally adopted people in Ireland have no records and no idea where to start searching for answers. They spend their lives searching and get nothing but heartache and sorrow. For those who have never been told that they are adopted, legally or illegally, the situation is worse again, because they are unaware of their medical history. I had to sit in a maternity hospital with my wife when we were expecting our first child and reply to a midwife's request for my medical history that 'I'm adopted'. I still remember her little double-take and shock: I felt embarrassed for her and personally humiliated. Innocent people have died as a result of illegal adoptions or adoptive parents withholding the truth from their children. Those who facilitated or arranged illegal adoptions have pocketed enormous sums of cash and many of them are still alive. The present government has no plans or the political will to deal with the problem for fear of being held liable in the civil courts. As always, Irish citizens' lives and health take second place to financial constraints.

The problems with illegal and with secret adoptions (where the adoption is legal but kept secret from the adoptee) are huge. Thousands of adoptees have discovered when going through old paperwork after their parents' deaths that they are adopted either legally or illegally and the shock is intense and life-changing. These 'Late Discovery Adoptees' around the world are far more common than is generally realised and there are books about the subject and special groups for support. Being told one is adopted at a family funeral or social event by a drunken uncle or cousin is also more common than people realise. Late-discovery adoptees always feel utterly betrayed by their own parents and usually have no chance of resolution or finding out the truth. They spend the remainder of their lives both hating and loving their deceased parents, and the emotional and mental stress has led to breakdowns and decades of suffering.

Tens of thousands of birth certificates have been legally and illegally faked since 1922. In the case of the legally faked certificates, the words 'Birth Certificate' were printed on the top of what was really an Adoption Certificate. Around 100,000 Irish mothers lost their babies to forced adoption or separation since 1922, both legal and illegal. Approximately one in every eight families in Ireland is directly affected and there are hundreds of thousands of such cases in Ireland.

Despite constant lobbying by representative groups, the government, and particularly Minister Zappone, is refusing to recommend that the current Inquiry into Mother and Baby Homes should include all illegal adoptions in its remit. James Reilly, as Minister for Children, initiated a comprehensive Adoption Bill that included considerable acknowledgement but limited help for illegally adopted people, but the Bill is currently a low priority for Minister Zappone and she has stalled at every opportunity to advance it. The official policy is to do nothing and steadfastly ignore the thousands of victims or, as the author Mike Milotte has described it, to 'deny till they die'.

St. Gerard's Mother and Baby Home

St. Gerard's was the smallest of the nine Mother and Baby Homes and the shortest-lived. (St. Gerard Majella is the patron saint of expectant mothers.) It was opened in 1933 by St. Patrick's Guild in a four-storey-over-basement, terraced Georgian house at 39 Mountjoy Square, Dublin 1. Intended to cater for fee-paying private cases and 'select destitute cases', it was approved by the Minister for Local Government and Health for twenty mothers and twelve babies. Little is known of this smallest of the homes as it closed in 1939 after just six years and there are no former residents known to the online or real-world survivor community, as is the case for Kilrush.

From July 1933 to the following March, sixty-one girls were admitted to the home and twenty-seven babies were born in the nearby Rotunda Maternity Hospital. One of the babies died there. Even though St. Gerard's was a terraced house in a busy square, surrounded by flats and tenements, there were ten births in the house and all the babies survived. The Interdepartmental Report in 2014 recorded that a final total of forty-five births were registered in St. Gerard's. Residents stayed on average for six months. They learned the standard array of skills such as sewing, knitting, dressmaking, cooking and domestic chores.

The very low infant mortality rate in St. Gerard's indicates that it was well run, as was to be expected in an exclusive, fee-paying home where wealthy families paid handsomely for their daughters, and for discretion. A bad reputation would have destroyed its ability to remain open. It may emerge as the best of the homes and is being fully investigated by the current Inquiry into Mother and Baby Homes.

Second-Layer Institutions

As the Mother and Baby Homes grew and the county homes created hundreds of babies and children, a network of smaller subsidiary centres developed around the country. These held unaccompanied children who were too old for the homes but too young for industrial schools. Many commentators and writers have classified the industrial schools and Magdalene Laundries as 'tiers' of a vast institutional system. However, most writers were unaware of the Mother and Baby Homes network until the Tuam 800 story broke in May 2014, and the industrial schools and laundries are now viewed as a third tier. In fact, there are four layers that could accommodate any woman or child of any age both before and after the county homes were finally closed in the 1950s or were rebranded to other functions.

The interlocking system began by producing babies to begin the life cycle in the Mother and Baby Homes and, at the other end, the Magdalene Laundries were the privately owned and run fourth tier for adult women over 16 years old. Before the laundries, children were placed in industrial schools. While there are exceptions to all the age rules, including industrial schools taking children as young as 2 or 3, or girls as young as 12 in the laundries, the system generally stuck to the age limits. The problem was that this left a gap between the children who were too old for the homes but too young for the industrial schools.

The unseen second tier of mini institutions for children from a couple of weeks old up to 8 years has been only partly investigated. Many of the old orphanages were examined by the Ryan Inquiry, but the role of the Mother and Baby Homes and two sizable second-tier holding centres escaped attention. It is still a common myth that children in orphanages had no parents: the majority were there because the State had prevented their parents from caring for their own children. Poverty or the death of a single parent was enough to have children and babies placed in 'care'. A sizable number were illegitimate and many of the second-tier places were reserved for them. Children were transferred from Pelletstown when they reached the age of around 4.5 years to two such places: boys and girls to St. Philomena's in Stillorgan/Kilmacud in Co. Dublin, and boys to St. Theresa's in nearby Blackrock. Protestant children were transferred from the Bethany Home to similar placements in Westbank in Greystones and Avoca, both in Co. Wicklow, and Braemar House in Co. Cork among others. Dún Laoghaire and Monkstown in Dublin seem to have been rife with Protestant orphanages of all sizes over the years. The enormous Temple Hill holding centre in Blackrock was an integral part of the network and used as a temporary holding facility by many of the Mother and Baby Homes, private nursing homes, and public as well as private maternity hospitals. Babies stayed from days to weeks to years.

Conditions varied considerably over the years and from one home to the next. In some, particularly Protestant orphanages, children were not moved on and grew up in places like the 'Birdsnest' in York Road, Dún Laoghaire, and 'Westbank' in Co. Wicklow, staying until they were adults in some cases. Catholic orphanages were mostly reserved for middle-class legitimate children of all ages. Some of these children were lucky to find long-term foster placements and had good lives, although many others suffered at the hands of uncaring families who simply wanted the money and free labour.

Times changed and the destinations where children went after their stay in a second-tier institution also changed. In the early days of the State, the children born in the homes generally ended up either in the county homes or industrial schools. These options were principally reserved for poor children with no family support, and illegitimate children fell into that category, albeit at an even lower level. They had miserable lives because they were singled out as an inferior class of human being and were regularly cursed as 'bastards' by the religious in the schools. Many of the 16-year-old girls who left industrial schools were starved of love and attention, making them easy prey for predatory men. Sadly, many of them ended up in the Mother and Baby Homes after quickly becoming pregnant outside marriage, surely a direct result of being ejected at 16 years of age into an alien environment without a shred of sex education and desperate for love after a lifetime of deprivation. Many women were doomed to a lifetime of misery and heartbreak in institutions because, if they became pregnant before marriage a second time, they were transferred from the Mother and Baby Homes directly to whichever Magdalene Laundry needed a new penitent to be punished with years of backbreaking labour. About one in every twenty-five women who entered a Magdalene Laundry was transferred directly from a Mother and Baby Home. The final chapters of *Children of the Poor Clares* (Mavis Arnold and Heather Laskey, 1985) record the heartbreaking testimonies of some of the girls who had been in the industrial school in Cavan and ended up in bad marriages or Mother and Baby Homes.[2]

The Registration of 1934 Maternity Homes Act

When Éamon de Valera came to power in 1932 there were four huge Catholic Mother and Baby Homes and one medium-sized Protestant home, but at least one more was needed so that in future all single mothers could be finally removed from the county homes and hospitals. However, the appalling mortality rates in the homes had finally come to the attention of the Dáil and a Bill was brought forward to regulate not just the Mother and Baby Homes but all private nursing homes, by requiring them to register and keep proper records. The Bill also provided for regular inspections. The Registration of Maternity Homes Act 1934 is like many of the Acts passed in Ireland: a fine piece of legislation if it had been enforced, but it was not. The Church had free rein to do as it pleased and was rarely challenged by State officials and inspectors.

The final responsibility for how the Act was enforced lay with the Cabinet and ultimately with the Taoiseach, but no politician was going to challenge the Church. Whatever internal divisions there were in the Church, they behaved like a fighting family when an outsider intervened: they suddenly forgot their differences and turned on the interfering stranger. It was political suicide for any minister to order his officials to enforce the law to its spirit, let alone its letter, so the reality was that nothing changed. The slaughter of the innocents continued for at least another ten years until something far more powerful motivated the nuns to stop the extensive carnage – cash.

Castlepollard Mother and Baby Home

In September 1934, Mother Superior General Laurence Daly of the Sacred Hearts bought the third and last of their Mother and Baby Homes in Ireland, another large house, this time in Castlepollard, Co. Westmeath. The 15-year-old girl who had left to become a nun in France had returned many years later as the head of a rich and powerful Catholic congregation but, since this was her home territory, Mother Daly did not want to be embarrassed on her own turf. As a result, Castlepollard was radically different from the other big institutional Mother and Baby Homes of the time. It is worth taking a close look at Castlepollard for several reasons.

The original estate house in Castlepollard was the seat of the Pollard family. It was built by Walter Pollard in 1716 with an accompanying jailhouse at the top of the nearby row of farm buildings. The Sacred Hearts bought it with 110 acres of land in September 1934, bringing their total Irish landholdings to over 900 acres. They immediately applied for yet another grant from the Irish Hospitals' Sweepstake and Éamon de Valera's government obliged them with £68,000 (€5.3 million at 2016 values). The cash paid in full for St. Peter's, a three-storey maternity hospital, constructed between 1937 and 1939. Castlepollard was the penultimate Mother and Baby Home, opened in the rush to remove single mothers from the workhouses. One more home was opened twenty years later in 1955 and that was the end of the building phase.

St. Peter's Mother and Baby Home, as Castlepollard was correctly called, was designed and built from 1937 to 1939 by architect T.J. Cullen. Cullen also designed and built the laundry extension at Temple Hill and the Chapel at Sean Ross Abbey. St. Peter's was Cullen's biggest project and it remains the only custom-built Mother and Baby Home of the nine original homes.

St. Peter's is concrete grey and painfully austere. The interior is equally plain and has a grim, institutional feel. It was officially certified for 80 mothers or mothers-to-be, and 125 babies and children. Like many of the other homes, Castlepollard could accommodate an excess of forty-five babies and children without their mothers. While there were slight variations over the years, depending on numbers, the ground floor usually contained the babies' and children's wards. The boys and girls were separated into different wards and kept in cots, approximately eight to sixteen at a time in each room. From the chapel end, the youngest were in the first wards and the babies increased in age along the ground floor. An old red swing set from the time still stands rusting away on the lawn.

Above, on the middle floor, the mothers slept in dormitories, six to ten in a room. Some of the large rooms on these two floors were used for 'mothers only' or 'babies only', depending on the need at any given time. The top floor had two large rooms in the centre of the building overlooking the back, and these were used as the delivery rooms. There was a small midwife's station in between with glass partitions into each room and blinds on the midwife's side. The rest of the rooms on the top floor were 'lying-in' and 'recovery' rooms. Some were also used by private patients as single or dual occupancy rooms. There is a small, standalone building on the back lawn. Officially it was the mattress-washing room. Its unofficial use will be discussed in the section on giving birth at Castlepollard. The canteen was a single-storey extension out the back, known as the 'refectory'. The kitchens and large pantry were also housed there.

The nuns added a medium-sized chapel, St. Joseph's, paying for it themselves at a cost of £11,000. It was also designed and built by Cullen, and has a centrepiece stained-glass window, invariably attributed to the famous Irish stained-glass artist Harry Clarke, but in fact Clarke died in 1931, over ten years before its construction. It is likely that the window was designed and built in the Harry Clarke Studios that Clarke founded with his father and brother. The back of St. Joseph's has a small balcony and there is a confessional box underneath it alongside the baptismal font where over 3,700 newborn babies were baptised.[3]

Mother and Baby Homes must be looked at individually and not solely as part of the 'system'. It is not the case that all homes were the same, even when run by the same order of nuns. A new Mother Superior, with a different attitude to single mothers and their babies and full of new and fresh ideas, could dramatically transform a home for better or worse within months. Each home was the personal fiefdom of the Mother Superiors and this was vividly illustrated during the early years in Castlepollard.

Castlepollard followed the general ethos of the other two Sacred Heart Mother and Baby Homes in that it was also an institution solely for so-called 'first-time offenders'. A girl or woman, who was unmarried and pregnant for a second time, was officially barred from returning but this rule was regularly broken over the years. One vitally important fact about Castlepollard is that it competed for the 'better class' of girl, meaning that it offered private care to wealthy 'patients', as opposed to 'inmates'. The more exclusive private nursing homes had the lucrative middle- and upper-class market sewn up and, while other private Mother and Baby Homes, notably Bessboro and Sean Ross, accepted some 'strictly private' cases, Castlepollard actively chased that market share from the beginning. St. Gerard's was pursuing the same market for a couple of years before Castlepollard and both homes actively competed for their share of that market. The princely sum of £100 would buy several weeks in Castlepollard. The girls had their own private or semi-private rooms on the third floor, although they were also put into the dormitories with the public patients if their parents, who were paying the bill, requested extra punishment. The private patients were technically exempt from work but were pressured to do light housework in the convent.

Castlepollard officially opened on 25 February 1935 when about fifteen sisters arrived from Bessboro to take charge, and they immediately prepared a small 'Angels' Plot' down a laneway past the farm buildings. It was blessed by the local parish priest, Father Joseph Kelly.[4] The plot was surrounded by ten- to twelve-feet-high granite walls, parts of which were already there as the remains of a ruin. The nuns' choice of location for the private cemetery was probably dictated by the fact that it was cheaper to incorporate the old ruin into the new surrounding walls. It was accessed through a small cast-iron gate embedded with a cross. A high wall ran across the interior of the plot with its own door, dividing the plot into two. The front section was for the nuns and the rear section was for the babies and children. A simple white cross, about three feet high, was erected at the very back of the babies' section, identical to crosses in the Angels' Plots at Bessboro and Sean Ross Abbey. The inscription says: 'Pray for the repose of the souls of the Sisters of the Sacred Hearts of Jesus and Mary.' The babies and children who died were buried in shoeboxes, a common enough tradition in Ireland at a time when grinding poverty was the norm. The nuns continued this practice until the home closed in 1971.[5] Local tradition has it that the workmen who dug the small graves hammered a homemade nail into the granite wall for every baby who was interred. Many of the nails remain in the wall today. The nails were hammered into the front section belonging to the nuns because the workmen had no key to open the permanently locked rear section once a baby had been buried.

The generous Sweepstakes grant which paid for St. Peter's Hospital in full, and the lure of easy money from wealthy, private patients, meant that Castlepollard was radically different from the other two Sacred Heart homes. The infant mortality rates throughout the entire lifetime of Castlepollard were dramatically lower than in the other large homes, particularly the other two Sacred Heart Homes. The Congregation of the Sacred Hearts of Jesus and Mary were more than capable of running a maternity hospital properly and of improving standards in their three Mother and Baby Homes. Before you read the tables below, take a silent moment to remember that these are not just numbers or evidence, they are human beings – the most innocent and vulnerable Irish citizens, some of whom should be alive today.

Table 1 below from just before Castlepollard opened is an indication of how steady the high mortality rates were in the homes at different ends of the country. These figures are for 'admissions', as opposed to births.

Table 1.

Institution	Admissions	Deaths	Mortality Rate
Pelletstown	155	53	34%
Tuam	120	42	35%
Bessboro	64	25	39%
Sean Ross Abbey	160	60	37%

Table 2.

ADMISSIONS, ETC.	Besboro' Home	Sean Ross Abbey	Manor House, Castle-pollard
Admissions—			
Number of expectant mothers ..	109	176	60
,,　　,, mothers with children	6	12	12
Births	96	157	38
Discharges—			
Number of mothers with children	29	80	10
,,　　,, mothers without children	81	102	5
,,　　,, children boarded out by local authorities	7	31	—
,,　　,, children adopted ..	15	12	3
,,　　,, children placed at nurse by mothers ..	1	80	1
,,　　,, children placed at nurse through a Rescue Society	—	3	2
Deaths—			
Number of mothers	—	—	—
,,　　,, children	25	54	4
Number in Institutions on the 31st March, 1936—			
Mothers	127	139	51
Children	79	129	33

Local Government Report 1935/36, p. 162. Comparative facts and figures for the three Sacred Heart Mother and Baby Homes.

Table 3.

Year	Bessboro, Cork			Sean Ross Abbey			Castlepollard		
	Births	Deaths	Mortality	Births	Deaths	Mortality	Births	Deaths	Mortality
1935/36	96	25	26%	157	54	34.4%	38	4	10.5%
1936/37	100	22	22%	120	60	50%	66	10	15.1%
1937/38	92	30	32.6%	138	54	39.1%	75	3	4%
1938/39	81	38	46.9%	148	27	18.2%	73	5	6.8%
1939/40	99	17	17.1%	143	19	13.2%	88	13	14.7%
1940/41	87	38	43.6%	162	58	35.8%	117	34	29%
Average			31.36%			31.78%			13.35%

Extracts and comparison of the three Sacred Heart Mother and Baby Homes from the sections of the *LGRs* on 'unmarried mothers' 1935 to 1941.[6]

The contrast between Castlepollard and the two other Sacred Heart Homes over six years proves beyond any shadow of doubt that the deaths of hundreds, and possibly thousands, of babies and children were entirely avoidable in Bessboro and Sean Ross Abbey, and most of the other homes too. If there is a single 'smoking gun' piece of evidence that destroys all the excuses the nuns make, such as underfunding, lack of understanding of hygiene, and victim blaming, then the Castlepollard mortality rates are that evidence. The tables above also shows that Tuam and Pelletstown were every bit as bad as Sean Ross and Bessboro.

However, while Castlepollard was considerably better than its two sister homes, it was still a cruel and harsh institution. There was little or no respect for mothers and babies even when their families had paid huge sums for extra care and discretion. For the first five years, infant mortality rates were still over twice the national average but in comparison to the other five main Mother and Baby Homes – Sean Ross Abbey, Bessboro, Bethany, Tuam and Pelletstown/St. Patrick's – Castlepollard was certainly the least horrific.[7]

All the babies were baptised within days of their birth in the baptismal font in St. Joseph's Chapel. This was common in all the homes: babies were baptised as soon as possible. I was born in Castlepollard on 4 December and a baby girl Ann was born two days later. My crib mate Ann and I were baptised together on 7 December 1964. The standard practice among the Sacred Hearts and all the homes was to wait until a couple of days after the birth, remove the newborn babies from the wards, and bring them to the chapel or a local church. Local priests baptised the baby or several babies at a time. Godparents were sometimes listed in accordance with the wishes of the natural mothers, even though they were not present. Most of the time the people named were unaware that they were formally the godparents of a baby. At times, the nuns simply listed random people or other natural mothers as the godparents.

There were 3,763 live babies born in Castlepollard and their births were officially registered in the General Registry Office or one of its local branches.[8] However, under the Registration of Maternity Homes Act 1934, stillbirths were simply notified to the local authorities where the natural mother originated. This was done by registered letter but most of these letters have been lost or have deteriorated in County Council archives around the country. Many of these babies, who never had a chance at life, have no record of their existence other than in the Mother and Baby Home ledgers and, even then, were rarely named.

The small chapel in Castlepollard saw at least fifteen marriages over its thirty-six-year operation. If a boyfriend showed up, Reverend Mother Rosamund McCarty, one of the last Mother Superiors in Castlepollard, would famously declare 'No time like the present!' and send for an available priest to marry the couple at once. After a cup of tea and a slice of cake, the newlyweds were shown the door.

Mother Superior General Laurence Daly was unable to visit Castlepollard in the years before her death owning to wartime travel restrictions, her poor health and advanced age, but without her direct input, standards slipped quickly in Castlepollard. Infant mortality rates from 1938 to 1941, the year of Daly's death, literally doubled every year thereafter. They increased from just below 7% to almost 15% and finally a shocking 29% in the year Daly died, by far the worst year ever in

Castlepollard. Shortages and rationing because of the war must have played a role but the same can be said of Bessboro and Sean Ross Abbey. As mortality rates went up, Castlepollard's reputation went down. On her deathbed, Daly made a farewell speech to a gathering of her senior sisters, and included the following advice: 'Be loyal to your community. Whenever you hear anyone speaking ill of it, have no respect for them or what they say.'[9]

Another Irish nun, Antonia (originally Mary) Phillips from Kilmuckridge, Co. Wexford, replaced Daly as Mother Superior General. She ruled for twenty-two years, until 1963, before stepping down. During her time, the Sacred Hearts expanded to California and Zimbabwe, and agreed to multiple vaccine trials in their three Irish Mother and Baby Homes.[10]

Castlepollard closed on St. Patrick's Day 1971 and was sold to the Midlands Health Board as a residential centre for adults and children with severe learning difficulties, and patients were moved in from nearby St. Loman's in Mullingar. This centre closed in 2015 after being run down over several years in favour of care in the community. Castlepollard is currently empty and boarded up. All three buildings are protected as listed buildings of historic interest.

The Angels' Plot is open to the public. Research by the Castlepollard group was published in 2017 with a list of the names of the babies, children and mothers who died there. Five mothers died and one is buried in the plot. At least 198 babies died and Freedom of Information requests show that there are a further 77 stillbirths recorded in the ledgers. However, it seems the nuns either kept no ledgers for twelve of the first sixteen years or they existed but are now missing. There are certainly a considerable number of stillbirths now completely missing. In total there are over 300 bodies buried in Castlepollard. A nun's death is also recorded in the home and two nuns are buried in the front section of the plot. Castlepollard is fully included in the current Inquiry into Mother and Baby Homes.

CHAPTER 5

Behind the High Walls: Daily Life in the Homes

As time passes, our ability to look more closely at the homes improves by degrees. The unvarying similarity of the personal testimonies from numerous women who were in the homes is undeniable. These accounts added to the infant mortality rates for the homes provide indisputable proof of the daily routine and conditions, especially regarding diet, medical personnel and equipment.

The road to the homes began with a girl or woman, with an average age of 19 or 20, tearfully confessing her 'condition' to her mother. Such matters were considered 'women's business' and in many cases the girls' fathers were not informed, or feigned ignorance. The first and preferable solution was to bring the guilty father of the crisis pregnancy to a church to be married as soon as possible. So-called 'shotgun weddings' were common. Other options included the girl's parents pretending that the baby was theirs.

If those preferences were ruled out, then the girl's mother, or occasionally both parents, would speak to their local priest or doctor. Sometimes they approached a relative who was a member of a religious order. Doctors would refer families to the local priest. The Catholic priests of Ireland were the primary entry point to the system and all of them had the address (and later phone numbers) of a Mother and Baby Home. The priests wrote to or phoned the home and made the necessary arrangements. Sometimes the priest would become personally involved and drive the pregnant girl, and sometimes her mother, to the chosen home. The priest and parents together would invent a cover story to explain the girl's sudden absence. Nine out of ten stories involved a sudden and lucrative job offer in England.

Girls as young as 13 or 14, who had never spent a night away from home, were banished to an unknown future and sent to giant, grey institutions in remote locations. In many cases this was the last time a girl would see her parents and family. Thousands of girls were instructed to leave and never return after 'shaming the family's good name'. Others were told not to even think of returning with their 'bastards' but to return without the baby. On rare occasions, older girls who showed genuine remorse and could be trusted were dispatched to a major city or town clutching their battered, cardboard suitcases or just an old bag with a few clothes.

Nuns or trusted girls from the homes were sent in plain clothes to meet unaccompanied girls off the bus. This was to ensure that the girls did not stay on the bus and possibly vanish to England. Many former residents have commented on bus drivers' attitudes; some were cold and aloof while others were sympathetic, offering wan smiles and wishing the girls good luck. All the girls and women carried a letter of reference from their local parish priest or occasionally from a relative in a religious order. Their ages ranged from at least 12, and possibly 11 in one case, and there were also women in their thirties and very occasionally in their forties, but, most of the women in the homes were aged a few years either side of 20.

The fathers of the babies were sometimes decent men or boys who were prevented by their families from marrying their pregnant girlfriends because of class and age differences. Many, however, were liars, cowards, rapists, a girl's own father, brother, neighbour or married man; some were priests or even bishops. The Irish State, the Catholic Church and society allowed the fathers, almost without exception, to suffer no consequences of their exploitative actions. The age of consent varied slightly in Ireland over the years but there is not one single story anywhere about a proper Garda investigation into numerous clear cases of statutory rape. Even allowing for the fact that the nuns always blamed the girls for their pregnancies and ignored stories of rape as an 'excuse', underage sex was a serious crime and yet the nuns withheld that information from the Gardaí.

On arrival in the home, the pregnant girls were 'processed'. Details of their lives were recorded in the gargantuan and intimidating ledgers and the rules were explained. Harsh lectures about lust and sin marked the beginning of months and years of verbal abuse and daily preaching. The residents were assigned 'house names', typically after saints. Contrary to popular belief, the names of the fathers were sometimes recorded in the books and files of the Mother and Baby Homes at various times, although this differed from one home to the next and in individual homes over time. In the 1930s, and presumably since independence in 1922, the new arrivals were generally provided with a shapeless uniform made of rough cloth, drawstring underwear and hard clogs. Bras were forbidden. Their hair was clipped short, often roughly, to purge them of their vanity and pride and to ensure they could not escape. The girls were strictly forbidden to speak to one another or form friendships. The 'inmates', as they had become, were systematically underfed and undernourished and forced to do hard work as penance.

Each day commenced between 5 and 6 a.m. The nuns began the daily routine of endless prayers recited out loud by the nuns and girls together. Rosaries were repeated ad nauseum. In Castlepollard during the 1960s, a cheap loudspeaker system was installed throughout St. Peter's to wake the girls so they could begin the daily round of prayers. After washing in cold water, they dressed themselves in their uniforms for the daily Mass. In the chapels they were subjected to regular 'fire and brimstone' sermons from the local priests, with a heavy focus on sins of the flesh and lust. Ingratitude to the nuns was singled out as a terrible and selfish sin. Girls sat at the back of the chapels, separate from the nuns at the front or sides. In Castlepollard, the nuns entered through the corridor from the house and sat in a side area of the church while the girls and women occupied the main section. Girls often fainted at Mass because they were forced to fast from the night before so they could receive Communion. Those who did faint were later punished for their 'disrespect'.

After Mass, the residents were ushered back to the wards for twenty to thirty minutes to feed, wash and change their children. The babies were always in a distressed state after spending the entire night alone in their cots with nothing but the cries of other distraught babies for company. The babies' backs were invariably covered with semi-dried excrement and urine, resulting in severe nappy rash and bedsores.

In many of the homes, the mothers were deliberately kept nearby and could hear their babies screaming all night. This was a planned part of the punishment and torture. When the girls' time with their babies was up, it was straight to breakfast in the refectory. Meals were basic. Breakfast and supper often consisted of just two slices of baked brown bread with a smear of cheap margarine and a mug of lukewarm tea or cocoa: sometimes, a thin porridge or gruel was dished out as breakfast during winter. Dinner, the main meal of the day, was around midday as was customary in the countryside. It was usually a potato or two in a greasy, watery stew with small grisly lumps of mystery meat and vegetables. The best produce from the three homes that also ran farms was sold at commercial rates for profit and any inferior products that were unfit for sale became the girls' dinners. Although the government was paying generously for the care of the residents, the nuns considered them to be unworthy of proper food. In Bessboro, the nuns had their own farm shop yet only 'allowed' the girls and women two eggs a week from their 210-acre farm. The Sacred Hearts sold top-quality butter and then bought in large tubs of the cheapest margarine they could find for the residents.

The length of time girls and women stayed varied. In the beginning, it was two to three years, but by the 1960s it had fallen to between ten to eighteen months. The nuns' priority was to ensure that sufficient free labour to work the farmland, do the commercial laundry or make religious regalia. Residents were in effect closely supervised slaves, the equivalent of prisoners in a low-to-medium security jail. Before giving birth, they generally worked in the buildings, cleaning, polishing, scrubbing already spotless floors and surfaces in the kitchens, or were assigned to a ward for the day to look after ten to sixteen babies. However, nuns brought their own style to assigning duties and pregnant girls could end up working anywhere.

After giving birth, the work varied according to the different homes and working-class girls were invariably assigned to the farms or the in-house laundries. Sean Ross Abbey had its own commercial laundry. Residents cut the lawns, sometimes as a group, on their knees, working backwards; they were forced to snap each individual blade of grass with their fingernails. They collected fallen trees and branches and cut them with large saws. When the logs had been seasoned, they chopped them into firewood used first to heat the convents and then sometimes the Mother and Baby Homes. They weeded the potato fields, picked fruit and wild berries and made jam, and were occasionally hired out locally, anything to repay the 'debt' they owed for their care. While many stayed an average of two years, there are numerous records that show mothers staying up to five, and on one occasion even six, years. Some women never left. They had their babies who were adopted or fostered out and spent the rest of their lives as unpaid help. They were known as the 'Old Girls'. There is no record of any of the Old Girls being properly paid; they received room and board and occasional pocket money.

After their day's work, residents were again allowed about twenty to thirty minutes to feed, wash and change their babies, or play with their children when they were older. The few hours left before bedtime were used to knit and sew clothes for their children and write letters home. The letters were collected and most of the homes sent them to Britain. The Sacred Hearts owned a hospital in south Wales in the 1950s and 1960s and the letters were stamped there and sent back to Ireland, to maintain the fiction for their extended families that they were working abroad.

Working days were twelve to fourteen hours, six days a week, without change or variety. Sunday was a day of rest, although the nuns made sure that residents were kept busy in some way. Sunday-morning walks around the grounds of the homes were common, with nuns at the front and back of the girls and women to ensure no one escaped. If there was one thing the nuns hated, it was idle residents.

Birthdays were ignored. Christmas was not celebrated in the festive sense but was much the same as the standard Sunday routine. There are reports of the odd Christmas tree in some homes in later years but, in most of them, there were no trees and certainly no presents on the day. There were no holidays of any description. It was a soul-destroying, grey, monotonous grind, day in, day out, with little variation.

When people talk about the appalling conditions in Mother and Baby Homes, they often miss the damage done by both the daily preaching and the low quality and quantity of food. These factors, combined with the forced work, resemble many of the characteristics one would now associate with a modern religious cult. The identical uniforms erased any individuality, and the segregation from the outside world and isolation from one another inside the homes led to fear and extreme vulnerability. Residents were ground down by the hard work and substandard food. The girls were systematically dehumanised and were highly susceptible to the message preached at early-morning Mass by authority figures. Constant verbal humiliation was part of the penance and system of control. Once a week, while still pregnant, the women and girls were forced to line up in front of the midwives who shaved their pubic hair, supposedly for hygienic reasons, in the three Sacred Heart Homes – a further humiliation to break down their personalities.

Nontheless, residents occasionally ran away. Sunday mornings were a favourite time for escape attempts during the walk after Mass. One added incentive was that they were wearing their 'Sunday best' clothes instead of uniforms, which might maintain their cover. Girls who ran away were quickly recaptured by the local Gardaí and returned. The nuns reported the girls for 'stealing' their uniforms or shoes or clogs or anything the nuns had provided as part of their uniform. They used the same excuse when reporting runaways from the Magdalene Laundries. After being returned, they were often beaten, had their heads shaved and were locked into a room on their own and put on bread and water. It was solitary confinement exactly as in the prison system. The local Garda station in Castlepollard was, and still is, across the road from the front entrance to the home.

Lifelong emotional and mental scars were the result of this existence for the vulnerable young women and many never recovered.

Despite all the rules and the strict regime, some of the residents managed to sneak the time and space to chat and make friends, while some of the other girls kept the rules rigidly. The friendships were especially important when their babies and children disappeared forever. There is almost no evidence of these illicit friendships surviving the homes. It appears to have been too painful to maintain contact once they left.

The homes all had different attitudes to doctors. Most never employed doctors or professional nurses and it was only in the 1960s that some were engaged on a part-time basis. A doctor was employed full-time in Pelletstown/St. Patrick's in the 1960s and possibly a little earlier. There is no evidence that one single, properly qualified nurse was ever employed in any of the homes. During its thirty-six years as a maternity hospital, Castlepollard never employed a single doctor or nurse. Initially the nuns employed just one fully qualified midwife at a time, as legally required under the 1934 Registration of Maternity Homes Act. However, at some point in the 1950s, after changes to the quality of care in the homes, some of them employed a second midwife. The midwives were generally in as much fear of the nuns as the residents and most of them quickly adopted the tone or ethos of the home. In common with the nuns, the midwives reacted to how an individual behaved. Submissive and obdient women would be largely left alone, except for verbal abuse. However, any sort of rebellion or standing up for oneself would lead to constant supervision and punishment; 'wilful', 'disobedient' or 'sinful' girls were targeted for closer supervision and the worst jobs.

If a serious problem arose during labour, an outside doctor was called, normally the local GP. If the situation was a matter of life and death, an ambulance was called, or in the very early days, girls in labour were transported to the hospital in the back of a car if one could be found. In the case of Castlepollard, which was in a remote location, Mother Superior is known to have accompanied girls in distress in the back of the local taxi to Dublin. Sometimes an ambulance was called from Dublin, which involved a wait of some two to three hours. All the Mother and Baby Homes were associated with a public maternity hospital; for Castlepollard, it was the Coombe Maternity Hospital, a mile west of Dublin city centre, which received the emergency patients. On occasion, Holles Street National Maternity Hospital was also used. St. Kevin's, on the site of the old workhouse in Dublin's James' Street, was associated with Pelletstown, then renamed St. Patrick's. St. Finbarr's in Cork was Bessboro's partner maternity hospital.

Many inmates were offered 'training' to become qualified nurses. None of the girls and women ever received formal training. It was a cost-saving ruse, allowing the nuns to use them to staff the wards and look after the babies and children during the day rather than employing properly qualified, paediatric nurses.

The treatment of the pregnant girls and women when it came time to give birth was basic and cold. Residents were expected to keep working until the last possible minute and not make a fuss. One of the hardest parts of the ritual punishment during labour was the enforced silence. Any expression of pain was strictly forbidden. At various times, and depending on the different nuns and midwives in charge, girls were often expected to give birth squatting over a stainless-steel bedpan. In later times, especially after the late 1960s and 1970s, the girls were permitted to lie on a bed. The delivery rooms had little or no medical equipment of any description, apart from the stirrups attached to the hospital beds and possibly some forceps. Religious pictures or statues adorned the otherwise bare rooms. There was no pain relief such as gas and air or pain medication available under any circumstances unless the doctor had to be called and he/she prescribed it. Several former residents recall the doctors being as cold and aloof as the nuns. Even when it was necessary, there was no stitching allowed afterwards. That was a luxury they did not deserve.

Girls who screamed during labour were ordered to be quiet, and different homes had different punishments for those who just could not help screaming. In Castlepollard, the Sacred Hearts found a unique solution for the screaming girls; they were removed to the mattress-washing room on the back lawn, where the nuns installed a hospital bed with stirrups and often abandoned terrified girls and women in labour for hours at a time. The building has been nicknamed the 'Screaming Room' by former residents and adoptees.

In all the homes, it was common for the nuns and some of the midwives to wander in and out of the various delivery rooms and berate the patient writhing in silent agony with well-worn phrases such as 'This is your punishment for your sin', 'This will teach you to keep your legs closed', 'Give your pain up to the Lord', 'Your bastard is born in sin', 'Serves you right!' and the seeming favourite of many of the nuns: 'Well? Was the five minutes of pleasure worth all this?'[1] After the birth, babies were sometimes taken away without their mothers ever seeing them, but usually the new mother and her baby went to a lying-in room for a couple of days. Ultimately, everything depended on the whim of the nuns in charge or the rules set down by the Mother Superiors. In private cases, parents who had paid £100 could, to some extent, specify exactly how their daughter was to be treated and whether she might be allowed to see her baby.

Bonding between mothers and their babies was strongly discouraged and they were kept apart as much as possible. New mothers and babies were separated after anything from days to a couple of weeks, depending on the home. The girls were returned to their dormitories while the babies were sent to the wards, where other girls in different uniforms spent long days trying to cope with a roomful of screaming, highly agitated babies. Many adoptees have lifelong difficulties with various parts of their digestive systems, including irritable bowel syndrome, and although no definitive evidence has yet emerged, many blame their medical conditions on their treatment in the so-called wards. One mother who worked in these wards in Castlepollard has gone public about her time assigned there in the mid-1960s when the official policy of the nuns was to move babies onto solid food after only six weeks to prevent mothers bonding with their babies.[2]

Funding and Finances in the Homes

There were two types of Mother and Baby Homes in Ireland and it is important to understand the differences between them. Pelletstown/St. Patrick's in Dublin was the first Mother and Baby Home and it was in *public* ownership. It was overseen by various public or quasi-official local groups over the years. Other homes, including Tuam and Kilrush, were also owned by the State under various names. The public Mother and Baby Homes were all public workhouses that were converted to accommodate single pregnant women and girls. The other type of Mother and Baby Home was *privately* owned and officially termed an 'extern institution'. These were sub-contracted by the government to care for single mothers and their babies. There is much confusion surrounding this arrangement because the government-owned homes were invariably run by nuns: from the outside, both types of home appeared identical. Both were run by nuns and the regime and the ethos of the nuns were similar from one home to the next. The government and officialdom treated them the same.[3]

All three Sacred Heart homes were privately owned by the congregation. Payments were in the form of a weekly capitation grant from the relevant local authority. There were increases in the capitation grants over the years; for example, in the early 1950s, the nuns received £1 per week for a mother and 2/6- (two shillings and sixpence) for a baby/child, to cover the cost of their care.[4]

The Irish Hospitals' Sweepstake funded many of the homes and related organisations, such as St. Patrick's Guild and the Regina Coeli Hostel, received several sizable grants. The total amount allocated to the Mother and Baby Homes and the related groups was over £300,000 (over €23 million at 2016 values). Many of the groups and religious orders dealing with single mothers pursued the grants vigorously. The largest grant went to the Sacred Heart nuns, who received a grant of £68,000 for the full cost of building St. Peter's Hospital in 1937. Their other homes in Bessboro and Sean Ross Abbey received another £67,000. St. Patrick's Guild and the Sacred Heart nuns each received over one-third of the total: over £100,000 (nearly €8 million at 2016 values) and £135,000 (over €10 million at 2016 values) respectively.[5]

The nuns have consistently cited 'underfunding' as an excuse for the poor conditions and high morality rates in their Mother and Baby Homes. However, the weekly amount paid to the nuns for the upkeep of each girl was the approximate equivalent of about half to two-thirds of an average farm labourer's wage.[6] Out of their meagre wages, labourers had to pay for rent, food and clothes for themselves, their wives and several children and send their children to school until at least the age of 12. The nuns, on the other hand, had practically no overheads except electricity bills and a derisory amount for minimal heating for the homes. The 'underfunding' excuse remains one of the Sacred Heart's primary defences alongside the now well-worn list the Catholic Church has perfected, including 'victim blaming' whereby the Church accused those making the accusations of being greedy confidence tricksters. It is now a standard Catholic Church tactic to attack the victim rather than address their issues, although the aggressive questioning is often done by unofficial proxy through lay Catholic organisations such as the 'Catholic League' in the United States.

Apart from State funding and Sweepstakes grants, there were several other sources of income for the nuns, including the leasing of farmland, income from laundries, making religious regalia and farm produce shops.

Even though the taxpayer was paying in full for residents at the homes, the nuns also aggressively solicited donations from the girls' families. The amounts varied depending on the individual family's circumstances but in many cases every penny of the family's savings was used to pay for their daughter's upkeep. It was generally the equivalent of two to three months' wages upwards. After the introduction of legal adoption in 1952, a 'donation' for an adopted baby could amount to several weeks' or months' wages. Many adoptive parents, especially in America, were told inventive tales by the nuns. Adoptive parents were emotionally blackmailed into handing over huge sums of money. Many of the different homes kept lists of easy targets, both at home and abroad, and sent Christmas cards with letters and notes blessing the adoptive parents and then outlining the hardships they had to endure in the name of the Lord. The pounds and dollars flooded in.

The nuns were ruthless in their use of the residents as free labour and made substantial profits as a result. In her book about Bessboro, June Goulding recounts witnessing, with her fiancé who had called to collect her, heavily pregnant girls and women filling in potholes in the driveway, using a fire to heat buckets of hot tar, adding shovelfuls of gravel, and finishing with a hand roller that required three heavily pregnant girls to pull it.[7]

Mike Milotte, author of *Banished Babies*, published an article in the *Sunday Business Post* magazine in September 2012 where he estimated the total sum of money (updated for inflation) that went to the various orders of nuns and adoption agencies involved in the banished babies trade at between $30 and $50 million dollars.[8] Overall the Sacred Heart Sisters dispatched 814 babies, more than any other group, or about 42% of the total, meaning that some $20 to $21 million flowed into the Sacred Heart coffers from the banished babies trade *alone*.[9]

Since Castlepollard was the most 'prestigious' of the three Sacred Heart Homes, it was particularly prolific and banished 278 babies or over 14% of the entire total to America to be adopted. Castlepollard earned a minimum of $4.2 million from the trade and possibly over $7 million in today's money.

In reply to a Dáil question on 27 November 1980, Minister for Justice Gerry Collins stated that the Sacred Heart Adoption Society operating out of Bessboro had received over £39,000 since 1974 and that was only a part of the total.

Two of the three former Mother and Baby Homes belonging to the Sacred Hearts, Bessboro and Sean Ross Abbey, are still occupied by the congregation and continue to provide services directly, or through sub-contractors, to the government. These services include the care and protection of vulnerable woman and children. From 2009 to 2013 in Bessboro, where the Sacred Hearts still operate after ninety-four years, they received about €10 million from the Health Service Executive (HSE). Approximately €5 million of that was for 'Adoption Research Services'.

Irish taxpayers' money formed part of the Sacred Hearts' total income over those same years. This amounted to over £57 million pounds sterling, partly from tax-free sales of some land and buildings around the world, including London and California. There are currently about 130 surviving Sacred Heart nuns and they have a pension fund of over £163 million.[10]

And because the Sacred Hearts and all the other orders are religious orders, their income is, and always was, completely tax-free.[11]

Leaving the Mother and Baby Homes

It was heartbreaking for expectant mothers to leave their homes and families, often never to return. However, a far worse trauma followed when their babies and children were taken from them, either for long-term boarding out before being sent to an industrial school aged anything from 3 or 4 years old until age 8, or for adoption after 1952. There are many records of mothers and children being transferred together to the county homes before they were split up when the child reached 6 or 8 years of age, at which point they were sent to an industrial school until they reached 16 when they were ejected. This was the fate of many of the children born before adoption was properly legalised in 1952. The official policy of separating single mothers and their babies was traumatic, with extreme life-changing consequences for both parent and child.

Adoptions and transfers generally happened with little or no warning. Sometimes mothers returned from their work assignments to be bluntly informed that their baby was gone forever. Mothers were normally called to the office and ordered to return to the wards to prepare their babies by dressing them in their best clothes. They were then instructed to carry them to the front room in the convent. Any protestations were met with a battery of standard responses common to all the homes. Mothers were told to 'Get over it! You knew this day was coming. What else did you expect? How can you possibly look after a child on your own? Isn't your child better off with a good Catholic mother and father? They can give your child a real life where he/she will have a proper and respectable upbringing and not be stigmatised as an illegitimate bastard. This is your punishment for your sins and lust. Now do as you're told!' The children could be any age up to 3 to 5 years old and usually sensed something frightening was happening. The traumatic final journey of mother and baby together was an integral part of the punishment and was nicknamed the 'walk of shame'. It was a deliberately cruel finale to the homes' regimes, a practice common to many of the other Mother and Baby Homes, but particularly favoured by the Sisters of the Sacred Hearts.

In Castlepollard, mothers would often run back into St. Peter's to one of the bathrooms on the end of the second-floor corridor. There they clambered onto a radiator and peered out the high window through their tears to watch a car leaving with their baby. The marks on the radiator from their shoes were visible up to as late as 2017. Most mothers never saw their children again.

Once the baby was gone, arrangements were made to release the women and girls as soon as possible. Sometimes their families would accept them back but, if not, the nuns arranged menial jobs as domestic servants or farm girls. Occasionally they were sent to England and Wales to work as staff in the order's other premises. The nuns carefully selected hardworking women and girls whom they had effectively institutionalised, and made docile and obedient. They received little more than room and board and pocket money.

On very rare occasions, parents or family relatives came and paid to have their daughter or niece released with her baby, promising to rear the baby as their own. The sum paid to the nuns varied, depending on how long the resident had been in the home. The nuns generally charged a 'release' fee of approximately one pound per week to cover their 'loss of earnings'.

Before leaving, women were sternly warned never to try and trace their children. They were told it was illegal to search and they could go to jail and end up being written about in the newspapers. They were told it was a mortal sin and they would go straight to hell if they had any sort of relationship with their son or daughter, even if their grown children were the ones who initiated contact. They were often told their children had gone to America when they had not. Some women who phoned or wrote or went back to the home were told that their children had died when they were in fact still alive and well.

Sadly, because of the threats of the nuns and a deep sense of shame, the friendships formed in the homes rarely continued in the outside world, as previously stated. There are several sad stories of old friends from the homes recognising each other, months or many years later, and turning away to continue their solitary paths of silence and isolation.

Today, the active adoption and survivor community is online and almost entirely based on Facebook. In many of the twenty or so groups there, natural mothers have met up and become good friends. In the groups that include both adoptees and mothers together, all the survivors have formed close bonds of friendship and mutual support, both online and in the real world.

The Records from the Homes

When Castlepollard was sold to the Midlands Health Board in 1971, the nuns burned much of the paperwork and letters that had built up over thirty-six years. No one knows if the bonfire included the financial records but it is known that they used an outside firm of accountants to manage their cash. A similar bonfire has been confirmed at Sean

Ross Abbey when it was closed as a Mother and Baby Home in 1969. While the main ledgers and antenatal notes were spared along with the adoption files, it seems that everything else was burned. What was left from Castlepollard and Sean Ross Abbey was sent to Bessboro to join the records there. There are currently no reports or records of a similar bonfire at Bessboro or any other home but it is likely that something similar occured. Pelletstown/St. Patrick's files were handed over to the government, as were Dunboyne's. We shall return to the records from the major homes later to see what transpired when it was time to hand them over to the government, as legally required under the Registration of Maternity Homes Act 1934.

The Castlepollard and Bessboro files have been located and investigated by this author and the journalist Conall Ó Fátharta in the *Irish Examiner* respectively. What is left of the Castlepollard files is in reasonable to very good condition. However, all the entries outside of the main ledgers were originally recorded in pencil and some are badly faded so they are extremely difficult, if not impossible, to read, including all the antenatal notes. The files from the homes are scattered around the country: the Bessboro files are in the custody of Social Services in Cork while the Sean Ross records are in Waterford. Pelletstown/St. Patrick's are in the Adoption Tracing Unit in Blanchardstown, Dublin. The Bethany Home files are in private hands with the adoption agency PACT.

The Castlepollard records are currently held by Tusla, the official body with branches around the country dealing with matters relating to children. Tusla is also responsible for adoption records and tracing in Donegal and it is worth detailing these records, as Castlepollard is otherwise the only home where full details of the records are known. They are:[12]

Admissions Book 1935–49[13]

Admissions Book 1943–57

Admissions Book 1955–70

Admissions Book (Private patients) July 1961–March 1970

Ante-natal notes 18 December 1939–17 June 1942[14]

Ante-natal notes 18 July 1942–late 1944

Ante-natal notes 16 January 1945–December 1946

Ante-natal notes 2 January 1947–January 1952

Ante-natal notes 24 January 1952–May 1957

Ante-natal notes 14 January 1957–9 September 1960

Ante-natal notes 6 May 1960–14 June 1963

Ante-natal notes 6 March 1963–21 June 1965

Ante-natal notes 5 February 1965–2 September 1966

Ante-natal cards. One box for 1966[15]

Ante-natal cards. Two boxes for 1967

Ante-natal cards. Two boxes for 1968

Ante-natal cards. Two boxes for 1969

Ante-natal cards. Two boxes for 1970

Maternity Book 15 April 1943–13 August 1947[16]

Maternity Book 10 June 1951–2 May 1956[17]

Maternity Book 4 May 1956–13 November 1961

Maternity Book 15 November 1961–14 February 1966

Maternity Book 24 February 1966–2 June 1969

Maternity Book 9 June 1969–10 January 1971

Wasserman [*sic*] Reaction Test Results 9 June 1947–15 October 1962[18]

Particulars of Patient to be entered on reception into the Home

Age Years	Date of reception	Condition on reception	Number of previous pregnancies. (Full time or otherwise)
(4)	(5)	(6)	(7)
20 yrs. 10·11·64.			

Author's personal entry beginning at the top left corner of Admissions Book Number 4 (Private Patients) July 1961–March 1970, page 33.[19] Note the custom design for maternity hospitals complying with the 1934 Regulation of Maternity Homes Act, Section 10 (1) and the handwritten 'St. Peters'. The numbers in brackets (1), (2), etc. go across the two pages up to (18) under the heading 'Whether born alive or stillborn'. Number (19) continues underneath back on the left-hand side and again goes across the pages up to (35) under the heading 'OBSERVATIONS' with comments such as 'Mother home' written in block capitals in the same handwriting as the main 'St. Peter's ...' entry at the top of the page. Other spaces provide for the father's names and occupation; dates and times of births, miscarriages and deaths, where the infant was discharged to, and who took them.

Donation of Bodies to Medical Science

RTÉ's flagship current affairs programme, *Prime Time*, sporadically broadcasts special episodes about issues concerning the homes. In late 2011 it revealed a new and previously unknown but officially authorised fifth vaccine trial in Sean Ross Abbey in 1965. *Prime Time* exposed for the first time that the nuns in St. Patrick's Mother and Baby Home (Pelletstown) and its associated hospital St. Kevin's (now St. James's), had 'donated' 461 dead bodies of babies and children to various medical institutions for routine dissection practice and anything else they wanted to do with the bodies. The practice began in 1940 and continued until 1965. The nuns steadfastly deny that they received a penny for the bodies. It should, however, be noted that Pelletstown/ St. Patrick's did not have its own Angels' Plot. The nuns had to pay for undertakers to remove all the bodies and further pay for a grave to be opened at Glasnevin with all the associated expenses. The Daughters of Charity saved themselves the cost of hundreds of funerals and burials by 'donating' the bodies. The *Prime Time* programme won an award. In 2017, Minister Katherine Zappone spoke in the Dáil and raised the figure to 474 bodies donated. To date there is no evidence of consent being sought or received from the natural mothers. It is yet another example of the attitude of the nuns to illegitimate babies.

PART 2

IN LIVING MEMORY, 1944–1990

CHAPTER 6

Changing Times: Disappearing at the Crossroads

By the end of the Second World War, the system for managing single mothers and their babies was struggling to cope. There was a sharp increase in numbers because of the war, and travel to Britain by single pregnant women was prohibited due to wartime security restrictions. The number of illegitimate births grew year on year and there was an increase of 47% from 1939 to 1945 – from fewer than 1,800 to over 2,500. An international comparison from this time is illuminating. In 1939, 8% of all illegitimate babies died in England and Wales. In Ireland the following year, 26% died. The nation that had promised to cherish all its children equally had betrayed the ideals of the 1916 Proclamation.

Alice Litster, the National Inspector of Boarded-Out Children, wrote a report in 1939 whose content was not widely publicised:

> The chance of survival of an illegitimate infant born in the slums and placed with a foster-mother in the slums a few days after birth is greater than that of an infant born in one of our special homes for unmarried mothers. I except the Manor House, Castlepollard, in which the infantile death rate is comparatively low. In theory, the advantage should lie on the side of the child institutionally born. Pre-natal care, proper diet, fresh air, sufficient exercise, no arduous work, proper and comfortable clothing, freedom from worry, the services of a skilled doctor, the supervision and attention

of a qualified nurse, all should be available and should make for the health of the expectant mother and the birth and survival of a healthy infant … Cleanliness, medical attention, dietetic knowledge, all the human skill may continue to preserve child life should be at hand. Yet any infant born in any other circumstances appears to have a better chance of life.

I have grave doubts of the wisdom of continuing to urge Boards of Health and Public Assistance to send patients to the special homes so long as no attempt is made to explore the causes of the abnormally high death rate.

The illegitimacy birth rate shows an upward trend. In 1916 it was 1530; in 1925 it was 1662. We cannot prevent the birth of these infants. We should be able to prevent their death.[1]

The old workhouses/county homes were still the primary places of detention for single mothers but they were full and conditions were appalling. The amount of time women stayed in the homes was reduced, thereby increasing turnover. The effects of the Second World War on supplies bit deeper with each passing year and the death rate of illegitimate babies that had gradually decreased since 1922 was now on the rise again.

Only 22% of pregnant Irish women entered the Mother and Baby Homes in the late 1920s, but by 1940 the network had expanded to include Sean Ross and Castlepollard, so this figure increased to nearly 56%. There were small numbers in each of the county homes scattered around the country. In 1941, for example, there were ten in Wicklow, eighteen in Wexford and sixteen in Sligo. There were eight in the Westmeath county home, despite the fact that Castlepollard was available only a few miles away. On the last day of March 1941, 451 single mothers were in the county homes, while 567 were in the Mother and Baby Homes. The county homes were gradually abandoned or converted to other uses. The Mother and Baby Homes were taking over.

Taoiseach Éamon de Valera introduced children's allowance in 1944 for the same reasons it was pioneered in Europe: to encourage population growth and assist the large families of the time. The allowance in Ireland was initially for the third child and subsequent children, and over the years it grew to apply to all children – but illegitimate children were excluded from the payment.

Before the 1940s there are no personal accounts of life in the Mother and Baby Homes, but post-1940 'Memories and Memoirs' play a vital role in filling in the blanks. The memoirs were written forty or fifty years later, still within living memory, and active survivor and adoption communities hear many testimonies dating from the mid-1940s up to the present. A tiny minority of women have spoken out in the media about their time in the homes and county homes. Sometimes their grown children relay stories from their mothers.

Despite adjustments from within, external forces transformed every aspect of the system. This began with Dr. James Deeny, a man regarded as a hero by the active survivor and adoption communities. However, Dr. Deeny's attack on the nuns was just the beginning of a deep and fundamental reform that was driven by the financial aspects of adoption.

Dr. James Deeny

James Deeny made a profound and lasting difference, not just to the women in Mother and Baby Homes in Ireland, but to people throughout the country. Appointed Chief Medical Officer for Ireland in 1944 aged just 38, he was vigorous in his pursuit of a public health-monitoring programme and eradication of tuberculosis. His appointment increased the pressures on local-authority medical officers to improve preventative health services and expand hospital care. He was that rare combination of intellect and energy and was a deeply compassionate man who dedicated his life to the advancement of public health. He undoubtedly saved hundreds of thousands of lives in Ireland and around the world through his later work with the World Health Organisation.

Deeny pioneered the 'medical survey' by working tirelessly in his native Northern Ireland to conduct surveys of infant and child mortality. Regarded as an early expert on the subject, he discovered that breastfeeding fundamentally improved the chances of survival for infants. Deeny's drive and energy revitalised Ireland's healthcare to the point that he reduced the number of deaths of Irish children under the age of one from over 4,000 per year to well below 2,000 during his tenure.

His autobiography *To Cure and to Care* spoke modestly about his many achievements, including his proposal of a scheme in Ireland to provide free medical care for women and children. His 'Mother and Child' scheme was accepted by de Valera's government and included in the landmark 1947 Health Act. It sought to reform all aspects of public health, as Britain was doing after the Second World War ended, but, before the plan could be enacted, there was a general election in 1948. After sixteen years in power, de Valera and Fianna Fáil were out of office. The first Interparty Coalition Government inherited the Act but the medical profession and the Catholic Church joined forces to resist providing women and children with free healthcare. The battle was the ultimate proof of the power of the Catholic Church at the time. The Minister for Health, Dr. Noel Browne, who championed the scheme, was forced to resign in April 1951.

The following day Taoiseach John Costello declared that when his government received 'directions' from the Church, the Church would receive 'our complete obedience and allegiance'. Costello went on to declare: 'I am an Irishman second, I am a Catholic first, and I accept without qualification in all respects the teaching of the hierarchy and the church to which I belong.' He resigned on 13 June 1951 and called a general election. Costello lost and de Valera was back in power again.

In his autobiography, Deeny talks about his early years as the newly appointed Chief Medical Officer for Ireland.[2] He discovered that something was badly wrong in Cork, where the infant mortality rate was considerably higher than the national average of just over 7%. He traced the problem to the Sacred Heart-run Bessboro Mother and Baby Home and noted that: 'in the previous year some 180 babies had been born there and [that] considerably more than 100 had died'. This is an infant mortality rate of more than 55%. Babies born in Bessboro were dying at more than seven times the national average. It later emerged that Cork's County Medical Officer had carried out a follow-up investigation into the mortality rate and it was actually a staggering 68%.[3] Almost seven out of every ten babies born alive died in Bessboro, just short of ten times the national average.

In 1944, Dr. Deeny arrived unannounced at Bessboro and insisted on examining the babies and inspecting the buildings. It was unknown for the Chief Medical Officer of Ireland to undertake such a personal inspection. He reported that the buildings were spotlessly clean and that he could not figure out what the problem could be. On a hunch, he ordered some of the babies to be stripped and was appalled by what he saw: 'Every baby had some purulent infection of the skin and all had green diarrhoea, carefully covered up. There was obviously a staphylococcus infection about.' Deeny sacked the Matron and then sacked the medical officer. He ordered Bessboro to be closed down but that never happened. Most tellingly, Deeny continued, 'The deaths had been going on for years. They had done nothing about it, had accepted the situation and were quite complacent about it.'

The Sacred Heart nuns ran for support to senior clergy, enlisting a priest and then a monsignor and the Bishop of Cork to destroy Deeny. Finally, the Papal Nuncio was also enlisted and he went to see the Taoiseach, de Valera. The Papal Nuncio was shown Deeny's report – and sided with Deeny. Many years later in 2014, it was also pressure from *outside* Ireland that finally saw the 'breakthrough' the survivor community had been seeking for years. Change must often come from outside Ireland when institutional abuse is involved. The battle that Deeny began dragged on for years, but slowly the mortality rates dropped, not only in Bessboro but in all the Mother and Baby Homes. While there were other decisive factors over the next several years that significantly affected and improved the quality of care in all the homes, Deeny's intervention may have saved hundreds, and possibly thousands, of lives. The bravery of his direct action against the largest and most powerful order in the homes, the Sacred Heart nuns, must be seen in the context of the time. He put his job, his career and his entire future in Ireland on the line for illegitimate children, when practically no one else in the country cared.

In the year following Deeny's intervention, the national infant mortality rate in Ireland was less than 7%, but in Bessboro it actually rose to a merciless 82% before slowly beginning to fall.

Deeny's activities did not end with Bessboro. Frank Duff's Regina Coeli Hostel for single mothers and their children was next. On hearing at a medical meeting that 'the Regina Coeli Hostel was in a terrible state, that babies were dying there and that conditions were abominable', Deeny took immediate action: 'The next morning I went along to have a look at the place.' Duff naturally 'resented any interference' but Deeny inspected Regina. He discovered that many babies were suffering from enteritis and, when Duff reacted with his legendary stubbornness, Deeny persisted until he agreed to cooperate and accept help. Deeny's secretary, Miss Howett, organised a collection of £25 among the civil servants in Dublin's Custom House and the money was used to furnish a room that Duff made available. This became a quarantine station and all new arrivals at Regina were initially accommodated there for five days. The survival rate for the children improved right away.

Deeny traced the primary source of the infections in Regina to the Rotunda Maternity Hospital. He confronted the Master of the Rotunda, Ninian Faulkner, while he was lying sick with flu. Deeny spoke forcefully to Faulkner and his paediatrician Bob Collis and conditions subsequently improved at the Rotunda.[4] Deeny remains a beloved hero to the survivor community.

Banished Babies

While many details are known about the 'Banished Babies' trade, its precise origins are unknown. The general understanding is that, in 1945, United States airmen still stationed in Britain after the end of the Second World War discovered that it was easy to adopt babies in Ireland. Back in America, the system was well regulated and strict age limits applied. There was also a very limited number of white babies available for adoption there, and this was the root cause of the banished babies' trade. The United States was still a deeply segregated and predominantly racist society in the 1940s. White people feared that if they adopted an apparently white baby, the child might later display mixed-race characteristics inherited from a secret grandparent or great-grandparent who might have been black or mixed-race. Irish children were guaranteed white, and the Irish nuns in the homes and agencies were happy to effectively 'sell' babies to wealthy Americans.

Mike Milotte was an investigative reporter with the RTÉ programme *Prime Time* whose 1996 report shocked an astonished public.[5] Following a mammoth investigation, his definitive and excellent book *Banished Babies* was published in 1997 and there was a second, expanded edition in 2012.[6] Aside from the stories from the banished themselves, almost everything known about the banished babies trade comes from Milotte's investigations and writing.

From 1945 to 1973, between 3,000 and 4,000 babies and children born in Ireland were sent abroad for adoption in other countries. The vast majority went to the United States. However, at least fifty babies were sent to other countries including Britain, Germany, Libya, Egypt, the Philippines, India, Australia, South Africa and Venezuela.

The government began keeping official statistics in 1949, four years after the trade began, and 2,132 babies and young children were in effect sold before it ended. The true figure is significantly higher when the unknown numbers of the first four years of the trade are included. There is also a great deal of circumstantial and anecdotal evidence to show that there was a thriving black market in Irish babies, facilitated not only by the nuns but by many midwives and nurses operating private nursing homes, eager to jump on that profitable bandwagon.

An official report into Bessboro and Tuam was prepared in 2012 for possible use by the McAleese Inquiry into the Magdalene Laundries, but was never used. It strongly suggested that many deaths in the Mother and Baby Homes were faked so that the babies could be sold on the underground black market. Every Minister for Children since then has vehemently denied ever seeing this report. Milotte also investigated St. Rita's nursing home in Dublin, which ran a lucrative and booming trade in illegal adoptions and baby-trafficking for years.

Éamon de Valera was Taoiseach in 1945 when the banished babies trade began but he was also Minister for External Affairs and therefore directly responsible for issuing passports. It is unknown if the matter of issuing hundreds of passports to nuns on behalf of babies in their legal guardianship was brought to his attention but, either way, they continued to be approved on his authority as

Minister despite the growing unease of the senior civil servants who administered the passport office. The legality of de Valera's action has been questioned. There is nothing in Irish law or the Constitution to explicitly outlaw the export of Irish babies, but there was certainly no legal basis for the trade, either. At best it was semi-legal child-trafficking on a vast scale.

The unregulated trade expanded rapidly and soon came to the attention of the media at home and abroad. Senior civil servants were angry that they might be used as scapegoats for issuing passports and possible legal challenges. Many survivor activists firmly believe this negative publicity was the underlying reason for the 1952 Adoption Act. That Act legalised the lucrative, international baby-trafficking market and the practice continued until 1973 when the supply of babies dried up. By the early 1960s, Ireland had actually reached a domestic equilibrium in terms of the number of babies available for adoption and the number of people wanting to adopt in the country, yet the trade continued for another ten years, albeit at a reduced rate. Archbishop McQuaid ordered a media ban on reporting anything related to the practice, including the Mother and Baby Homes.[7] It was an extraordinary command and once again demonstrates the power of the Catholic Church during that period.

The Mother and Baby Homes effectively disappeared from public view and did not re-emerge until the Tuam 800 story that broke on the front page of the *Mail on Sunday* in May 2014. The homes' 'vanishing act' from the 1950s onward was helped by the fact that, while the Magdalene Laundries always existed in towns and cities, Mother and Baby Homes tended to be mostly in the countryside or occasionally on the edges of suburbia and were therefore away from the public eye.

Milotte has estimated that the Church earned between $30 and $50 million (adjusted for inflation) from the trade in babies. The Sacred Heart nuns dispatched at least 814 babies from 1949, followed closely by St. Patrick's Guild with at least 515.

One of the many disturbing aspects of the export trade is that the Church refused to allow US Social Services to vet potential adoptive parents. The Church in the US insisted on its own vetting system, via a patchy network of voluntary Social Services groups. The system was chaotic, and dreadful mistakes were made. People who should never have been allowed near children under any circumstances were certified as fit to be adoptive parents.

The Catholic volunteers who vetted potential adoptive parents had two main criteria: Catholicism and money. The child had to be given a Catholic education, it had to be confirmed that the potential adoptive parents were not using contraceptives, and the mother had to give up work, a particular obsession of McQuaid's. When it came to proof of wealth, the American Catholic volunteers, on behalf of the Irish nuns and agencies, demanded deeds of houses, payslips, certified copies of savings accounts and share certificates.

In some cases, so-called 'suitable' adoptive parents were subsequently discovered to be paedophiles and child abusers. In other cases, the adoptive parents sold on or simply gave away their child, who then disappeared into the black hole of child-trafficking.

The majority did, however, go to admirable homes and had first-class lives because their adoptive parents desperately wanted children, were invariably wealthy, and therefore had the means to provide a good-quality life. The children went to superior Catholic schools, often private, and then on to college in almost all cases. This author knows many of the banished, however, who despite having excellent lives, experience a deep sadness and a longing for home. They return to Ireland regularly and attend annual reunions in Mother and Baby Homes and are highly active in Facebook groups. The banished baby support group was formed in 2013. Many of them are campaigners and some are as angry and militant as the hardcore domestic activists. Milotte's book *Banished Babies* is still widely available online for those interested in learning more.

June Goulding

In 1951, 23-year-old, newly qualified midwife June Goulding accepted a position as the resident midwife at Bessboro for nine months until June 1952 when she left to get married. Goulding was appalled by what she witnessed and later wrote a book called *The Light in the Window*, which was published in 1998.[8]

Like Deeny before her, Goulding did her best in the context of the times to stand up to the nuns and treat the 350 residents as human beings. As a result of her professionalism and empathy, the mortality rate in Bessboro dropped to under 2% during her nine-month tenure: down from a high of 82% just six years before.

Many of the stories carried in the Facebook adoption groups and later in the media are sourced from Goulding's book, most notably the story about pregnant girls putting down tarmac on the driveway in Bessboro. Another famous incident was Goulding witnessing an unnamed 'Sister', one of the Sacred Heart nuns, lining up the pregnant women on the lawn, ordering them down on their knees and to cut the grass with their fingernails one blade at a time. (It should be noted that this practice extended to other institutions, including the industrial schools at Goldenbridge and Artane.[9])

Goulding was obliged to carry on the practice of shaving the residents' pubic hair every week but tried to be gentle, unlike previous midwives. The delivery room contained no medical equipment except for a tiny cabinet attached to a wall containing surgical thread and needles to stitch up the girls after they gave birth. Goulding discovered that the cabinet was kept permanently locked and Sister refused to open it under any circumstances. The famous quote from 'Sister' asking women in labour 'if the five minutes' pleasure is worth all this?' is also from her book.

Goulding is often referred to as 'Saint June' by the survivor community and some of the babies she delivered are active members. The Sacred Heart nuns were furious at their portrayal and solicitors' letters were sent out to Goulding threatening legal action if the book wasn't withdrawn. Thankfully June Goulding stood her ground and the nuns never followed through with their threats. They hired an 'expert' of their own to try and disprove some of the facts in the book but this endeavour failed.

The film *Sinners,* released in 2003, was loosely based on June's book and is by far the most realistic portrayal of an Irish Mother and Baby Home to date.[10] It is grim and depressing, yet the book itself is ultimately a story of redemption for June and all the women and babies she helped. June Goulding sadly passed away in 2010.

St. Clare's Holding Centre (aka St. Joseph's Home)

The Sisters of the Poor Clares ran St. Joseph's industrial school in Cavan where a fire on 23 February 1943 killed thirty-five girls and one adult employee. It later emerged that they had been locked into their rooms. There was a skewed inquiry afterwards.[11]

The same order of nuns established a holding centre similar to Temple Hill in Dublin, in an extended Victorian country house in Stamullen, Co. Meath, in 1952. Babies and children up to four years old were sent to Stamullen from a variety of sources, including nearby Castlepollard, local hospitals, home births and even foundlings. The capacity of Stamullen was sixty babies and children. Mother Mary Aloysious Durkin, who died in 2010, ran the home for many years until she was replaced by Mother Marie Louise, who was there until Stamullen closed in 1985.

A number of women who worked there have come forward to describe conditions from the early 1960s until the 1980s. By all accounts Stamullen was run firmly but well and mortality rates were probably low. They cared for a number of special-needs babies at a time when adopting such babies did not happen. Some vaccine trials took place between December 1960 and November 1961. Stamullen has been repeatedly called a Mother and Baby Home but it was not. There were no mothers and no births there. It is not being investigated by the current Inquiry into Mother and Baby Homes.

Probable numbers, estimated at about sixty babies at any one time and an average stay of about six months, allowing for a severe drop-off in numbers towards the end, meant that anywhere from 3,000 to 4,000 babies went through Stamullen. Father P.J. Regan was closely associated with the home and 130 babies were sent to the United States for adoption from Stamullen.

There is an Angels' Plot in Stamullen Cemetery believed to contain the remains of 50–100 babies, although this seems a very low figure. Séamus Reilly Junior spoke publicly about his father Séamus Senior, who worked in Stamullen as caretaker for ten years. Séamus Junior sometimes accompanied his father to work and remembered that his father was the man designated to dig the graves and bury the babies.[12] No nuns or priests attended and it was left to Reilly to say prayers for the babies. While Stamullen formally closed in 1985, it seems to have continued on under a different name or under a different certification and has been used as a residential care centre for adults or children ever since. Because of its exclusion from the Inquiry into Mother and Baby Homes, it is doubtful that the full story will ever emerge.

Until the current author's privately published reference book *Mother and Baby Homes in Ireland, A Standard Reference Guide and Timeline* in 2015, Monsignor Cecil J. Barrett's book *Adoption: The Parent, The Child, The Home,* published in 1952, was the first and only general book about adoption in Ireland. This short tome is highly peculiar and contradicts every cliché about the treatment of single mothers and their babies. Barrett portrays the Church as benevolent, compassionate and doing its best to keep single mothers and their babies together, and he constantly claims that it is the mothers themselves who are desperate to relinquish their babies. Even when reviewed in the context of the many other factors softening the regimes in the homes, as well as the upcoming Adoption Act of 1952, the motives for writing this counterintuitive book remain deeply suspect. It certainly allowed McQuaid and Barrett to present themselves as the country's foremost authorities on adoption and therefore influence the Act to suit their preferences.

1952 Adoption Act

By the late 1940s and early 1950s, pressure increased on the government and the Church to pass a proper adoption Act. Most countries in Europe had enacted such legislation in the aftermath of the First World War and the flu epidemic of 1918–19 that killed 40 million worldwide. In Ireland, 800,000 were infected and 23,000 died. As a result, hundreds of thousands of children became orphans and were informally adopted. European governments brought in legislation during the 1920s to regularise the lives of these new families.

While the Irish government had no ideological objections to legal adoption, the Church was extremely reluctant to endorse such an Act because it feared that Catholic babies would be adopted by

Protestants. This bigotry left Ireland decades behind international best practice. Archbishop McQuaid and Monsignor Cyril Barrett found themselves in the middle of an increasingly complex muddle. On one side, the government and senior civil servants were becoming increasingly anxious about the banished babies trade and the issuing of thousands of passports at the behest of the nuns. On the other side, the nuns were dedicated to carrying on with the flourishing banished babies trade and this was having a profound effect on the ground, where mortality rates had plummeted since the end of the Second World War. For example, the difference in the Castlepollard infant mortality rates after 1950 is startling. From 1951 to 1966, there are only 12 deaths recorded in the Home's maternity books from the 1,951 recorded entries: an average annual mortality rate of just 0.6% over 15 years.[13] A range of other pressures were also coming to bear, including the tiny 'Legal Adoption Society' which wanted a modern Act to replace the 1899 Poor Law and legislate on issues such as inheritance rights and the right to grant permission for medical procedures.

McQuaid hated the idea of the government interfering in social matters that he regarded as the Church's business alone, but he finally agreed to legislation. The reason he conceded was simple: the government more or less allowed McQuaid to write the Adoption Act. It was famously sent to him five times for his 'comments' and, alongside his expert on adoption, C.J. Barrett, they finally got the safeguards they required to ensure that Catholic babies went to Catholic families only.

The Adoption Act of 1952 was Ireland's first standalone adoption legislation and the Adoption Board was set up to manage the new system. The Act provided for the court-ordered, permanent severing of all relationships between single mothers and their illegitimate children, but made it clear that only illegitimate children over six months old and not more than seven years old at the date of the application could be adopted. The Act circumvented the strong provisions in the Constitution protecting the family by claiming that single mothers and their children were not a 'family' as defined by the Constitution. The courts could now grant permanent, irreversible custody of adoptees to their new families, including full inheritance rights. After an adoption order was granted, the full legal status of the child was transferred irreversibly to their new adoptive parents. Under the Act, adoption files were sealed for life to all parties involved. Natural mothers had no further rights of any description, not even the right to know if their son or daughter was dead or alive. Even in cases where there was a medical emergency, the Adoption Board refused to release medical information or history to an adoptee and/or to their adoptive parents and that remains the legal position today.

Fraudulent 'birth certificates' were issued to adoptive parents and their new children. A person who did not know they were adopted would never be informed otherwise by the State. Today if adoptees go to the General Registry Office and ask for their birth certificate, they will receive a fraudulent birth certificate. If adoptees asks for an adoption certificate, they will be given a similar piece of paper with 'adoption certificate' printed on the top but containing identical information to their fake birth certificates. The Act also legalised the banished babies trade, with some minor restrictions concerning the age of the babies who were exported.

One bizarre aspect of the new Adoption Act was Schedule 8, Paragraph 14 (1), requiring all adoption orders from the courts to be published. The Adoption Board chose the obscure government publication *Iris Oifigiúil* to fulfil its legal obligations. *Iris Oifigiúil* is the official State newspaper for the purpose of publishing public notices such as the beginning and end of hunting and fishing seasons, and matters concerning wills, where beneficiaries cannot be found. It has been published twice a week since the foundation of the State in 1922. It still exists and is of real interest only to the legal and accounting professions.

From the time the Act came into force on 1 January 1953, the Adoption Board published the court orders in random batches of 200 to 300 names every few months. However, under Paragraph 14 (2), no pre-adoption identifying details could be published, including the natural mother's name, the former name of the adoptee, and his/her place of birth.

The full names and addresses of adoptive parents and adoptees were published until the 1988 Adoption Act rescinded this provision. The lists can be used by natural mothers to trace their children with a little detective work, and this was why the former President of Ireland, Mary Robinson, fought to have the publications stopped in the 1980s. She even wanted all copies of *Iris Oifigiúil* dating back to 1953 removed from the shelves of the Dáil, universities and the National Library of Ireland. The former President's name has cropped up several times in relation to the Adoption Machine since the 1960s. One feature of the publication of adoption orders that has consistently confused the adoption community is that they did not include the banished babies, as their adoptions were endorsed by US courts. *Iris Oifigiúil* contained some 900 to 1,400 court-approved domestic adoptions per year and approximately 35,000 to over 40,000 adoptees' new names and addresses.

The published batches were generally listed in rows of several girls, followed by several boys. They were sub-grouped around geographical areas such as a batch from Cork and then Louth, but there were no hard and fast rules governing the lists, just generalisations, as the Adoption Board undoubtedly intended. In the lists, almost all adoptees went to a couple named as 'Mr. and Mrs.', the odd one to a 'Mrs.' only (a widow) and a very rare one to a 'Miss'. The occasional entry was in Irish.

The Adoption Act made adoption acceptable and even fashionable from the mid-1950s. There were several other Adoption Acts over the years but with no substantive changes; they mostly updated the original Act and closed certain loopholes.

CHAPTER 7

Welcome to the Machine

The twenty years after the Adoption Act came into force on 1 January 1953 were a Golden Age for the nuns who ran the Mother and Baby Homes and the adoption agencies. The combination of Dr. Deeny, the banished babies industry, Goulding's improvements in Bessboro and the Adoption Act had transformed the Mother and Baby Homes along with all the secondary institutions that serviced the network. The entire system reinvented itself as a smooth, well-oiled and extremely efficient machine hidden from the public behind high walls and legally sheltered behind the sealed-for-life provisions of the new Adoption Act.

Ard Mhuire Mother and Baby Home

Things were going so well for the Adoption Machine in the 1950s that a ninth and final Mother and Baby Home opened a full twenty years after Castlepollard was founded in 1935. 'Ard Mhuire' was opened in Dunboyne, Co. Meath, in 1955 and operated as an 'extern institution' by the Sisters of the Good Shepherd, originally of French origin, who also ran four of Ireland's largest Magdalene Laundries in Limerick, Waterford, New Ross and Cork. The new mid-sized home opened in a converted manor house, but the total numbers are a mystery as the *LGRs* had long ceased to report facts, figures or statistics about the homes. The average length of residency, only three to six months, was very short compared to the other homes and so numbers are difficult to estimate, but it is likely that from 2,000 to 3,000 women and girls went through its doors.

'Dunboyne', as it is known, was an attempt to increase quality standards in the now lucrative and competitive Mother and Baby Homes industry and, in that respect, it was similar to St. Gerard's, in Mountjoy Square, Dublin. Dunboyne was a relatively genteel, middle-class home and the nuns expected a generous 'donation' of cash in advance from their residents' families. It opened after the sweeping changes of the previous decade and was intended for a specific type of single mother. It was a little like Castlepollard in that part of its remit was to bring in middle- and upper-class paying residents.

The Good Shepherd nuns continued the old system of having no delivery rooms of their own and outsourcing all births. They purchased their own minibus and one of them drove it to Dublin every Friday. Sister Paul is widely remembered as the driver for many years. The first stop was in Sean McDermott Street at the Magdalene Laundry to drop off their week's soiled linen and clothes and collect the previous week's cleaned laundry. The next stop was Holles Street Maternity Hospital. The women were brought into a section of the hospital where they were segregated. They were examined every week and reports are that this experience was mixed. Some doctors and midwives were professional, occasionally even friendly and sympathetic, but others were cold and judgemental.

Dunboyne was in operation until the early 1990s and attitudes towards the unmarried mothers had improved over the years. A couple of weeks before a woman was due to give birth, she would remain in Holles Street, where most births took place. When the interdepartmental report was released in 2014, it recorded just seven births in Dunboyne and they were almost certainly premature deliveries.

After giving birth, the mothers and babies remained in Holles Street for about two weeks. The mothers then returned on the Friday bus to Dunboyne while the babies were generally transferred to Temple Hill holding centre in Blackrock and adopted through St. Patrick's Guild until 1974 when some babies did return with their mothers. Mothers remained in Dunboyne for only two or three weeks before being discharged.

Conditions in the home are well-known through a Facebook group and information on the internet. The testimonies reveal Dunboyne as by far the easiest of the homes. There was no forced labour and a little light housework was all that was expected from the residents. Local women were hired to cook and, as stated, the laundry was outsourced.

The residents spent most of their time knitting and sewing clothes for their babies. They were allowed a great deal of freedom and many recall walking arm in arm into Dunboyne to a local wool shop, to purchase supplies. They also bought toiletries in other shops as well as cigarettes and treats. There was a coin-operated phone in the back hall of the building for the women to receive and make calls, and visitors were allowed on Sundays.

Dunboyne reflects the new attitude and conditions that prevailed since the tumultuous eight years that preceded 1953. While the other homes did not match the relatively relaxed atmosphere in Dunboyne until the late 1970s, conditions improved completely from the early 1950s. Dunboyne closed in 1991 and it is now a luxury hotel called Dunboyne Castle.

The Blame Game

Since the first revelations of institutional abuse in Ireland in the 1990s, there has been a concerted and well-organised effort by the Catholic Church to deflect blame away from itself. The integrity of survivors was questioned and undermined. Later, the Church claimed that the whole of society was to blame because we, as a nation, had abandoned the pregnant girls, orphans, illegitimate and 'destitute' children. In fact, the Church claimed, they were the only ones who cared enough to shelter them in their hour of need.

Enda Kenny, as Taoiseach, declared of the Mother and Baby Homes that 'no nuns broke into our homes to kidnap our children' and he is not alone in that framing of the issue. Many people in the present Church and State apparatus, and Irish political parties, clearly have a vested interest in blaming others rather accepting responsibility. Enda Kenny never met survivors of Mother and Baby Homes although meetings were requested on several occasions.

The nuns may not have personally broken into our houses to kidnap children, but priests, members of the Gardaí, and those acting on behalf of the Irish Society for the Prevention of Cruelty to Children, knocked on the doors. Some children were sentenced by the courts to terms in industrial and reformatory schools, mostly for the crime of being poor.

Women and girls were sent to Magdalene Laundries. Terrified pregnant girls were ordered out of their homes by their fathers because the local parish priest had instructed them to do so. This author personally knows some of those women who never returned home, and never saw their families again, because of the commands of local priests. A number of those same priests were the fathers of the babies and wanted to bury the evidence.

The media in Ireland ignored the infant mortality rates from the homes even though the government published them annually and made them freely available. Investigative journalism did not really exist in Ireland until the 1990s and, even then, committed and passionate journalists were rare. The legal profession also failed to protect human and civil rights, with only the very odd exception.

In modern-day Ireland, Garda Sergeant Maurice McCabe and other whistle-blowers have been subjected to ridicule, concerted harassment, and threats of criminal charges, despite acting out of genuine and legitimate concerns. Church and State had even an greater social power in the 1940s that most ordinary parents could not resist in order to keep a pregnant daughter at home. The local Gardaí would not dare interfere with the local parish priest. No solicitor would even consider the case. No politician would risk his re-election and career by standing up to the Catholic Church. On the rare occasion when a woman did manage to hold on to her baby, sooner or later there was a knock on the door and the illegitimate child was taken and sentenced by the courts to spend his or her childhood in an industrial school.

The Nuns

Many people still defend the nuns as 'doing their best in the circumstances' but most of these apologists are the nuns themselves. Some have defended the nuns, on the grounds that they too were victims who were brainwashed by their teachers and superiors as soon as their training began. It is true that there was undoubtedly a great deal of pressure, from both their superiors and their families, on individual nuns and many had crises of faith from their earliest days. Another important point is that the nuns took a solemn and formal vow of obedience and it was often unimaginable for them, in the context of Catholic Ireland, to break their vows. It is possible to define all these factors as a form of brainwashing. There are several books by former nuns who left their orders. They express deep regret and often bitterness at what they regard as their wasted lives and tell stories of former colleagues in the orders who felt trapped and unable to leave.[1]

However, it should also be noted that the nuns were very well educated and universally respected in Ireland. It was one of the only 'careers' with serious social standing for women up to the 1980s. There is no question that nuns in old Ireland yielded considerable power and authority. The orders themselves not only treated inmates in their institutions according to their class, but that same class structure was applied within the orders themselves. Many of the orders had two different 'classes' of nuns, depending on their background.

One fact is undeniable: the nuns were familiar with the Bible and the words and deeds of Jesus Christ. While it is easy to selectively pick and choose from the Bible to back up a bigoted or prejudiced viewpoint, the New Testament teaches self-sacrifice, forgiveness, compassion, mercy and love. The many parables that Jesus taught, such as that of the Good Samaritan, contain messages of love and compassion for all people, regardless of their religion or beliefs. The principle of 'Let he among you without sin cast the first stone' is also a central theme. Jesus personally reached out to those in society who were marginalised and desperate, and he forgave and aided them. The nuns in the Mother and Baby Homes cannot have been unaware of their 'Christian' duty in the truest and most charitable sense of the word.

Yet they chose not only to remain in the homes but stood by and watched as babies and children suffered and died in their thousands. They witnessed hundreds of distraught mothers weeping and suffering when their babies were taken away, and they did nothing. It is those people who had a choice who must accept the responsibility that goes with that choice. Any nun could have packed her bags and left the home. It would have been an extremely difficult decision, but the right one. It is depressing to accept that the nuns, choosing a life serving a God who preached compassion and forgiveness, were the cause of the wilful neglect, starvation and deaths of dozens of mothers and thousands of babies.

Most nuns do not seem to have had any doubts or crises of faith, even though they all had plenty of time alone with their thoughts, to reflect on their actions and inactions as human beings and as Christians. Many were benign, but a substantial number are remembered as judgemental, arrogant, vicious and devoid of empathy. Former residents recall little in the way of kindness but an avalanche of hubris, preaching and cruelty.

One aspect of these nuns' lives that is never mentioned is that they had chosen a life of chastity and childlessness, but were surrounded by pregnant girls and women and their illegitimate children. The sensitive issues of chastity, periods, pre-menstrual tension, 'biological clocks' and the menopause, all experienced while living alongside pregnant women and babies, would make for a very interesting study. How much of the nuns' malice was caused by jealousy, resentment and bitterness? They spent their lives surrounded by women and girls who had sex, were pregnant, and had babies, while all the time knowing it would never be them. It must have had a powerful and entirely negative effect on their lives. Ultimately, they choose to remain in the homes. Unlike the so-called inmates, no one locked them in their rooms at night and supervised their waking moments. Gardaí were never going to snatch an escaping nun off the street and return her to a home.

Two other aspects of institutional 'care' are never or rarely highlighted. Firstly, the religious mirrored how they were themselves treated by the residents. Nuns in the homes generally reflected the treatment they received. Most residents entered the homes as devout Catholics and were genuinely contrite about their condition. They kept their heads down, obeyed all the rules and worked hard. As a result, they were left alone by most of the nuns to 'do their own time' as the prison cliché goes. Secondly, there is a telling quote from a woman who was in St. Joseph's industrial school in Cavan. Mary says that 'The nuns treated us according to our background' and that experience is well recorded across the homes.[2] The unique combination of Victorian morality and Irish Catholic hubris in the nineteenth century combined to form a toxic atmosphere in Ireland that reached its high point in the cliché of 'Holy Catholic Ireland' from the 1930s onwards.

Many residents were naturally rebellious in spirit or angry at being punished because of something that was neither their choice nor their fault, such as rape, incest or a gutless boyfriend. Their anger and high spirits were a red rag to the nuns, so those residents were targeted to be 'taught manners'. 'I'll beat the devil out of you!' was a favourite catchphrase. There was a small minority of nuns who were just naturally vicious, heartless, abusive and corrupted by power, and who were often deliberately chosen by the Mothers Superior as the enforcers of discipline and punishment.

One cold, hard fact remains above all others. There is not one recorded case of a nun leaving the homes and speaking out about the criminal mistreatment of vulnerable women and girls. None of the orders of nuns who ran the Mother and Baby Homes have apologised or offered to provide help or redress to their former inmates. The Sufi saint, Ziaudin Jahib Suhrawardi, wrote that 'self-justification is worse than the original offence'. This is proved daily by the nuns, whose multiple justifications and excuses clearly demonstrate that they have learned nothing. They continue their tactical silence and hide behind lawyers and never, ever accept responsibility for their premeditated actions.

Priests and the Homes

Each of the homes was assigned a priest to advise and assist the nuns when problems arose. Father Patrick J. Regan, originally from Enfield, Co. Meath, is the best known. After his ordination, he was moved around for a few years before being appointed Administrator in the Diocese of Mullingar in 1951. His duties included the general supervision of Castlepollard and he voluntarily worked with another Mother and Baby Home and one holding centre. Regan later became fully involved with adoptions, particularly foreign adoptions to the United States.

Regan founded and was president of the 'St. Clare's Adoption Society', which handled adoptions from a variety of sources, including Castlepollard, Dunboyne and St. Clare's holding centre in Stamullen. Although Castlepollard and Stamullen holding centre each sent large numbers of babies to the United States, there is no record of a single foreign adoption from Dunboyne. Many commentators are baffled but the reason there are no records is that the women gave birth in Holles Street and their babies were sent for adoption, both foreign and domestic, from Temple Hill, through St. Patrick's Guild.

Regan is vividly remembered by former residents of Castlepollard Mother and Baby Home as a dour, aloof and arrogant man. In 1976 he was appointed parish priest in Castlepollard. There are several stories about him in *Banished Babies* where he is portrayed as petty and mean-spirited, which dovetails perfectly with how natural mothers and adoptees remember him.[3]

He died in 1995, not long after the local community had thrown a lavish party to celebrate his golden jubilee (50 years) as a priest. Regan is buried in the local parish cemetery in Castlepollard under a headstone that reads, 'He is fondly remembered by local people as a decent and kind man.'

Lifelong Consequences

By the 1950s, adoption was well-established in many countries around the world and a number of small adoption rights groups started to form in America. Academic institutions began to conduct surveys into the long-term consequences of separation for mothers and their babies, and between the findings of the rights groups and the academic research, a great deal is now known.

Although the sudden exit from the Mother and Baby Homes could be deeply disorientating, it was in the months and years afterwards that the full impact of losing their babies hit the women. The emotional and mental trauma remained with them for the rest of their lives. The babies separated from their natural mothers were also affected to a greater or lesser extent: a range of well-documented psychological issues shaped and marked them for life.[4] These issues included many adoptees' denial of their situation (the so-called 'good-adoptee' syndrome), 'primal wounds', genetic bewilderment, reactive attachment disorder, and a sense of loneliness, isolation and grief. Babies separated from their mothers shortly after birth often displayed lifelong, deep-seated insecurities because of what is known as 'premature ego development'. It is now understood that a 'pregnancy' lasts for about twelve to fifteen months because a baby takes a further three to six months after birth to slowly realise that he or she is a separate human being. Separating babies before this time causes them to realise prematurely that they are individuals, which is deeply disturbing and frightening for them on a subconscious level. The fact that medical histories are sealed and therefore unknown can also result in potentially lethal consequences.

There are radical differences between the experiences of mothers and adoptees. Adoptees are affected from the moment of adoption and so their childhoods and therefore their lives are defined by adoption. The situation is different for mothers, in terms of loss, since they had the mental framework to comprehend what was occurring and to recognise the injustice of their situation. Losing a baby to adoption is now recognised as a traumatic event similar to the death of a baby in practically every case. Some maintain it is even worse because it is a constant state of limbo and never-ending grief. Most are haunted by the unknown fate of their children, constantly wondering where they are and what has become of them. The majority suffer from post-traumatic stress disorder ranging from severe to mild symptoms including nightmares, anxiety, panic attacks, suicidal ideation, depression, secondary infertility, parenting issues and a fear of losing subsequent babies.

Many, if not the vast majority of the former residents of the homes, kept their secret and indeed remain silent out of fear of the nuns, the law and their families, and to safeguard their personal reputations. Some women go into denial as a form of self-protection from the pain, and suffer from selective amnesia. Family occasions such as Christmas, Easter, Mother's Day and their lost children's birthdays can trigger intense sadness and often depression. On average, mothers who lose their children to adoption die three years younger than the statistical average in their own countries.[5] The redoubtable natural mother and formidable researcher Lizzy Howard in Australia and the international adoption rights organisation Origins have made significant progress in collating and publicising this research. When Australia officially apologised for its history of forcing single mothers to 'relinquish' their babies, they also published substantial accredited research that remains a primary source about the effects of separation of mothers and children.

Many, if not most, of the women had mixed feelings, particularly in Ireland. They were torn between love for their babies and the judgement of the Church and their families. Many women ignored the threats from the nuns and social workers and still tried to trace their children but those who did were met with silence and disapproval. The closed and sealed nature of Ireland's adoption legislation was a convenient, legal shelter for a system ideologically and religiously opposed to the very idea of reunions. By the mid-1980s, younger and more enlightened social workers agitated for change but this was firmly resisted by the religious orders and older, conservative members of the civil service. Progress has been painfully slow and, while attitudes have changed considerably over the last thirty years, the waiting lists have not. Securing a first appointment with a social worker can take months and sometimes years. Even when a social worker finally makes contact, people can be unlucky and can find one of the 'old school' brigade frowning across a desk, radiating disapproval and a dismissive attitude. At one point in 2009, people adopted through the Rotunda Girls Aid Society were waiting up to eight years for an appointment with a designated social worker.[6]

Sadly, the heart-warming stories of reunions after forty or fifty years, occasionally seen in the media, are not the norm. In the majority of cases, neither party wants to meet and sometimes one party or the other will desperately want a reunion while the other wants no contact. While it may seem callous, many activists call the human interest stories in the media 'reunion porn' and utterly despise them as misrepresenting the real situation. Reunions fail for a variety of reasons and are emotionally complex on both sides. These include the legal and religious threats the nuns issued to natural mothers, personal circumstances where a new husband or a child is unaware of the situation, post-traumatic stress disorder, fear of disloyalty to adoptive parents, fear of rejection (also known as 'secondary rejection'). The issues adopted people face are now commonly referred to as the 'primal wounds', after a book published in 1993 and often referred to as the 'Adoptees' Bible' by the active community.[7] The effects of separation are the subject of hundreds of books and ongoing long-term research studies.

Hidden among the other issues is the 'love that dare not speak its name' in modern society. 'Genetic Sexual Attraction' is a phenomenon that is rarely discussed even among the active international adoption rights groups and has been buried deep underground by the multibillion-dollar international adoption industry. All of us as human beings are attracted to a certain 'type' of mate and we all tend to subconsciously choose mates similar to ourselves. Therefore, it makes sense that the people to whom we should feel the most attraction are our own siblings and parents. However, close relatives who intermarry will often have babies with mild to severe genetic deformities, as has been recognised for millennia. From a very young age, therefore, it is drilled into children that they cannot marry their parents or siblings and thus they grow up without feeling any sexual attraction towards immediate family members. This learned injunction is called 'reverse imprinting'. However, when adoptees meet their natural mothers or siblings in adulthood, that reverse imprinting is non-existent and there is sometimes a powerful and occasionally overwhelming sexual attraction between them. This includes natural fathers and daughters as well as brothers and sisters.

There are many stories about what the reality of this situation means to the adoption community and what happens next. For example, a common story in the Irish adoption community is about a priest who discovered that two people who wanted to get married were in fact at least half-brother and sister and possibly full siblings. The priest checked the background of the couple and sought 'letters of freedom' from both of them. He discovered the truth but went ahead and married them anyway. When the couple in question later discovered the truth and confronted him, he claimed he felt bound by the Data Protection Act not to inform them. How true that story is, this author does not know, but there are numerous confirmed stories of natural cousins marrying each other, and multiple proven stories around the world about half- or possibly full brothers and sisters accidentally marrying and later discovering their relationship. The best-known case is a German couple who met at college and fell madly in love. They later discovered they were brother and sister and that Genetic Sexual Attraction explained the overwhelming attraction they felt towards each other. They fought Germany's incest laws and even went to the Bavarian Supreme Court for the right to marry but they lost their case. They have four children.

The growing wealth of knowledge about the consequences of adoption is steadfastly ignored by those who seek to adopt in Western societies, and are aided and abetted by the profit- or religiously driven international adoption industry. Trans Racial Adoption was forced on society in the 1950s and 1960s and any person who spoke out was smeared as 'racist'. All research shows that the further an adoptee is removed from their native culture, country and ethnic background, the less successful the adoption will be. It is important to point out that the differences are relatively slight but grow as each further step away from an adoptee's origins is taken. 'Matching' is well understood as a method of ensuring successful adoptions and should be best practice today. However, it is widely ignored and sacrificed on the altar of political correctness and selfishness on the part of 'prospective adoptive parents'. Until the widespread availability of the internet, adoptive parents were innocent victims as much as adoptees and natural mothers. Prospective adoptive parents were informed by both Church and State that they were saving babies from a life in the industrial schools and were praised as generous and Christian by social workers and nuns. There was no information to counter this self-serving and disingenuous orthodoxy. Nowadays there are no excuses to be ill-informed.

Today, people automatically consider adoption to be a worthy and benevolent act especially when 'rescuing' orphans from poor countries. This is despite the fact that the majority of foreign adoptees are not orphans at all. They are simply from poor families who take the heartbreaking decision to temporarily place their children in orphanages until their circumstances improve. Parents in the poorest countries in the world return to orphanages to find that their children are gone forever, effectively sold by corrupt employees and local officials. The religious-based adoption industry has dishonestly claimed there is an 'orphan crisis' in the world, but they do not mention that their definition of an orphan is the biblical definition, that is, a child without a father. Single mothers are not viewed as parents by the right-wing religious fanatics.

Many people feel that these children are better off with their adoptive families. Without realising it, they mean *materially* better off. Emotionally and mentally, the adoptees are far worse off. Adoptee rights groups often wonder if the foreign adopters, who ignore the accredited evidence widely available, would so easily sell their own mothers for the latest iPhone or a private education. Although Irish people are outraged by what happened to the banished babies in Ireland, they can see no correlation with what wealthy Irish people continue to do to the poorest and most vulnerable women in the poorest countries in the world. Adopting a baby from abroad costs at least €40,000 to €50,000 and the adoption rights community points out that if the prospective adopters really cared about the 'best interests of the child', they would hand that money over to the poor families to keep them together, rather than taking their children. A slogan in our community is 'family preservation rather than separation'. Another slogan is that 'adoption is about finding homes for children and not about finding children for homes'. Anyone who cannot understand the difference is not fit to adopt a child.

The commercial surrogacy industry in India, Nepal and many other underdeveloped countries around the world is exploitative and grotesque. It costs around €70,000 upwards to obtain a surrogate baby or twins and it is presently legal for Irish citizens to adopt foreign babies. If it happens that too many of the implanted and fertilized eggs are viable, then the participants can opt to abort one or two or three of them and keep the remaining baby or two. The natural mothers, usually in desperate poverty, sign binding, legal contracts agreeing to relinquish all rights and to never look for their babies. Then they are given about €2,500 to €3,000 each for their services.

Miscarriages and the Foetal Mortality Rate

There are many aspects of the Mother and Baby Homes that have been ignored, including miscarriages and foetal deaths. Before a pregnancy has passed its twentieth week, a premature loss is called a miscarriage. Any loss after this time is called a foetal death, which includes stillborn babies. Detailed records exist in many of the Mother and Baby Home ledgers of every miscarriage and foetal death (including full-term stillborn babies) as required by the 1934 Registration of Maternity Homes Act. Stillborn babies were not officially registered and the nuns had to notify local authorities of any stillborn babies by registered post. After the forthcoming Commission of Inquiry into Mother and Baby

Homes, when the ledgers of some of the homes are examined in detail, it will be possible to ascertain the numbers of miscarriages and the foetal mortality rates (unless the ledgers are missing or falsified). They are expected to be considerably higher than the national average. In some cases, the nuns did not bother registering the birth and death of a baby who had survived for only a few hours; they simply declared it a stillbirth and reported it as such to the local authorities.

There are twelve years of records missing from Castlepollard during the first sixteen years of its operation. The surviving ledgers record seventy-seven stillbirths. Research released by the Castlepollard group records the names of 200 babies and children who died in Castlepollard. It is certain that when the stillbirths from the twelve missing years are included, the figure of seventy-seven for the other twenty-four years would be well above 100. If the figures for Castlepollard are applied to all the homes then, at an ultra-conservative minimum, all recorded figures for the Angels' Plots should be at least 50% higher – and probably more.

The babies who died without a chance at life are rarely mentioned. This is deeply unfair and dishonourable. Many of those babies would undoubtedly have lived if their mothers had received proper care, including a healthy diet and medical attention. Every one of them counts, in the homes and the holding centres and the secondary institutions. The Tuam 800 story will always be the Tuam 1,200 story to this author. The Castlepollard 200 will always be the Castlepollard 300. They were my crib mates and I refuse to forget them and the lives they never lived.

Vaccine Trials

In the 1990s, word began to leak out about experimental vaccine trials in the Mother and Baby Homes. The full story has yet to emerge and for many years it was believed that three trials had taken place in the three Sacred Heart homes and two other homes. The British-based pharmaceutical company Burroughs-Wellcome (now a part of GlaxoSmithKline) commissioned the trials. Most of the confirmed trials were carried out on behalf of the company by Professor Patrick Meenan and Dr (later Professor) Irene Hillary, both of University College Dublin medical school.

The Laffoy/Ryan Commission to Inquire into Child Abuse investigated the three trials, but Hillary went to Court in 2003 to prevent the investigation and won the case. The voluminous historical documents about the trials, which Glaxo had given the Ryan Commission, were returned to them.

When the Tuam 800 story broke in May 2014, Neil Michael was the chief reporter with the *Daily Mail* and when he searched for evidence about the homes he came into contact with Michael Dwyer, a professional historian and researcher in University College Cork. Dwyer had a long-standing fascination with the vaccine trials and decided to personally investigate the matter using a painstaking, old-school approach of methodically examining thousands of back issues of medical journals in search of articles about the trials. He was well advanced in his endeavours and writing a book on his findings when the Tuam 800 story broke. Dwyer was the recorded source behind the 6 June headline, one of the now famous 'Mail 9 Headlines' over eighteen days that resulted in the current Inquiry into Mother and Baby Homes.

The *Daily Mail* report and a subsequent article by Dwyer revealed that 2,051 children in twenty-four residential institutions had been test subjects between 1930 and 1935 in a Wellcome APT anti-diphtheria vaccine trial.[8] The three Sacred Heart homes were included in these trials, and Dwyer further confirmed that various other trials continued until 1977 and stated clearly that the nuns in the homes may not have been fully informed about what was occurring. Dwyer is resolute that the medical professionals who carried out the trials are the people directly and almost wholly responsible. Many activists in the survivor community, including myself, respectfully disagree with Dwyer and hold the nuns completely responsible, since they had a legal duty of care to safeguard the babies in their custody.

It is important to note that it is certain that no laws were broken, simply because there were no legal prohibitions on such experiments. Another important point is that Britain had strong legislation to prevent such human and civil rights abuses and no similar trials occurred there. However, it was easy for British-based pharmaceutical companies to cross the Irish Sea and pay Irish medical professionals instead.

One of the most controversial issues concerning the trials was consent. Natural mothers are adamant that they never agreed to any trials and never would. Indeed, it is universally agreed that they never even knew about the trials, let alone agreed to them. The issue has dogged the controversy and the position of the two professors involved is unclear because Meenan is dead and Hillary has long refused to discuss the matter. It would appear that the government, and in particular medical officers attached to the homes, had the right to give consent because the children were wards of the State.

Once a baby was selected for the research, he or she was kept in the Mother and Baby Home for up to a year and a half so the trials could be completed, before being adopted. This fact is seen by the survivor community as proof that the nuns must have known about the trials. There was no monitoring of the babies afterwards although the professors, doctors, pharmaceutical companies, government and nuns collectively insist there was no harm done to any of the people involved. How they know this remains one of the great mysteries in the history of Mother and Baby Homes for, without following up, how could they possibly know? It is a fact that *so far* there has been no evidence of anyone being adversely affected by the trials, but they were in direct contravention of the 1947 Nuremberg Code, issued after the trials of Nazi war criminals to prevent the type of experiments conducted by doctors such as Josef Mengele ever reoccurring. The State and medical professionals simply ignored the international code.

Between 1960 and 1973 there were three confirmed trials of experimental and modified vaccines carried out in the three Sacred Heart-run Mother and Baby Homes. Many of the trials were written up as scientific articles in respected medical journals, such as *The Lancet*. The three known trials began in December 1960 when an experimental 4-in-1 vaccine was tested on a number of babies and children in the Sacred Heart Homes in Castlepollard (6), Bessboro (25), Pelletstown/St. Patrick's (14), Dunboyne (9) and Stamullen (4). The trials were carried out on groups of babies up to two years old. The second trial was in St. Anne's industrial school in Dublin in 1970 for a Rubella vaccine given to sixty-nine subjects. Finally, there was Trivax, a 3-in-1 vaccine tested in 1973 on fifty-three children in children's homes in Dublin.

The total number of babies used as human guinea pigs in the three known trials that were first revealed is 211, and 123 of those were in the homes. The information available at present suggests that the children outside the homes may have been a 'control group' who were given placebos or previously tested vaccines, although this has not been confirmed. There are other indications that schoolchildren and even army recruits were used to trial other vaccines.

Up until 2011, GlaxoSmithKline were only admitting to these three trials but an investigation by RTÉ's *Prime Time* programme forced Glaxo to admit a fourth trial in Sean Ross Abbey in 1964. Then it emerged in late 2014 that Michael Dwyer had found an article in *The Lancet* on a fifth trial in 1965 with a measles vaccine being prepared by Glaxo Laboratories. Thirty-four children, aged between eight months and two years, were used as test subjects; although there is no mention of exactly where the trial took place, it was almost certainly some kind of home that housed many children. Glaxo currently denies that the fifth trial took place in a Mother and Baby Home. However, there is a recorded case of a baby in Bessboro receiving a 5-in-1 test vaccine in that same year.[9]

The vaccine trials are included in the current Inquiry into Mother and Baby Homes and perhaps we will finally learn the truth. However, there is one final twist to this tale that does not bode well for the survivors of the trials who are seeking answers. In 2015 Conall Ó Fátharta, reporting in *The Examiner*, revealed that he had made a Freedom of Information request and had uncovered irrefutable evidence, in the form of written proof generated by the Sacred Heart nuns themselves, that they had altered records relating to the stays of mothers and babies who were included in the 1960 vaccine trials. Through the online community groups, it is now also clear that a high proportion of the vaccine-trial survivors were banished babies.

Signs of Change: The Early 1960s

Tuam Mother and Baby Home closed in 1961. The Department of Local Government and Galway County Council had discussed a major renovation of the building, but they decided that it was not economical and the home was to be closed. In early 1961, the Bon Secours began transferring their residents from Tuam to Sean Ross Abbey and Bessboro. Anecdotal evidence suggests that some went to Castlepollard and as far away as Pelletstown/St. Patrick's in Dublin. By the summer of 1961, Tuam was empty. The buildings were later demolished and a housing estate was built on the site. The original Angels' Plot remains surrounded by houses. It is walled off and clearly delineated. A children's playground has been built beside the cemetery. However, many people, including Catherine Corless, the acknowledged expert on Tuam, are adamant that there are more burials outside the walls and the area should be properly excavated and examined.

From the early 1960s, the only sign of change was within the different departments of state which were fighting with one another over the future of the industrial and reformatory schools. The issues were controversial; in 1962 a committee recommended complete closure or, failing that, implementing multiple recommendations on improving standards. Both options were ignored. The politicians and senior civil servants tried to pass the responsibility over to another department to close the schools or reform them, and there was no central well-defined policy. Although a substantial number of the schools did close down in a piecemeal fashion, many continued into the 1970s and even the 1980s, until the remaining few saw another change of use.

In 1962, Archbishop McQuaid commissioned an American Jesuit priest named Biever to carry out a survey into the Catholic Church's position in Ireland and how ordinary people perceived the Church.[10] The results by today's standards seem astonishing. Nine out of ten Dubliners said they would side with the Church if there was a conflict between it and the State. The vast majority of people were devoted to the Church and considered the hierarchy to be the true leaders of the country. Biever declared Ireland was 'virtually a Theocracy' with all social legislation vetted in advance by McQuaid and his colleagues.

Séan Lemass became Taoiseach in 1959, and gradually began to modernise Ireland, economically if not socially. Socially, he walked a fine line between an all-powerful Church and an increasing desire among young people for radical social change. Televisions arrived and the foreign stations showed people a world of colour beyond Ireland's grey existence. The spirit of the 1960s was progressive and demanded individual freedoms and equal rights, but while Irish people saw the changes abroad being implemented, they knew that action on issues such as contraceptives, divorce, homosexuality and the lifting of censorship were years, if not decades, away in Ireland.

My Story, Part I

Over the years the nuns created many abusive terms for single mothers and children, but the Sacred Heart nuns seemed to delight in one particular phrase. They called illegitimate babies 'the spawn of Satan'.

I was born in Castlepollard in 1964. I have always been very private about my personal story and have spoken about it to the media on two occasions and only then because of particular circumstances.

The Dominican nuns have never had anything to do with adoption in Ireland and their primary mission is education. They run several very middle-class schools for girls along the east coast of Ireland, including Sion Hill in Blackrock, Co. Dublin, and Muckross Park in Donnybrook, Dublin 4. From some point in the mid-1950s and possibly earlier, the Dominicans unofficially appointed one of their nuns to make the necessary arrangements if any of their girls 'got into trouble'.

Sister Marcoline Lawlor was one of two sisters from Wicklow who joined the order. She qualified as an English and Drama teacher and moved around the Dominican schools, but taught mainly at their Wicklow convent. My natural mother, Adeline, was a former Dominican schoolgirl when she discovered she was expecting me around the time she turned 20. Her parents contacted her old school principal for advice and she contacted Marcoline. My natural maternal grandparents were wealthy and, as such, my mother's time in the system would be very short.

Marcoline was living in the Dominican Convent in Cabra at the time and it was about a ten-minute walk to St. Patrick's Mother and Baby Home. She sent most of her schoolgirls there as public patients. However, because my grandparents were among the select few who could at the time afford £100, Adeline was sent to Castlepollard as a private patient and she arrived just four weeks before I was due. Because of their money,

Adeline's parents had options for their daughter that were unavailable for public patients. They could have requested a single or shared room on the top floor instead of the dormitories on the middle floor. Adeline could have been exempted from work at their request. My grandparents also had the choice to allow their daughter to see her own baby after I was born. I was born on 4 December 1964 and my natural mother and I remained in Castlepollard for thirteen days. Adeline named me Jude with no middle name. I was baptised with a girl named Ann three days later without my mother present. One of the nuns, probably Sister Aidan, inserted the name Peter in front of Jude and I was named after the Mother and Baby Home itself, St. Peter's.

On 17 December, my mother and I were transferred to St. Patrick's (Pelletstown), Navan Road, in Cabra. I believe we were driven to Dublin in the local Castlepollard taxi by Mr. Murray, who doubled as the nuns' part-time janitor in the home and looked after many transfers for them. When we arrived in Pelletstown, Sister Agnes received us and I was taken from Adeline's arms while she was ordered to wait in the hallway. I have never seen her since. I was handed to someone, possibly a natural mother as part of her daily duties, who brought me to the wards occupied by hundreds of unaccompanied babies and children. Meanwhile, Sister Agnes went into her office and phoned my grandfather who was in the legal profession with an office in Dublin city centre. He was told his daughter would be waiting outside and to collect her immediately. Adeline was ordered to go outside and wait, and her father arrived about twenty minutes later.

Marcoline came to visit me and checked that I was healthy. I underwent a medical examination and was declared a 'normal healthy male infant'. My adoptive parents, John and Anita Redmond, collected me four days later. They were advised to bring a change of clothes and prepared bottled milk. Sister Agnes bustled out to meet them. They showed her a letter from Sister Marcoline. 'Oh yes,' Sister Agnes said and raised her eyes to heaven, 'another one of Marcoline's "specials"!' Marcoline was a genuine nun and tried her best to ensure proper care for her charges. I believe she was well aware of the cruelty in the homes. I later discovered that she had a habit of telling the nuns to take 'special care' of either a mother or a baby because they were 'very special'. Both the Sacred Heart nuns and

Daughters of Charity found this amusing and took to calling her charges 'Marcoline's specials'.

My adoptive parents brought me back to Pelletstown when I was 3 months old to meet Marcoline for tea and cakes. I was inspected and declared to be 'very special'. A casual remark by my father led to Marcoline making a mention of both my natural parents. That single sentence remains the only clue to the identity of my natural father.

I grew up in Dublin and spent ten long years in a Christian Brothers school in the suburb of Stillorgan. I had a happy childhood with my family as the oldest of five children. I have no memory of being informed that I was adopted, but I grew up always knowing it and understanding what it meant, and that is the only way to do it. In our community, we say that if you are old enough to remember being told you are adopted, then you were told too late.

I wondered about my natural mother for as long as I can remember. She was a shadow because I knew nothing about her and she seemed always just out of reach. When I turned to catch a glimpse, she moved but was still behind me just at the edge of my vision, tantalisingly close. I tried so hard as a child to put colour or shape on the mysterious lady who haunted my life. I wanted to turn and face the shadow and fill it with colour and life, but it was always out of reach. It was not until I was in my early twenties that I could finally give my shadow a name and begin to bring her from behind me into the light. I was convinced, as only a child can be, that she would attend when I made my First Holy Communion. I have a vivid memory of lying in my bed on that Saturday morning in 1972, staring at the ceiling and contemplating seeing my shadow for the first time. On my way into the church, I scanned the back looking for a kindly lady with strawberry blonde hair. I did the same on my way out in the procession. She was not there.

The Second Vatican Council (1962–5) dragged the Catholic Church into the twentieth century, although there was significant resistance within its own ranks. Meanwhile, in the background, the Adoption Machine silently continued behind the high walls, invisible, extremely efficient, and utterly ruthless in the forced separation of single mothers and their babies. In 1967, the Western world listened to the Beatles' seminal album *Sergeant Pepper's Lonely Hearts Club Band*. The new generation sang along to the first live, satellite, television broadcast, featuring 'All You Need Is Love'. That same year, the 'Summer of Love', the number of children born to single mothers in Ireland and then adopted peaked at a staggering world record of 97% as the highly polished Adoption Machine reached its zenith.

CHAPTER 8

The Beginning of the End

The county homes were gone by the late 1960s and other changes were affecting the network of Mother and Baby Homes. The first indications that something was happening came from the Sacred Heart nuns. Mother Superior General Antonia Philipps, from Kilmuckridge, Co. Wexford, had run the order for twenty-two years since Mother Superior General Laurence Daly had died. Philips was awarded the Order of the British Empire in 1956 by Queen Elizabeth for her 'valuable services … to the care and education of handicapped children and adults'.[1] There was a General Chapter in 1963,[2] a meeting of all available nuns in the order, and she was replaced by Bernadette Flavin who served for only two years before her sudden death. Shortly after she died, a new mission she had accepted came to fruition and the Sacred Hearts dispatched two nuns to Zimbabwe to help staff a new school there. The two nuns, Sister Anne Ahearn and Sister Mary Sarto Harney, flew from Heathrow in December 1965. Sarto, who is still alive and living in Cork, is very well-known to the Irish survivor community because she later became Mother Superior of Bessboro and ran the Sacred Heart Adoption Society.

Flavin was replaced in 1965 by Etheldreda Gleeson, who ruled until 1978[3] when she was in turn replaced by Oliver Kinane. Gleeson was faced with a serious challenge when many nuns began leaving the order with few new vocations to replace them. The sudden and acute shortage of personnel in the aftermath of the Second Vatican Council, and the spirit of the 1960s that was liberalising British society, combined to spell the end of the Mother and Baby Homes. Gleeson saw the writing on the wall and decided to close them down. She began with Brettargholt in the Lake District and Kelton in Liverpool in 1968. St. Pelagia's in

London, the first Catholic Mother and Baby Home in the world, closed its doors in 1970.

In Ireland, Sean Ross Abbey was closed in 1969 and the remaining residents were transferred to Bessboro, although the nuns kept possession of Sean Ross and occupied it for many years. Castlepollard stopped receiving new patients in the mid-1970s and it finally closed on 17 March 1971. Any remaining residents were transferred to Bessboro. The Castlepollard complex was sold to the Midlands Health Board. St. Peter's became a residential centre for adults and children with severe learning difficulties and began to receive patients from St. Loman's in nearby Mullingar.

Next to close was the Protestant Bethany Home in 1972. Now there were only three remaining of the original nine: Pelletstown/St. Patrick's in Dublin, Bessboro in Cork and Dunboyne in Meath. The nuns reduced the average length of time residents stayed in the homes and once again eased the regimes.

A similar phenomenon affected the private nursing homes around the country. The 1972 Health Act caused near panic in the private homes. According to the website of Adopted Illegally Ireland, the highly respected campaigner Theresa Hiney Tinggal wrote:

> 42 mother and baby homes, mainly run by nurses involved in this informal or illegal … [adoption] … practice, closed suddenly in 1972 when the new Health Act came into force. An astounding coincidence I would say. But what's even more astounding is out of those 42 nursing homes, there is reportedly not one set of files available, which is statistically unrealistic. Somewhere these files are hidden away in archives and informal adoptees should have the right to access these files.

Regina Coeli was still quietly scraping by. The Dublin Health Authority inspected the hostel for single mothers and children in 1963 and condemned the buildings. It was scheduled for closure, but Frank Duff fought back. At 74 years of age, he declared he would chain himself to the building if it were closed. He was interviewed by *The Irish Times* and on RTÉ television as part of a media campaign to prevent the closure.

The battle dragged on and took a toll on Duff's health, but he finally won. Regina Coeli was granted money for an extensive renovation and it continued to operate. The threat of closure remained until 2007 when the Legion of Mary was finally granted outright ownership of the hostel. Duff wrote in 1971 that Regina has accommodated 'about three thousand, five hundred children' since its foundation in 1930.[4] The two holding centres, Temple Hill and Stamullen, also survived the cull and continued into the 1980s and 1990s.

In 1970, the Garda ban on illegitimate people joining its ranks was abolished. The reason was simple. The first people legally adopted after 1 January 1953, under the 1952 Adoption Act, were turning 18 and therefore were eligible to join the Garda Síochána but they would have been automatically refused because of their illegitimacy. Legal adoption had made illegitimacy acceptable and the discrimination had to end. There was no such move by the Catholic Church and illegitimate people are still banned from becoming priests.

Cherish (including Gingerbread and One Family)

In retrospect, it is astonishing that Maura O'Dea and her small group of single mothers managed to achieve so much in such a short time. O'Dea gave birth to her son in 1970 in a private nursing home; shortly afterwards she left her comfortable flat in Ballsbridge, Dublin, and ended up living in a mobile home in Tallaght. O'Dea's parents were dead but she had a good job and bought herself a small house in Kimmage. She reached out and connected with a handful of other single mothers and they joined together and established a representative group in 1972. Another of the founder members, Colette O'Neill, suggested the name 'Cherish' and they all agreed that it was perfect; the symbolism is clear. It was well over fifty years since several similar groups had formed in Britain. Considering the repressive atmosphere and hostility towards single mothers and their babies, it is a testament to their bravery that they banded together to fight the Church and State.

O'Dea wrote to the newspapers, asking them to spread the word about Cherish, and courageously included her name, address and phone number. The media arrived on her doorstep. The resultant publicity ensured that Cherish took off in spectacular fashion. There is nothing more powerful than an idea whose time has come. In spite of resistance and even abuse on the streets, Cherish began to raise funds with flag days and raffles.

Cherish began lobbying the government immediately and, after only one year, scored a major victory when an 'unmarried mothers' allowance was introduced in 1973. It was a paltry £8.50 per week, but it gave single mothers something they had lacked for generations – a choice. This meagre allowance, more than anything else, transformed the future for single mothers in Ireland. Maura O'Dea rightly won the *Irish Times* 'Person of the Year' award in 1975.

Cherish has gone through major changes over the years and amalgamated with other groups, including 'Gingerbread', and is now known as 'One Family'. This new name reflects their commitment to all single-parent families and they still do Trojan work assisting single mothers in dozens of ways. Cherish was also largely responsible for the Status of Children Act in 1987 which abolished illegitimacy as a legal concept and a discriminatory label. It remains another milestone in the fight for equality for babies born out of wedlock.

The one great regret about Cherish is that the organisation did not, and does not, deal with the past. They have never campaigned for an investigation into the previous treatment of single mothers or into what occurred in the Mother and Baby Homes. In fairness to Cherish, the organisation always looked forward and put the pressing needs of single mothers and children above all else. That minor quibble aside, their outstanding courage and commitment over the decades have been extraordinary. More than any other group, Cherish achieved sweeping changes in how Ireland perceives and treats single mothers and their babies.

Kennedy Report

In 1967, Judge Eileen Kennedy was appointed to investigate the industrial and reformatory schools. To her credit, her Inquiry included a visit to each and every one of the approximately thirty to forty surviving schools and was scathing in its assessment: the schools were staffed with members of the religious orders who had no qualifications in childcare. The Kennedy Report was highly critical of the conditions in general: the inadequate clothing, the poor food, substandard sanitary facilities and lack of real education. The draft section on 'discipline' was so grim that the entire section was removed from the final report. What was particularly disturbing was that the report revealed that some of the schools had never once been visited by the Department of Education's official inspectors. Many of the civil servants within the department were openly hostile and obstructive to the Inquiry. A number of the schools remained open until 1984 when they were recertified but with hugely improved standards of care. The Magdalene Laundries were briefly mentioned in a bad light in the Kennedy Report but the omission of references to Mother and Baby Homes was an unfortunate lapse.

The Kennedy Report was the first in a number of inquiries and investigations over the years. What is noteworthy is that not one of these inquiries addressed the Mother and Baby Homes or the wider issue of the forced separation of single mothers and their children since 1922. This is inexplicable given the numbers involved. Around 50,000 children went through the industrial schools since 1922, another 16,000 through the reformatory schools and approximately 16,000 women and girls were in the Magdalene Laundries, a total of about 82,000 women and children.

About 100,000 women in Ireland lost their babies to forced separation since 1922. Some 35,000 went through the homes. It is difficult to state even an approximate figure for the workhouses/county homes because figures are unavailable for many years after the mid-1930s, but it must be well over 20,000 and possibly as high as the total numbers from the Mother and Baby Homes. In short, at least 55,000 single mothers went through the institutional 'care' system between 1922 and 1996. The figure is well over 100,000 Irish citizens when the babies are included, a total higher than all the other institutions combined. Equally, the number of deaths in the Mother and Baby Homes alone is likely to be over 6,000 at a highly conservative estimate. Yet since the Kennedy Inquiry, all the institutions have been investigated (albeit that some of the investigations were rushed and incomplete, such as the interdepartmental McAleese Magdalene

Inquiry). The homes remained hidden from public consciousness until 2014 when tens of thousands of survivors had already passed away. They were denied justice in life and in death. One of the notable results of the Kennedy Report was the Church's ferocious counter-attack. A litany of excuses followed as one individual after another blamed 'underfunding' as the cause of the neglect. The Catholic Church demanded that both the government and the people of Ireland should in fact be 'grateful' to them for their selfless work.

Minister for Justice Paddy Cooney gave a speech at an adoption conference as late as 1974 and stated that adoption 'is better for the illegitimate baby than to be cared for by its mother', but it was too late. The impetus for change was outpacing the slow-moving political and Church attitudes, and the numbers of single women having babies continued to increase. Adoption numbers peaked in 1973 at around 1,500, an increase of 50% on numbers in the 1960s, but, after that, it is a story of sharp decline. Ten years later, it was extremely difficult to adopt babies, and waiting lists were growing. Twenty years later, there was only a handful of babies available for adoption and Ireland has now been transformed from an exporter, to an importer, of babies. The battle for single mothers to retain custody of their children and raise them was part of a long social war between an increasingly secular Republic and Catholic Ireland. The war continued into the 1990s before it became clear that the Irish people were rejecting old-school Catholicism and embracing new freedoms and international norms.

In 1975, Britain passed the Children Act and opened all the previously sealed adoption records in England and Wales. Despite some voicing of fears at this development, after an initial surge of applications, mostly by adoptees to see their files, everything settled down and life went on. In 2017, Ireland's adoption files are still sealed.

By the mid-to-late 1970s, the three remaining homes were practically unrecognisable except for Dunboyne where the relatively liberal regime continued to improve. In Bessboro and Pelletstown/St. Patrick's, the former inmates and offenders were now 'residents' and 'patients' and they knew their rights. Many of them stood up to the nuns and successfully demanded to leave with their babies. A couple of the nuns in Pelletstown even helped new mothers to source accommodation so they could leave with their babies. By the late 1970s, between Bessboro and Pelletstown, there was a pool table, a jukebox, televisions and a smoking room. The residents were allowed their own small transistor radios and rock and roll music echoed through the corridors and dormitories. The women in Pelletstown held weekly dances just for themselves, although they were still closely supervised by the nuns. The residents there also began leaving on a daily basis to go out and work locally as domestic cleaners. Many saved their earnings for deposits on flats for themselves and their babies.

The nuns adapted to the new circumstances and used a variety of psychological tricks to entice women into giving up their babies for adoption. Emotional blackmail was common and the nuns and associated social workers frequently asked vulnerable and confused women, often suffering from post-natal depression, if they wanted the best for their babies – didn't they want their babies to have a good home with a mother and a father who could provide the material comforts they could never provide? Many women caved in but an ever-increasing number left Pelletstown, Bessboro and Dunboyne (via Holles Street Maternity Hospital) with their babies and children. Women who lost their children to adoption in the 1970s often feel a great deal more guilt than women from earlier times. They witnessed some of their fellow residents fight for the right to leave with their children and often blame themselves for not fighting hard enough to keep their own. They are entirely innocent victims, of course, but they blame themselves nonetheless.

An ever-increasing number of single mothers never went near the three remaining homes and chose to attend public maternity hospitals where the staff generally disapproved but nevertheless provided proper care. From 1970 to 1980 the number of babies born to single mothers more than doubled from 1,700 to over 3,400. Some were convinced by social workers to relinquish their babies, but many insisted on keeping their infants. Waiting lists for children available for adoption kept growing.

In 1977, it was brought to the government's attention that the Adoption Board had usurped the court's authority in 'rubber-stamping' adoptions, rather than going through the courts and, because of this, thousands of adoptions were probably invalid. The government was forced to hold a referendum in 1979 to immediately legalise all adoptions. The turnout was very low but it passed with an almost unanimous 99% vote and became the Sixth Amendment to the Constitution.

My Story, Part II

I remember that referendum well because my parents were going out on a Thursday night and that was not their usual routine. I asked where they were going. My mother briefly explained that they were going to vote and why. She said that I could be taken away from them at any time if the referendum did not pass. This was not a reassuring thing to hear as an awkward and insecure 15-year-old teenager. I do not remember when exactly, but around this time I finally did something about tracing my elusive shadow. I looked up the address of the Adoption Board in the phone book and cycled about six miles into Dublin city centre. I chained my bike to the railings outside an imposing Georgian house. Probably bright red with embarrassment, as I blushed easily as the time, I knocked and explained to the man who answered that I was looking for information relating to my adoption. He went off to get someone and a dour woman appeared and asked me to step inside. I again explained myself in the gloomy and echoing entrance hall. She brusquely informed me that I had to wait until I was 21 before I could be given any information, and had hardly finished before spinning around and marching towards the front door. I followed in confusion and when she stopped suddenly, I passed her and found her hand on my lower back firmly guiding me out. I turned but the door was already closing in my face. Not slammed, just very firmly closed.

Over the next few years I poked around here and there and occasionally asked questions about my adoption, but I got nowhere. The years of youth are slow and it seemed an eternity to wait five or six years until my 21st birthday when I could go back to the Adoption Board and get my shadow's name. Along the way, the odd article in a newspaper about adoption made me realise that the records in Ireland were sealed and unless my shadow wanted to get in touch, I would learn nothing. During my teenage years, I had discovered that I was a collector by nature. I'd loved soccer-trading cards as a child, and kept scrapbooks of my favourite team, Liverpool. That was followed by a Star Wars *obsession, then the Beatles. Record-collecting led to first meeting my best friend, Peter Fitzpatrick, in an underground bootleg shop; he introduced me to my beloved Siobhán whom I would later marry. Collecting has both defined and shaped my life in many ways.*

During my adult years the focus of my obsessions changed, and I began studying subjects that fired my imagination – the Dead Sea Scrolls, early Christianity, Quantum Mechanics, the assassination of John. F. Kennedy. This obsessional impulse ensured I would never stop searching for answers, and I searched for thirty-three years before I finally had a phone call with my shadow. I am still searching today and probably always will be. And in a lonely Angels' Plot in the midlands in 2011, this defined my reaction to a new mystery that demanded answers.

A More Enlightened Era: The 1970s

A new type of sub-institution appeared over the course of the 1970s and 80s. Supervised 'flatlets' were similar to private nursing homes but were generally run by nuns. The name is self-explanatory. Most of them were clustered around the area between the Dublin suburbs of Donnybrook and Ranelagh, the same area where numerous private nursing homes had accommodated wealthy single mothers for generations. This area was also previously known for nursing homes carrying out illegal adoptions. Because the numbers were so small in the flatlets, there was very little first-hand information about them. What is known, from the few people who have related their experiences, is that the women who stayed in them were generally middle-class and well educated. They were mostly professional women who had made the personal choice that the time was wrong for them to start a family. They either did not agree with abortion (in Britain) or they had left it too late. There is no evidence they were ever forced to stay or relinquish their babies. Neither is there a whisper of abuse about the flatlets other than the psychological tricks the nuns, social workers and lay workers used to convince the residents to relinquish their babies when the time came.

These flatlets are included in the current Inquiry into Mother and Baby Homes.

The 1980s were a time of slow and uncertain change in Ireland. Despite the Troubles continuing in Northern Ireland and a grinding recession throughout the decade, there was an increasing demand for change from young people. A new generation came of age and, although they had grown up in an Ireland still under the control of the Catholic Church, they were also exposed to overseas television, Punk Rock and New Wave music and they were intensely aware that Ireland was decades behind international norms in social progress and personal freedoms. Economic circumstances may have been bad from the late 1970s but many teenagers and young adults had benefitted from free secondary school education. They were infinitely more educated and enlightened than their parents' generation and keenly aware that the Catholic Church was the primary source of their repression. An ongoing and heated debate in public life and the media included such topics as feminism, equality, the decriminalisation of homosexuality, the influence of foreign television, abortion, divorce and contraception.

As more and more single women and girls kept their babies, the issue became increasingly controversial and the subject of a bitter, class-ridden and divisive public debate. In several working-class areas from the late 1970s, there was an explosion of single teenage girls choosing to raise their own children. Young people's attitudes had changed but the older generation was still repeating the same arguments that had existed for over 200 years. The British government granted large sums of money to Captain Coram's Foundling Hospital shortly after it was opened in 1739 and an argument raged about granting public money to institutions. Centuries later, Ireland's hard-pressed taxpayers were outraged that their taxes were going to support 'sinners and bastards', in effect forcing 'decent' taxpayers to involuntarily support vice and indolence.

The new revolution was led to some extent by Bob Geldof, the lead singer of the Boomtown Rats, the most popular of the crop of new Irish bands that formed in the punk era of the late 1970s and early 1980s. In spite of his trademark scruffiness, Geldof was in fact from a solidly middle-class background. He was intelligent, well-read, articulate and highly critical of both Church and State. Geldof voiced the feelings of young people and he was joined by plenty of other angry bands from Dublin and other cities in Ireland to lead a long overdue social revolution.

The conflict dragged on throughout the 1980s. The Church was still a powerful entity and politicians remained wary of public condemnation. The older generation was often alarmed by the pace of change and fought to maintain the status quo with their votes and attendance at Sunday Mass. Any doubts about who was ultimately in charge were dispelled by two referenda in the 1980s. The final vote tallies reflect Ireland's stunted social progress. The first in 1983 was passed with a 67% majority, ensuring that abortion was constitutionally barred in Ireland. There was endless controversy over the right to even give information about abortion to pregnant women. Another referendum in 1986 to remove the constitutional prohibition on divorce also failed, with 63% of voters rejecting it. Contraception was re-legalised in 1985 for the first time since its ban in 1935, but was severely restricted and often impossible to obtain.

The Catholic ethos was so deeply embedded in the Constitution and legislation that change would have to be generational. Several major controversies and events during the 1980s brought the older generation of still devout Catholics into conflict with the younger population. Many of the issues centred on single motherhood. The controversy centred around what was still called the Unmarried Mothers Allowance and taxpayers' 'rights' versus single mothers' 'rights'. Two dreadful incidents brought that debate to a head.

Of all the tragedies that have affected single mothers over the years there is still something unbearably sad and poignant about Ann Lovett's death. On a cold, wet winter's day on 31 January 1984 in Co. Longford, 15-year-old Ann left school and went to a nearby grotto dedicated to the Virgin Mary. She gave birth to a son who died and Ann was barely alive and bleeding heavily when she was discovered by passing schoolchildren. After they had alerted a farmer, Ann was brought to the local priest's house and then to her parents' house. She died before the ambulance arrived.

Bessboro Mother and Baby Home, Cork. Courtesy of Sharon Lawless.

Castlepollard Mother and Baby Home, Co. Westmeath. Courtesy of Kim Haughton/*Sunday Times*.

Author at 17 days old on his Adoption Day, shortly after leaving St. Patrick's Mother and Baby Home. Courtesy of the author.

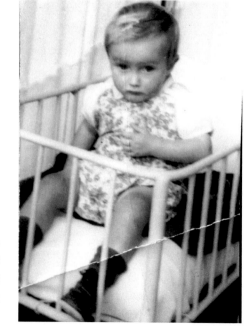

Crib mate of the author, Brian Lockier, in a cot at Sean Ross Abbey. Brian was adopted out to American adoptive parents and still lives in the US. Courtesy of Brian Lockier.

Sign at the rear of Castlepollard Mother and Baby Home, with St. Joseph's Chapel on right. Courtesy of Kim Haughton/*Sunday Times*.

Memorial stone at Castlepollard Angels' Plot erected by the Sacred Heart nuns. 'In memory of God's special angels/Interred in this cemetary'. Note misspelling of 'cemetary'. Courtesy of Kim Haughton/*Sunday Times*.

Memorial nail in the wall of Castlepollard Angels' Plot. Local workmen hammered a nail into the adjacent wall for each baby they buried. Courtesy of Kim Haughton/*Sunday Times*.

Angels' Plot at Castlepollard where an estimated 200 babies and children are buried. Courtesy of the author.

Memorial stone at Sean Ross Abbey Angels' Plot. Courtesy of Sharon Lawless.

National flags in the Sean Ross Abbey Angels' Plot, left by visiting survivors of the home. Courtesy of Sharon Lawless.

A shrine in the Tuam Angels' Plot, erected in memory of the estimated 800 children who were buried at the site. © Paul Faith/Getty Images.

Front page headlines breaking the story of Tuam 800, from the *Irish Daily Mail*, May 2014. Courtesy of *Irish Daily Mail*.

Author at Castlepollard Mother and Baby Home, with St. Joseph's Chapel and Convent in background. Courtesy of Kim Haughton/*Sunday Times*.

The media arrived in force and the public reaction was an outpouring of sorrow and rage. A public debate went on for months in the newspapers and on the airwaves. In previous years many teenage girls had died in childbirth but they died behind the high walls of the homes and no one ever knew except their immediate families. Ann Lovett's public death forced Ireland to face a heartbreaking reality that had been hidden since independence.

While the debate about Ann Lovett's death was dying down another event occurred and reignited the debate.

On 14 April 1984, the body of a newborn baby was found on a beach in Cahersiveen, Co. Kerry. The baby was born alive, washed and his umbilical cord cut. He had been stabbed twenty-eight times and his neck was broken. Joanne Hayes was a single woman, pregnant and due to give birth around the same time. Her baby was nowhere to be found and so Joanne and her extended family were charged with murdering the baby found on the beach. It emerged that Joanne's baby had in fact died shortly after birth and the body was hidden on the family farm. The problem was that before Joanne's baby was found, several members of the extended Hayes family had 'confessed' to being involved in the murder and disposal of the body. The focus moved immediately to the Gardaí and how they had obtained these multiple false confessions and details that could not possibly have been known to the Hayes family. The Gardaí investigating the case refused to admit to anything and came up with a theory that was widely ridiculed.

The two dead babies, who were found many miles apart, had different blood types and therefore could not have shared the same father. However, the Gardaí discovered a rare type of pregnancy whereby a woman can become pregnant with children from two different fathers if she has intercourse with both of them at around the same time. The Gardaí pounced on the explanation and started a vicious smear campaign to discredit Joanne Hayes. It backfired badly, resulting in the Kerry Babies Tribunal, which was critical of how the Gardaí had conducted the investigation but just as scathing towards the victims, the Hayes family.

Many women across Ireland were outraged at how the tribunal had treated Joanne herself and the country was split, not just on the truth about the Kerry Babies case but on the wider issue of women's rights and single motherhood. The fact that the government ordered a judicial tribunal that was held in Kerry with an all-male membership further outraged many women. The Kerry Babies Report was published in October 1985. It took until early 2018 for the Gardaí to review the case and confirm that DNA samples finally proved Joanne Hayes was not the mother of the Cahirciveen baby. The Gardaí publicly apologised to Joanne and announced they were going to re open the case.

Between Ann Lovett's unnecessary death and the vilification of Joanne Hayes, Ireland was forced to face its own prejudice and silent complicity.

St. Patrick's Mother and Baby Home (Pelletstown) on the Navan Road in Dublin, and St. Patrick's Infant Hospital, known as Temple Hill, in Blackrock, both closed quietly and without fanfare in 1985 and 1987 respectively. Contrary to popular belief, Pelletstown did not fully close; it downsized to a period house of supervised flatlets in Dublin 4. The old Pelletstown building, forerunner to St. Patrick's, was unceremoniously demolished and a middle-class, suburban housing estate named Kempton stands on the old grounds. At the same time, expectant mothers were sitting their Leaving Certificate exams at Bessboro.

My Story, Part III

My parents and I had not mentioned my adoption since I was 6 or 7 years of age and it became a taboo subject for us all. I was therefore very surprised, and mortified, when I was about 20 and they brought up the subject. They were clearly as embarrassed as I was. They explained that the Dominican nun who had arranged my adoption had been assigned to a convent in Lisbon for many years but was coming home from Portugal for a visit and wanted to meet me.

I met Sister Marcoline a few weeks later and she was a force of nature, tiny but brimming with energy and good humour. Sister Marcoline was one of those people to whom you just cannot say no and she never let anything slip about my background in all the years I knew her. She did, however, get my parents to write to my old adoption agency and then contacted the social worker who was handling the case. An appointment was made for me. Since it was with my parents' blessing and with Sister Marcoline's influence, I felt no guilt, which is often felt by adoptees searching for their natural mothers. The social worker was working out of an office in St. James's Hospital.

I was apprehensive and nervous when I went to the appointment. The office was cluttered and reeked of age. Mrs. R was rather austere and prim. She initially asked me some general questions about how my adoption was going. She then went through my details, blandly reading them from a file, which she held up in front of her face in case I snuck a glance at it. I was born in Castlepollard. I had never heard of the place. My natural mother was Catholic and over 21 when I was born. She was from northside Dublin. Then the big moment arrived. I was 22 years old and my shadow finally had a name. It was Adeline.

The rest of the interview was a blur. I vaguely remember Mrs. R. saying that she was going to write to the old address on the file, but that seemed a million miles away. My shadow's name was Adeline.

I remember leaving the building and walking towards town. The south side of James' Street was in shadow, so I ran across the road into the sunshine and bounced up onto the path. I wanted to run with excitement. I have a vivid memory of singing Van Morrison's song 'Bright Side of the Road'. It was like striking gold. I truly believed that I had enough to find my mother on my own without my social worker. I was on a high for weeks.

There was another meeting with Mrs. R. a few months later but only to confirm that there was no reply to the letter that had been sent. My social worker said I was not to worry because this was what usually happened and I should not feel bad. I would be much better off just moving on with my life now. I already knew that the woman in the Adoption Board had lied and that I could have applied when I was 18 years old rather than 21 as she had told me. I had an innate distrust of the establishment and I simply did not believe any of the 'no-reply-to-letter' stories. I fully intended to redouble my efforts.

I poked away once more with the limited information I had acquired. I knew Adeline was from the northside of Dublin and that she had been over 21 in order to sign the adoption relinquishment forms. I figured out *that since Adeline was over 21, she had to be registered to vote. Since I knew the voters' register was a public document, I only had to find a copy covering the year of my birth and go through the whole of north Dublin for women named Adeline. I tracked down a copy to the Dublin City Council's office on O'Connell Street and came up with a plan. I wore a Trinity College scarf a student friend had loaned me and explained to the manager that I was doing a research project on how first names reflect the values of our society. He gave me permission to access the registers to do my research. I returned several times and went through hundreds of thousands of names. I never found my natural mother.*

There were several other crazy things I tried, but nothing came of them. At one point I even did a correspondence course to become a private detective. I tried the General Registry Office once, but all I got was the adopted people's register, where I found some details under my adopted name but no new real information except some sort of code number that I faithfully wrote down. I tried a private detective and I'm sure he ripped me off. He probably did the same course I had done. Later I found out that, in fact, Adeline was only 20 when I was born. These 'minor' detail mistakes were often used to misdirect us back then.

Two things happened around 1988. One day I spotted a small ad in one of the evening papers: an offer to trace adopted people's identities that claimed to have a 100% success rate. I responded and a man named Leo responded. He was a gentleman and, months later, he finally came up with a surname! Now my shadow was becoming more substantial. He was meant to return with more information but I never saw him again.

Marcoline's visits became more frequent because flights were cheaper and we also wrote to each other regularly. I still have a stack of her letters. She was always pushing me to start again with Social Services, so I reapplied. I had moved house in the meantime, so I was now assigned to the Dún Laoghaire branch. To my surprise, I was assigned a social worker in no time. I later discovered that once again Marcoline had contacted Social Services and had used her influence on my behalf.

My new social worker, Nora, was brilliant. She was young and fresh and really went above and beyond what she had to do. She finally managed to track down Adeline – she was living in America. I realised

how little Mrs. R. had cared about my case now that I had someone to
compare her with. Nora was on my side and genuinely wanted to help me.
She decided in 1988 that the best and only way to approach Adeline was
through a personal visit to her door in the United States. Letters or phone
calls could be ignored. Then the bad news arrived. The visit must be by
a volunteer charity worker through a group called International Social
Services and there was a waiting list of up to five years.

In 1987, the British 'Children Act', which had become law in 1975 to open all adoption records in England and Wales, was extended to Northern Ireland. In the Republic of Ireland, the highlight of the year was the abolition of illegitimacy as a legal definition, thanks to Cherish, which was going from strength to strength while the once mighty network of Mother and Baby Homes was becoming a shadow of its former self.

Dunboyne was still in operation (certified for thirty babies) and Bessboro was hanging on with a skeleton crew of mostly elderly nuns and twenty-five babies. The downsized St. Patrick's flatlets were now simply called 'Belmont' and were still run by the Daughters of Charity in Belmont Avenue, Donnybrook (eleven babies). A couple of doors away from Denny House in Eglington Road (seven babies) was Eglington House run by the Eastern Health Board, forerunner of the HSE (eight babies). Miss Carr's flatlets were in Northbrook Road (eight babies) and the Castle in Co. Donegal run by the Northwest Health Board, another earlier name for the HSE (eight babies). Donegal also had an 'infant nursing home' (a holding centre) run by the Sisters of Nazareth (twenty babies). This meant there were 117 cots in total.[5]

As the fourth-largest of the original institutions, Castlepollard was certified for 80 mothers and 125 cots and was often overcrowded way past that number. It was the smallest of the three Sacred Heart Homes but in 1987 it was bigger than every home cumulatively in Ireland. Bessboro once held three times that amount – 350 women, at one stage. All the homes collectively were granted £873,000. The Sacred Heart nuns with just 21% of the total number of cots received more of the taxpayer's cash than all the rest put together, with £469,000 going to Bessboro.

Just twenty years before, the Adoption Machine had peaked at 97% of all illegitimate babies being adopted. While Ireland's legislation had not changed, the situation on the ground had. Single mothers were numerous, they were keeping their babies and it was becoming more acceptable all the time. Women were making choices for themselves and the trend rapidly spread up the social ladder. Very few women were talked into handing over their babies for adoption and, if they were, it was because of tragic circumstances. By the late 1980s, there were foreign adoptions into Ireland and the banished babies trade was reversed.

As the 1980s ended, Ireland was on the cusp of a decade of political change and legislation finally began to reflect the day-to-day social reality. The more liberal 1960s generation was mature and beginning to have families of their own and they were tired of waiting for the law to catch up with the widespread social changes. The next generation of young people were even more frustrated and impatient. There was a real hunger for change and a deep anger with the Catholic Church for blocking the road to a range of personal freedoms. The progressive, liberal vision of society did come to fruition by the year 2000 but it was primarily because the Church was about to have its sadistic and abusive past aired in public. Once the floodgates opened, it seemed to never stop. The hubris and lack of remorse from the Church killed the last vestiges of Catholic Ireland and very few people mourned its long-overdue death. Legislative changes soon followed.

One of the earliest scandals was relatively harmless and this author vividly remembers celebrating when the Bishop of Galway was revealed as having a son after an affair with a distant relative. Annie Murphy, an American divorcée, had sought Casey's advice in her recovery from a messy relationship and Casey had taken advantage of the vulnerable 24-year-old woman. When Murphy gave birth in a Dublin hospital, the nuns tried to convince her to relinquish her son for adoption. When that failed, Casey sent monthly payments through an intermediary to support his son, who was now back in America. Many years later, Murphy's new partner turned up on Casey's doorstep to confront him about it. Casey denied everything. Shortly afterwards, Murphy and her son were compensated with nearly

$100,000 of Church funds but without Casey admitting paternity. He met his son during the negotiations but barely acknowledged him. Casey was in further discussions to pay upwards of another $100,000 for his son's college education when Murphy's new partner went to the media. The resultant scandal saw Casey banished to Ecuador in South America, and the Vatican announced that Casey had resigned as Bishop of Galway.

PART 3

CAMPAIGNING, 1990–2013

CHAPTER 9

The Adoption Community

By 1990, there were only three Mother and Baby Homes and a handful of small-scale supervised flatlets still in operation. The adoption community began to take its first tentative steps. The first known group was called the 'Adult Adoptees Association' (AAA) and they began to hold meetings and discussion groups in Dublin and Cork. I went to a couple of the early ones. They were in Dublin city centre in a room of a small hotel. At the time, I was in a very different place from the adoptees who sat around drinking tea and coffee and sharing their feelings. I was the only male adoptee there and primarily interested in tracing my own natural mother so I went to only a handful of meetings.

My Story, Part IV

I had made progress with the surname Leo had found. Through more digging, I found an address and it was still occupied by Adeline's family. Adeline's younger brother lived there. In 1992 I made a huge mistake. I turned up on his doorstep. Our community has learned the hard way, through stories like mine, that a 'knocker-shocker' as it is called in the community is the worst type of approach and almost always guaranteed to fail. Slow is the only way to go, starting with letters, building up to phone calls and then, with luck, agreeing to meet on neutral ground. But I bulldozed up to the door. We sat down to talk, and it did not go well. He had not known about me and, looking back, I know he must have felt betrayed and deeply wounded that his parents and sister had kept such a huge secret from him. Between that and a follow-up meeting, I gave him all the proof he had asked for, but he ended it by divulging nothing about his sister and making it clear that he never wanted to see or hear from me again. I was very hurt. This is called secondary rejection in the literature, but this term does not adequately describe the loneliness and emptiness I felt when it happened to me.

Years later I got a letter asking me to attend an appointment with my social worker. Nora had been transferred, but my case was still active so at least I did not have to start waiting again. Still, I had little faith in my new social worker. She did not ask me any questions but just stuck to the basics. The meeting between my mother and the volunteer from International Social Services had taken place. I attended the meeting with a sense of dread. She told me that Adeline had answered the door and panicked when she realised what was happening; she said it must be a case of mistaken identity and hurriedly closed the door. My social worker was not exactly sympathetic. When Sister Marcoline died in 1996, I felt I had lost my number one supporter. Her funeral was in Blackrock, Co. Dublin and she was buried in the little cemetery at the Dominican convent in Wicklow Town.

After that I let things drift and months passed into years. The technical term used for this is 'limbo'. My shadow had again moved a fraction forward into the light but that was all. When I turned towards her, she was still only the edge of a shadow already disappearing; gossamer whispers, as elusive as ever. No colour, no photos, no smile, no welcome. I kept all my paperwork in a briefcase and while I occasionally reopened it, had a look and made plans for a new push, I was sidetracked by my busy life. Months became years and my adoption and my shadow faded further from my mind except for trigger occasions such as birthdays, Christmas Day and Mother's Day when it all came flooding back.

The Adopted People's Association (APA) that had evolved from the first community meetings became a political group campaigning to open the sealed adoption records. In 1993, a related group formed the Magdalene Memorial Committee. Its aim was to ensure that women who had died in the laundries would not be forgotten. In April 1996, the committee unveiled a memorial bench in St. Stephen's Green, Dublin. Ironically, the last Magdalene Laundry was still in operation in Sean McDermott Street, just across the River Liffey, closing only in

October that year. The Natural Parents Network of Ireland was formed in the mid-1990s and offered support for parents who had lost a child to adoption.

The story of the next twenty-five years is one of a community cursed by bad luck. One accidental decision in particular stands out from those early days and still has strong ramifications in our community today. Adoptees and natural mothers set up separate groups, despite the fact that our issues were almost entirely identical. This unnatural split has separated and damaged our community ever since.

The adopted people who began the early groups self-labelled themselves as 'adoptees' and focused almost entirely on the issue of opening the sealed adoption records. This is still the case on the websites of many of the current crop of adoption activist groups. Issues relating to Mother and Baby Homes and forced separation were ignored or relegated to the bottom of the list, if mentioned at all.

Another flaw was built into the nature of the groups. Activists in any arena are predisposed to get involved for personal reasons and therefore tend to focus on their own personal issues and interests. If any of them decide to investigate the hospital where they were born, or the agency responsible for their adoption, they invariably come up against a brick wall and do not realise the wider issues involved. Since information is still so hard to come by in adoption-related research, most activists stop before they have properly begun. The names of the two early adoptee groups both contain the word 'adoption' or a slight variation of it, and the word instantly limited their horizons. I would find out the hard way years later that these were traps; we were limited by our artificial divisions, narrow focus and lack of vision, and limited by self-imposed labels and personal experience.

In the United States, there have been activist groups since the 1950s. Most of the American groups were focused on opening records as a civil rights issue, but Ireland's treatment of single mothers and their children was especially damaging. Our issues went far beyond a civil rights matter and into a serious and sustained abuse of human rights. Consequently, the one-size-fits-all approach into which the Irish activists fell, which was partly lifted from their American counterparts, was doomed to failure from the very start. Vested interests in Ireland

who did not want the adoption records unsealed were infinitely more
powerful than their American civil counterparts.

Later experience during the storm that followed the Tuam 800
breakthrough in May 2014 would also expose perhaps the deepest flaw
in the twenty-five years of campaigning. There was and had been little
or no interest in research into the system as a whole for its own sake,
let alone as evidence for the campaigning work. The idea that horrors
beyond imagination had taken place in the system was unknown to the
adoptees and the split between natural mothers and adoptees stopped
both sides comparing notes, understanding the inhumanity of the
Mother and Baby Homes and fighting for justice together. There were no
local historians or passionate researchers among the early community;
there were no administrators who might have organised the community
to carry out a systematic research project. It was another piece of bad
luck.

There were other problems. The survivor groups, from the industrial
schools' survivors to the Magdalene Laundries, and including the
Mother and Baby Home and forced adoption survivors, have been
divided from the beginning. The bigger the community becomes, the
more the splits and infighting. It is in our nature, because we as a
community are affected by our forced separation, and that damage
disconnects us. It can manifest itself in several ways including simple
ego or sometimes a clash of genuine but powerful personalities. To this
day there is no united representative group for the survivors of any
particular form of institutional abuse or clerical sexual abuse. Every
group seems to manage to grow to a certain size and then implodes
and splits. Multiple small groups, with the activists from each group
joining together in mutual respect and working through consensus
via a loose umbrella group, have proven to be the way forward.

In defence of the early pioneers, there was no widespread internet
availability or 'how to' guides at the start of the 1990s and they did
their best with what was available to them. However, many thousands
of survivors died without a reunion or any acknowledgement or official
apology during twenty-five years of rivalry and an obsessive focus on
opening the adoption files to the exclusion of more important issues. This
became the Holy Grail for some, who refused to support or accommodate

new people who joined with innovative ideas or new fields of interest. The harshest criticism of those wasted years is the lack of published papers or reports, of any substance, involving adoption. There was certainly nothing about Mother and Baby Homes or infant mortality rates. There was no one buying 800 death certificates or photocopying dusty old documents in the National Library of Ireland, in university libraries or the National Archives.

While the activist community was establishing itself, the Mother and Baby Homes machine was spluttering to a halt. Dunboyne closed in 1991. The downsized St. Patrick's flatlets quietly closed in the early 1990s and then there was only Bessboro left, although it was unrecognisable when compared to its earlier self. Bessboro had morphed once again over the course of the late 1980s and 90s, this time into a 'refuge' for girls in 'trouble'. It officially delisted as a Mother and Baby Home in 1996 but in effect, nothing changed. The Sacred Heart nuns still ran the Sacred Heart Adoption Society from Bessboro for many years and they still received millions of euro from the government up to 2012 at least. It is currently open for business and owned by the Sacred Heart nuns. They also still own Sean Ross Abbey near Roscrea, but at the time of writing, it is up for sale, as is Bessboro.

In the early 1990s, around the same time as the Irish public was learning about the child abuse scandals and the industrial schools, the Sacred Heart nuns sent money to the Department of Health staff running Castlepollard to have the Angels' Plot cleaned up. They also arranged for a small memorial stone to be erected. It is made from cheap limestone and weathers badly. The last word on the stone, 'cemetery', is misspelled as 'cemetary'. There were similar clean-up attempts in Bessboro and Sean Ross Abbey.

The steadily increasing prosperity of the 1990s, combined with a well-educated populace and an increasing foreign influence, meant that Ireland made rapid social progress at a grassroots level. At the same time, the Catholic Church staggered from scandal to scandal, dragging its reputation further into the gutter. A wave of child sexual abuse revelations shocked and horrified the country. Well-known bishops and priests, including Ireland's 'singing priest', Michael Cleary, were revealed to have fathered children or stolen diocesan funds and some were living lives of luxury. But infinitely worse was to come as the brutality, rampant paedophilia and wanton neglect in the industrial schools began to leak out. There was a seemingly endless wave of scandals about priests sexually abusing children.

It emerged that the sexual abuse of children was not only well known at the most senior levels of the Church but the Catholic hierarchy was actively conspiring to cover it up by moving savage and inhuman paedophiles from one parish to another every time the families of the victims complained. The older generation at the time were shocked to their core. The Fianna Fáil–Labour government of 1993/4 collapsed over the extradition of paedophile priest Brendan Smyth.

Politicians across the spectrum sensed the change in the public mood. Legislation began to catch up as the political parties tailored their policies to take account of social progress. Landmark and long-overdue legislation was finally passed. The body politic was also happy to demonise the Church to distract from the endless tribunals uncovering one scandal after another in political life and costing hundreds of millions of pounds that Ireland could not afford. Contraception became widely available and less controversial and *Playboy* magazine appeared on top shelves in December 1995 after the Censorship of Publications Board lifted its ban. Church and State drew up battle lines for a second divorce referendum in 1995, which was passed by a margin of 50.1% to 49.9% despite fierce opposition from the Church. The close result reflected the gradual movement of civil society away from the influence of the Catholic Church, as well as the rural/urban divide in Ireland. It was a momentous day in post-Independence Ireland. The people had defied the Catholic Church and it was not just about divorce. The momentum for change picked up speed and within ten years the Church was a shadow of its former self, destroyed mostly by its own hubris and self-righteousness.

Within months of the divorce referendum, in early 1996, a documentary called *Dear Daughter* was broadcast on RTÉ Television. It became the first of a series of 'breakthrough' moments as the wall of secrecy and silence protecting the ecclesiastical institutions crumbled. Christine Buckley was mixed-race and had been raised in Goldenbridge industrial school in Dublin where she suffered not only the ordinary horrors but extra cruelty and hardship fuelled by casual racism. She spoke freely and movingly of her pain and her childhood of abuse and torture. A subsequent public debate turned bitter and divided the country over whether or not she was telling the truth, but other survivors and evidence supported her testimony. There were further revelations as a steady stream of survivors came forward to tell their own stories in the media. The nation was horrified.

Later that same year, on 20 June, RTÉ Television broadcast another short but explosive documentary and this time it was directly related to the Mother and Baby Home: Mike Milotte's investigation, *Banished Babies*, which shocked the nation.

But somehow the foothold was lost by the emerging activist community and the controversy faded.

The steady work of the Adopted Peoples Association had slowly placed the matter of opening the adoption records on the political agenda from this time, through political lobbying and media work. In early 1997, Frances Fitzgerald TD stood up in the Dáil and said:

> It is universally accepted that denial of access to information about one's origins is denial of a basic human right. That right is enshrined in the UN Children's Rights Convention and our own constitutional review group has recommended that Article 41 of the Constitution should be amended to make it abundantly clear that Ireland unequivocally subscribes to that view.[1]

The following year one of the most significant events to affect adopted people since the original Adoption Act of 1952 took place. Two de facto adoptees went to court and challenged the secrecy that had always defined adoption in Ireland, claiming that it was unconstitutional.

The now infamous I. O'T and M.H. v. Rotunda Girls Aid Society case in the Supreme Court ended on 3 April 1998. It was a controversial and complex court ruling that set adoption rights back to less than zero. Two women, who had been informally or 'de facto' adopted before the introduction of legal adoption in January 1953, went to court to seek their original birth certificates and their natural mothers' details. The Supreme Court realised that the adoptees and their natural mothers all had rights under the Constitution. This was a classic clash of competing rights: an adoptee's right to identity versus a natural mother's right to privacy.

The Supreme Court took the unusual step of tracing and contacting both the natural mothers and asking them for their opinions. In yet another stunning piece of bad luck for our community, both natural mothers were adamant that they knew exactly what they were doing when they relinquished his/her babies. They insisted that they had willingly signed the forms and they were both firm in their refusals to meet their grown-up daughters. The Supreme Court noted in its judgement that both parties had firm constitutional rights: adoptees had a right to their identities but natural mothers also had a right to privacy. However, it is in the nature of sealed adoption records that there can be no compromise, only a clear-cut winner and loser.

The Supreme Court ruled that a natural mother's right to privacy superseded the adoptee's right to his/her details. The records would stay sealed. The Adoption Board sought legal advice and it was clear; the lawyers interpreted the judgement to mean that all natural mothers who had lost their children to adoption by any name, legal or illegal, de facto or fostering, had the 'right' to privacy, whether they wanted it or not.

The effect was that adoptees and natural mothers had no rights to each other's information, an injunction that still remains in place today. Sealed adoption was copper-fastened by the Supreme Court in the judgement known as the I.O'T ruling. There are only two ways to overturn this ruling, a full Constitutional Referendum or another court case challenging the ruling, probably going all the way to the European Court of Human Rights. The adoption activists ruled out the referendum option as they were afraid they could lose. That left a court challenge as the only possible means to fully open adoption records but, they reasoned, that could fail as well and therefore the I.O'T ruling case has never been challenged to date. The fact that the various campaigners never took a case in the sixteen years before the Tuam 800 story has been the source of considerable bitterness in our community. Ruling out a referendum is one thing but never pursuing the only other option is unforgivable to many survivors.

That same year, 1998, Poolbeg Press published June Goulding's memoir about her time in Bessboro. June did some media work to promote the book and sparked a public debate. The Sacred Heart nuns denied everything that was said about them in the book and sent solicitors' letters to Goulding threatening to sue her for spreading lies. The fuss died down in the absence of further research by the activist community to back the facts in the book. Once again, the Mother and Baby Homes escaped attention and another opportunity was lost.

The single most determined and stubborn campaigner in the fight for justice had been working away on his own personal case for five years by 1998 and he was ready to take the next step. Derek Leinster (sometimes Linster) was born in the Protestant Bethany Home in 1941 to a 17-year-old Protestant mother. When his mother left the home, Derek remained there for nearly five years on his own, where his health was badly affected by the harsh treatment. He founded the 'Bethany Home Survivors' group in 1998, making it the oldest surviving representative group related to adoption and Mother and Baby Homes. Derek's legendary tough streak and strategic skills would bring the Bethany Home Survivors further than all the other representative groups put together. Derek is the proverbial dog with a bone, hardened by his many years as a champion amateur boxer and trade union representative. Unlike the limited tactics of the Adopted People's Association and the Natural Parents Association of Ireland, Derek Leinster has used every strategy available to further his case. His work includes research, Freedom of Information requests and appeals, political lobbying, media work, seeking a pro bono legal team and much more. His battle was, and is, all the more remarkable because he lives in England and has practically no formal education as a result of his circumstances, and he left school functionally illiterate. He emigrated to England as a young man and pulled himself up through sheer grit and determination. He founded a highly successful amateur boxing club that is still in existence. He also self-published a two-volume autobiography, *Hannah's Shame* and *Destiny Unknown*, in 2005 and 2008.

That same year also saw the Channel 4 television broadcast *Witness: Sex in a Cold Climate* about the Magdalene Laundries. It was an important milestone for the former residents in their fight for justice but once again it proved to be a failure in terms of political movement. The laundries were on the media agenda but the government argued that they were privately owned and operated and therefore nothing to do with officialdom. Successive governments stuck to that line of defence until the United Nations ordered them to hold a limited inquiry in 2011 following a complaint to the Committee Against Torture.

Meanwhile, the APA did try something new and launched the private and unofficial Irish Adoption Contact Register in 1999, sponsored by Tesco Ireland. I registered myself. The community also started to form online chat groups. Computers were becoming more common and social media platforms, such as Yahoo Groups, were launched, which allowed adoptees to meet one another online. The internet also proved to be a useful tool for searches and personal tracing. I observed, but very rarely participated in the early groups, and although they lacked proper leadership and responsible moderators to bring order to the chaos, there was some small comfort in their existence. These groups began to set up websites and the Adopted People's Association used the name 'Adoption Ireland' for theirs, while the Natural Parents Network of Ireland used the name 'Adoption Loss'.

While the Mother and Baby Homes seemed to be fading into oblivion, the industrial schools were laid bare in a landmark documentary series broadcast on RTÉ Television between April and May 1999. *States of Fear* was created by the remarkable journalist Mary Raftery and was made up of three one-hour episodes, detailing the abuse suffered by children between the 1930s and 1970s in Ireland's State childcare system, primarily in the reformatory and industrial schools. It rightly won the Irish Film and Television Academy Award for Best Documentary of the Year, as well as numerous other awards around the world. It was another pivotal 'breakthrough' moment and, in November 1999, Raftery and Eoin O'Sullivan published a follow-up book entitled *Suffer the Little Children*. Mother and Baby Homes were mentioned extensively and should have set off alarm bells in the media and the activist community, but once again they escaped public attention. This brilliant but harrowing book, alongside Milotte's recently published book about the banished babies and Goulding's exposé about Bessboro, should have been enough to open up a debate among the adoption community and change their narrow focus. Instead, the campaigners continued to obsess about opening the adoption records to the exclusion of all else. Their work kept the sealed adoption records on the political agenda, but it would take until 2001 to produce a Bill that exploded the whole debate in a spectacular fashion.

Raftery's efforts may not have brought the Mother and Baby Homes or the wider issue of the forced separation of single mothers and their babies into the public arena, but the public outcry and resulting pressure on the government led to a public apology to the survivors of industrial schools by the then Taoiseach, Bertie Ahern. This was a new type of problem for the government and neither the politicians nor the senior civil servants had any idea how it should be handled. In later years the standard practice of dealing with such sensitive matters followed a fixed timetable: deny the accusations for as long as possible, set up an inquiry, wait for the report, publicly apologise and finally set up a redress scheme. But in 1999 Bertie Ahern began with an apology, and then set up an inquiry followed by a redress scheme that was in effect long before the Inquiry reported.

Ahern and his government could not have foreseen the consequences or the enormous size of the final report, nor the high cost of redress that would finally reach well over €1.5 billion. Both the length and cost of the Ryan Commission and the cost of the Redress became a long-running, open sore in Irish politics for a decade. The fees of lawyers representing survivors ran into tens of millions. The lessons the government and senior civil servants learned meant that all future calls for a public inquiry or redress relating to any form of institutional abuse in Ireland would be fought tooth and nail, including calls for an inquiry into the Magdalene Laundries and the Mother and Baby Homes.

Not only was no one campaigning for a public inquiry into the Mother and Baby Homes but a succession of governments were hostile to even hearing about any form of institutional abuse, let alone doing anything about it.

While the Magdalene Laundries campaign continued to gain ground and the testimonies of the survivors flitted in and out of the media and public consciousness, the Mother and Baby Homes continued to sink deeper and deeper into oblivion.

At this time, many adoptees, including myself, believed that we had been born in Magdalene Laundries. There was considerable confusion and a general belief that single women and girls gave birth to their babies in the laundries, despite the historical fact that the Catholic laundries refused to admit pregnant girls and would routinely transfer them to Mother and Baby Homes or county homes as soon as their 'condition' was apparent. Even today, both the official Castlepollard website and the Wikipedia entry still refer to the Castlepollard Mother and Baby Home as a 'Magdalene Asylum'. The vast size and scale of the Mother and Baby Homes were completely unknown to the survivor community, the public and the media. The Protestant Bethany Home was better known than all the eight Catholic homes together, because of Derek Leinster's determination.

The redress scheme of 2002 was intended for the survivors of industrial and reformatory schools, although St. Patrick's Mother and Baby Home was included as a later addition. The adoption activists of the time knew nothing of the history or the central role of Pelletstown/ St. Patrick's and they never engaged with the Redress Board set up to administer the payouts. Derek Leinster campaigned relentlessly for the Bethany Home to be included in the redress scheme. He later discovered, through a Freedom of Information request, that the civil servants referred to him as the 'constant caller'. The Bethany Home was excluded and Leinster remains adamant that this exclusion was due to sectarianism and discrimination.

CHAPTER 10

Running to Stand Still

The Adopted People's Association and others had gained valuable experience and contacts over the years, in the media and in politics. It continued to campaign for open adoption records and made substantial progress towards the end of the 1990s. There was also finally some good luck on the activists' side. The cause of the industrial schools' survivors had powerful momentum and one of their demands was access to personal records. Their demands more or less matched adoptee demands and added significant weight to the adoptees' fight for open records, a key factor that led to the Adoption Bill 2001.

The Bill was Minister Mary Hanafin's brainchild and, bar one fatal flaw, it stands up to her claim that it was a 'major piece of social legislation'.[1] Hanafin trawled through global adoption legislation, searching for best practice. Her Bill was crafted to open the adoption records and give adoptees and natural mothers access to their names and birth/adoption certificates and even to the files themselves. Foster children, and children raised in State, private or religious institutions were fully included. Survivors of the industrial and reformatory schools were at the heart of this Bill as much as adoptees.

Hanafin said that the new Bill was designed to 'strike a balance between a person's right to information and a person's right to privacy', before admitting that it was 'a legal minefield'. Ominously, she said that she would be working with the Director of Public Prosecutions to draft the Bill. From a first reading of the press release, there would be a 'national veto register'. It is important to understand exactly how this system works. A 'national veto register' is used around the world in countries where previously sealed adoption records are opened by new legislation. Many natural mothers and some adoptees want to continue to have no contact with their adult children and/or parents so governments establish a register where those people who want to maintain their privacy can record their 'veto' on contact. Although that was common enough elsewhere in the world, it was a vital legal necessity in Ireland to cover the 'right to privacy' of natural mothers, as defined by the I. O'T and M.H. v the Rotunda Girls Aid Society Supreme Court ruling. The Natural Parents Network of Ireland welcomed the Bill.[2] However, Hanafin also mentioned in an *Irish Independent* article that there would be sanctions for anyone who broke the veto on contact with someone who wished to remain anonymous by contacting them anyway.[3]

The sanctions turned out to be up to one year in jail and/or a fine of €5,000. The APA and adopted people and their natural mothers were outraged and the APA (now known as Adoption Ireland) began a campaign to scrap the Bill in its entirety. It took two years but they won. It was a long-term disaster for the adoption community. The negative backlash Hanafin received sent ministers and politicians from all parties running from the issue for over a decade. Meanwhile, the increasingly elderly survivors were dying in their thousands.

My Story, Part V

I was vaguely aware of the controversy over the new Adoption Bill while it was in the media, but opening the adoption records now held no interest for me. I already had my natural mother's name and I was working on tracing her in the United States. The new millennium was a chance for a fresh start and in April 2000, I wrote to Social Services to start again. I knew that this time they had my natural mother Adeline's address and all I really wanted was a letter or phone call to see if she had changed her mind about meeting me. Without Sister Marcoline's influence, I had to wait over a year and a half until December 2001 before I received an appointment with my third social worker.

It was an unmitigated disaster. I met my social worker in Dún Laoghaire and she clearly had no interest in me, or my case. She gave the impression that I was just a nuisance to her. She did not ask me anything personal nor did she want to know anything about my feelings towards the trace. She simply launched straight into what she had already done without my knowledge. She had written to Adeline and, following that contact, had received a phone call from Adeline's solicitor. When all the legal language was removed, the message was clear: 'stay away'. I felt numb. When I pulled myself together and started asking questions, the encounter just got worse. She had taken action, based on the information in an old version of my file, without discussing it with me first. As a result, she had written to a previous family address where Adeline's brother still lived. This brother was Adeline's solicitor. I pointed out that the surnames of the solicitor and my natural mother were the same. She looked in the file and realised her oversight. Why had she not written directly to Adeline in the United States where she now lived? There was no such address, she coldly replied. Where was the rest of my file with all the information that Nora, my previous social worker, had painstakingly gathered over years? She knew nothing about it and it was not in the file in front of her. She did not even have the decency to say sorry.

I pushed her to find my file and suggested that she phone Nora straight away. She agreed reluctantly and I left in disgust, struggling to suppress my anger. This is one of the worst aspects of dealing with social workers. You are at their mercy because they have all the power and you have to abide by their wishes. I sent the social worker copies of all the letters Nora and I had exchanged, so she could phone her about my file. I included the details of International Social Services who had Adeline's address. A letter to them would have sorted out the mess. I put the issue with my social worker to one side and let her get on with it. I was engaged at the time and Siobhán and I were planning our wedding in August 2002.

I finally phoned the social worker in April 2003, nearly a year and a half after I had met her, and asked if she had found my missing file. No. Had she contacted Nora to ask where it was? No. Had she written to International Social Services? No. I was shocked that she had literally done nothing all that time. I began phoning every month and then every couple of weeks. Apparently, she was too busy to make a simple phone call or write a letter. After nearly two years of inaction and dozens of calls, I received a letter informing me that this individual was going on leave for two months from her part-time position – the first I'd heard of her being only a part-timer. What really made my blood boil was that in the time she had spent on the phone to me making excuses, and the time it took to write the latest sad excuse of a letter to me, she could have made the five-minute phone call or written the letter I wanted her to write many times.

I made a formal complaint to my social worker's manager in August 2003. The principal social worker finally wrote the letter to International Social Services, nearly two years after my initial request, but it was too late. International Social Services destroy all their files after five years and my file with Adeline's address had now been shredded. I was fuming and the fact that we were already past that deadline did nothing to calm me. This was war as far as I was concerned. I went to my solicitor, determined to sue my social worker.

The one positive thing from this latest shambles was that I had started tracing for myself again. With the new social media platforms burgeoning, I was trying all sorts of random searches, including trying to track down Adeline through her business. It was a needle-in-a-haystack search but I worked my way through it whenever I got the chance.

This sad and sorry tale with my social worker dragged on. A senior family law barrister researched my case and was very decent about it, as were my solicitors, but the end result was that I could not sue. The secrecy aspect of adoption legislation, apart from anything else, would be used to thrash me in court. The complaint I had made was investigated. The complaint itself was mishandled and broke the code of conduct of social services several times. When I did get a reply, it was hand-delivered to my letterbox over Christmas 2003, with no stamp. I do not know if it was an attempt to intimidate me or to spoil my Christmas, but it had the opposite effect. It was five pages of sad excuses and apologies, with the phrase 'not a satisfactory situation' used several times. However, no action was going to be taken against the social worker and my request for a new social worker was denied. I attended a meeting with the principal social worker in Dún Laoghaire and got nowhere. Then, just to top off this sorry fiasco, I received a call from him one day to inform me that both he and my social worker had spent two full days searching for my missing file but without success! I asked if they had spoken to Nora about the missing file. Maybe she would remember Adeline's address? They had not contacted her. I was expected to believe that two people had spent two full days searching through thousands of dusty old files rather than make a single phone

call to the person who had last seen the file. I hung up and had nothing
do with social services again apart from multiple Freedom of Information
requests.

I got married in 2002 and Siobhán and I had two gorgeous children
within four years. I found Adeline during that time but much of my
yearning was dispelled when I held my first child, Molly, in Holles Street
Hospital. Why should I chase a ghost when this angel was in my life and
her unconditional love was melting away my pain? My son Gavin's birth a
couple of years later also healed me to the point where I almost no longer
cared that I was adopted. My parents, wife and children, extended family
and good friends felt enough for me now, but a tiny hope still lingered in
the deepest part of my heart. Most of the time I just forgot about it and
moved on as a son, husband and, above all, as a father.

In 2004, thanks to a paid 'people tracer' website in the United States,
I finally found an address for Adeline's business. I discovered she had
changed the spelling of her first name with just a single letter. No wonder
it had taken so long. My initial ecstasy was followed by a horrible sense
of anticlimax. I now had the necessary information to contact my natural
mother myself and even had her picture from a Facebook page, but with
that came a huge risk of being rejected. Regardless of my mixed feelings, I
had found my childhood shadow at long last.

Mary Hanafin's replacement as Minister of Children in June 2002 was
Brian Lenihan. His style was a master class in how to deal with a hot
political potato in the aftermath of the 2001 Adoption Bill debacle. He
invited the activist community to committees to be 'stakeholders' and
offered funding. He provided plenty of tea and sympathy, but ultimately
failed to deliver. Nothing happened and the momentum had vanished
by the time other ministers replaced him. Every minister after Lenihan
either said 'no' straight out or made empty promises. They parroted
the well-worn official line that the Supreme Court I. O'T ruling was a
'complex legal minefield' and their hands were tied.

The one sop was the foundation of a National Contact Register
in 2005. The register was strictly voluntary and administered by the
Adoption Board. Leaflets were distributed to every household in the

country. If it so happened that an adoptee and his or her natural mother (or other family member) both signed up and a match was made, the two parties were referred back to their original adoption agency, which would supposedly facilitate the reunion. There were waiting lists of one to five years for tracing and reunion appointments in different parts of the country. Worse still, many of the agencies were still run by the same orders of nuns or Catholic lay volunteers, including St. Patrick's Guild and Cúnamh (the Catholic Protection and Rescue Society of Ireland until 1992), who had handled around half of all legal adoptions since 1952. The Sacred Heart Adoption Agency was still run by Sister Sarto Harney, former head of Bessboro, and no great supporter of survivors who returned for information. The sincerity of the nuns was frequently questioned and many of them were deeply unpopular with the adoption community. In one bizarre incident, a Freedom of Information request revealed that Sister Sarto had slipped into one of the online activist groups under an avatar name and was keeping close tabs on adoption activists. In response to criticism she also said, 'I think it is sad that it's come to this. We gave our lives to looking after the girls and we're certainly not appreciated for doing it.'

In 2007, the Adoption Support Network of Ireland was formed to offer peer support to adoptees and natural families, and the following year Theresa Hiney Tinggal founded 'Adopted Illegally Ireland'. Hiney Tinggal campaigned for action by the government on the specific issue of illegal adoptions and, in particular, to secure records illegally held in private hands and to press for criminal investigations. Theresa is petite and softly spoken but, like Derek Leinster, she is another self-confessed dog with a bone. Theresa drew support over the years from the multiple Facebook groups and, once she found her feet, became a force to be reckoned with.

APA/Adoption Ireland gradually faded away up to 2010, worn down by almost ten years of a relentless political run-around. Two former members, Susan Lohan and Claire McGettrick, went on to form the Adoption Rights Alliance in 2009. On its website, the organisation states that its 'main goal ... is to achieve equality and rights for adopted people in legislation'. The new Adoption Rights Alliance continued APA's strategy of political lobbying and raising public awareness through a media campaign. It has a large and professional website and there is a long list of aims and mission statements over two pages; a public inquiry into Mother and Baby Homes is still close to the bottom of the list. The history of the Mother and Baby Homes on its website is painfully thin and lacking basic facts. However, within its limited aims and old tactics, the Adoption Rights Alliance fought hard for open records. Yet once again, it was too late.

A new Adoption Act was passed in 2010, rolling all previous adoption legislation into one. It brought Ireland more or less into line with the international Hague Convention on Adoption. Little more needs to be said about the 2010 Act, passed under the guidance of then Minister for Children Barry Andrews, except that it contains nothing for adopted people or natural mothers, no open records and no post-adoption support. It was a disaster on several levels for the adoption community. The sheer depth of the nightmare was fully appreciated only by those familiar with adoption legislation. Our time and our chance had passed; possibly for up to eight or ten more years. The first decade of the twenty-first century, like the 1990s, passed with no progress on the Mother and Baby Home front.

In 2003 Aisling Walsh made *Sinners*, a film supported by the BBC and loosely based on June Goulding's book. It was first shown on RTÉ and three days later on BBC. *Sinners* is a dark and grim portrayal of the daily grind and casual cruelty in a Mother and Baby Home and is very difficult and disturbing to watch. In terms of accuracy, the great flaw in the film was to confuse the Mother and Baby Home with a Magdalene Laundry. In one scene which influenced my life and I am sure many other adoptees and mothers, a van pulls up to the back of the home to deliver laundry and there in huge letters on its side, and clearly meant to be seen by the viewers, are the words 'Magdalene Laundry'. At the time, I thought I must have been born in a Magdalene Laundry but I know now that Bessboro never had its own commercial laundry, only a hand laundry for its own use. Apart from that one historical flaw, the film remains the most realistic portrayal of daily life in a Mother and Baby Home. It was brutally honest and polemical; it deservedly won the Best Feature-Length Drama at the Celtic Film and Television Festival in 2003 and numerous other international awards.

In 2009 RTÉ's *Prime Time* broadcast a special called *Bethany, the Home the State Forgot*, with the full cooperation of survivors such as Derek Leinster. It is a powerful and damning indictment of the treatment of the Bethany survivors during the time of their exclusion, despite Leinster's ferocious lobbying, from the 2002 Redress Act.

The few opportunities of the early 2000s were lost just as they had been in the 1990s. The momentum fizzled out after each potential breakthrough moment. Successive governments simply refused to reopen and reignite the controversy over the final cost of redress at €1.5 billion and, for reasons unclear to the adoption community, no journalist or media organisation has to date investigated in any depth the issues of the Magdalene Laundries and the Mother and Baby Homes.

Many of the activists lost heart after the Adoption Act 2010. After twenty years there was nothing to show for all the campaigning. The National Contact Register paid lip service to the rights of the adoption community and the new Adoption Act was nicknamed a 'once-in-a-decade chance lost'.

Veteran campaigner since 2000, Susan Lohan, would later accuse Minister for Health James Reilly in 2014 of 'reading from the same speech delivered by every children's minister who preceded him'.[4] She continued by comparing her 14-year fight for open records as being like *Groundhog Day*, a film where the main character has to live the same day over and over again. One other fundamental flaw in the tired old strategies became apparent over the next few years. Even though many people had become involved via the postal service or online since the late 1990s, none of the veterans ever organised regular meet-ups or commemorations. This was later revealed as a major oversight. When Facebook arrived, it provided a simple platform for social interaction and facilitated the formation of private groups. From 2010, the various Facebook groups grew in size and strength, and a new group of activists organised meetings of all descriptions. They were small at first but highly successful in bonding people together and creating friendships that had been absent from the first twenty years of our community. Most importantly, survivors began sharing stories and educating one another. I was one of the new group and we were referred to by some of the veterans as the 'Facebook newbies' or 'the Young Guns'.

CHAPTER 11

Facebook and the Young Guns

While the 2010 Adoption Act was a disaster and set back the open adoption records cause by several years, there were more positive signs. Facebook is a simple-to-use media platform and ideal for an older generation not overly technical when it came to computers. A steady stream began joining from 2010 onwards.

Around this time, I was driving along one Sunday evening with *Global Village*, a Newstalk 106 show about human and civil rights, playing on the radio. The discussion included adoption and the right to adopt. I texted in a couple of times and my texts were read out. I complained loudly that there were no adoptees to put forward 'our' side of the story and I requested a programme entirely about adoption. To my surprise, the programme agreed and I found myself on live radio a couple of weeks later. I was very private about my adoption and rarely discussed it with anyone except three or four close friends, so I was 'Peter' on the show. I was honest about how I felt and the darkness that adoption had sometimes brought to my life. I shocked one of the pro-adoption representatives with my openness about the confusing times many adoptees go through in their teens, trying to figure out why they were adopted, and the possible horror stories that go through our minds, including rape and incest.

One of the guests was with an adoptee representative group and we went for a drink afterwards. I was invited to join their Facebook group and, while I was outwardly polite, I was inwardly sceptical. I hated social media and the mere idea of joining Facebook was alien, but I joined the group. For several months I dipped in and out every few weeks, reading but never posting or commenting.

One day in the summer of 2011 a man asked if anyone in the online group was born in Castlepollard. Several of us had been, and began to discuss our old home. This was a revelation. I felt an instant kinship with these strangers and, incredibly, I also discovered that my own meagre efforts over the years had left me knowing more about Castlepollard than any of the others. I was shocked that so little was known. Naturally we talked about visiting and I suggested we visit our old home together. One of the other people in the discussion contacted me and asked if I was serious about this idea. I said I was and I made a couple of calls. Before I knew it, seven of us had organised to meet up in Castlepollard in August 2011.

It was an odd situation. We shared so much and yet we were strangers walking into the unknown together. We were transfixed as we drove through the gates and down the driveway. We had all been born in this grey and depressing place. We had been with our natural mothers here and had lost them here. We were together, but each of us was also on a personal journey. It was a very intense experience. The complex was aged and ugly. One of the two people who ran the place, Sheila, met us at the appointed time and could not have been more understanding. Our little group consisted of two men and five women. The other man, also named Paul, and I had video cameras and we were determined to record everything.

We began with the old manor house the nuns had turned into a convent, then through to the attached chapel to see our baptismal font and out the back door of the chapel and over to the side door of St. Peter's Hospital and Mother and Baby Home. We saw the empty wards on the ground floor where we had stayed, the dormitories on the second floor where our mothers had lived and the rooms on the third floor where we had been born. The sadness seemed to drip from the walls. We were all in our own worlds a lot of the time, dropping back into reality now and then to discuss things and ask questions before drifting off again into pasts we could not even remember. Our video cameras continued to run.

Sheila told us about the steady flow of adoptees and natural mothers who had turned up over the past forty years since the home had closed in 1971. We found we were the first to visit as a group. Later I would discover that we were the first group of former residents to visit *any* of the Mother and Baby Homes together, a fact that both saddens and angers me to this day.

Michelle, who had nudged me into making the phone calls and organising the trip, had suggested planting a tree in the Angels' Plot and we had eagerly agreed. She had brought a support post and a seven-foot-tall tree in her car from Wexford, driving with the boot open the whole way. I'd brought my garden spade and a lump hammer for the post that was to be attached to the tree and off we went without a clue as to what the Angels' Plot looked like. We walked past the row of outbuildings that were used as a laundry and bakery for the home, and down a laneway for several hundred metres until finally arriving at a stone wall with a small, wrought-iron gate containing a cross in the centre.

'Is this it?' I wondered. I thought it would be a lot bigger. It was about a hundred metres long and no wider than an average back garden. There were supposed to be up to 500 babies buried here? It got worse when we were led to a pair of graves with headstones and surrounds. They were about halfway down on the right-hand side by the long stone wall, which ran to a height of fifteen feet along the right-hand length of the plot. We learned that an identical wall had run the whole way around the plot, but that the entire left side had been taken down years before. The marked graves belonged to two nuns. They had the entire front half of the plot to themselves. The foundation of another wall was pointed out to us just past the nuns' graves. The plot had been divided in two and there used to be a door in the dividing wall leading to the second half. The nuns kept the door locked.

The second half of the plot began with a small memorial stone on the right-hand side, about a metre high, with the inscription 'IN MEMORY OF GOD'S SPECIAL ANGELS INTERRED IN THIS CEMETARY'. The misspelling of the last word was already known to me from internet research, and I pointed it out. The rest of the Angels' Plot was painfully plain, with only one marked grave; it belonged to a named girl who had died in childbirth, we were told, aged 14 and a half. She was buried with her baby. Later I discovered she was in fact 28 and the local legends were incorrect. At the very end of the plot there was a plain, white cross about a metre high. The base mentioned the Sacred Heart nuns, but I had no interest in them at that moment.

We were all very conscious that we were walking on hundreds of bodies of babies and children buried just a few feet beneath us. I was lost in thought when Paul asked if this would be a good spot for us to plant the tree. He was holding it in the centre of the plot. I looked down and realised I was holding the spade.

I moved to where everyone had agreed to plant the tree and placed the spade to the ground. Then I froze. I just stood there with my foot on the spade for what seemed like an eternity. Paul whispered some reassuring words and, without thinking about it, I blessed myself, took a deep breath and began to dig. I had to dig about a foot square and about two feet deep to accommodate the large roots of the oversized tree. I knew we were all having the same thought: I was digging a grave-sized, grave-shaped hole in a forgotten baby cemetery that hadn't been touched for forty years. I reached into the hole to scoop out another couple of inches of loose earth and finally the tree fitted. I filled earth in around the roots and we all joined together in a circle to plant flower bulbs around the base. I was never quite the same person again. I changed in that Angels' Plot and I cannot explain exactly why or how, although I've thought about those moments many times over the years.

Before we left the Angels' Plot, I lingered a moment to be on my own. I filmed the other six of my crib mates leaving the cemetery and then I filmed the Angels' section. I had entered the Plot as an adoptee, but in my heart I left as a survivor, deeply connected with this garden-sized patch of sorrow and sadness.

My first instinct was to begin looking into Castlepollard Mother and Baby Home and how and why this tiny Angels' Plot existed. I would quickly discover that there was virtually nothing known about the place, even though it had radically changed the lives of the nearly 8,000 people who were born there and of the girls and women who had lost their babies. The last edition of *The History of Castlepollard* that I wrote was almost forty pages long with a hundred footnotes, photographs, a full list of all the surviving paperwork and a bibliography. Unbeknownst to me at the time, another couple of people were also beginning to do exactly what I wanted to do: research a Mother and Baby Home. My research led me very quickly to include all of the Mother and Baby Homes and the wider system that had deeply affected the lives of 200,000 people since 1922, and my focus from the start was the Angels' Plots and the infant mortality rates.

There were positive signs over the few years following the setback of the 2010 Adoption Act. Derek Leinster continued his research from Britain. He was joined by Dr. Niall Meehan, Head of Journalism at Griffith College, who became Secretary of the Bethany Home Survivors Group. Niall used the information that Derek had collected over fifteen years and combined it with his own independent research to write the very first history of a Mother and Baby Home. *Church & State and The Bethany Home* was published in the September–October 2010 edition of the highly respected *History Ireland* magazine. It was a scholarly article and included graphs, charts and reproductions of original advertisements from the Bethany Home. It stands as an irrefutable piece of hard evidence for anyone campaigning on the issue.

At the same time, a number of people in the media began to take an interest. In 2010, journalist Conall Ó Fátharta in the *Irish Examiner* wrote two articles about Tressa Reeve, whose baby had been illegally adopted via SPG, and followed it up with a detailed investigation of the Adoption Authority/Board.[1] Ó Fátharta's work won first prize in the daily newspaper category in the Justice Media Awards in June 2011.[2] He continues to pursue the subject and his independent research and multiple exclusives have marked him out as a pioneering journalist. He is a hero to many in the survivor community and presently acknowledged as the expert on Bessboro Mother and Baby Home.

In May 2011, Ireland's independent television station TV3 broadcast a two-part 'Adoption Stories' series written and directed by Sharon Lawless and produced by her independent company, Flawless Films. Following the success of the mini-series, TV3 commissioned a further six episodes, each twenty-two minutes long, which aired in early 2012. Each episode generally featured two stories. Sharon's lack of ego and willingness to take a back seat has allowed adoptees and natural mothers to speak for themselves. Sealed adoption records were revealed as a life sentence of emotional turmoil for almost all parties. Some of the illegal practices the nuns and adoption agencies perpetrated in the days of the Adoption Machine were also laid bare. *Adoption Stories* has become a regular fixture, and production is beginning on its seventh series. Sharon Lawless has been universally praised in the adoption community for her professionalism, understanding and sensitivity. *Adoption Stories* would later widen its scope to include adoptive parents, who were given the chance to talk for themselves. The programme kept up to date with new developments, such as people finding their natural families through DNA testing. In 2016, Sharon released a companion book also called *Adoption Stories*.

Overall the most positive effect of *Adoption Stories*, Ó Fátharta's articles and Facebook was that many people who had been suffering in silence realised that they were not alone. In the years from 2010 onwards, a steady flow of people joined the Facebook adoption groups. People bonded and began to meet at informal, social get-togethers. I personally founded, or assisted in the formation of, several of these groups, including the Castlepollard, Bessboro and one of the two St. Patrick's groups, where well over 1,000 people have joined to share their stories and connect with other survivors.

Shortly afterwards, there was a gathering related to our cause. A Sinn Féin party member who worked for Mary Lou McDonald TD wanted to commemorate and remember the Magdalene women who had died in the Magdalene Laundries and were buried in Glasnevin Cemetery. The first 'Flowers for Magdalenes' event was organised for 4 March 2012. When I arrived, I stopped at the gates to chat to the 'Two Séans' who were two well-known survivors of childhood abuse. One of them had made the famous yellow Magdalene banner often seen in media reports. They asked me to carry one side of the banner while the two of them alternated between the other side of the banner, and photographing the event with the banner always in the background. When the Two Séans finally gave me a break, I met Clodagh Malone and her husband Paul for the first time. We were Facebook friends and I was a member of the group she had founded, 'Beyond Adoption Ireland'. Clodagh is a 'Search Angel', one of several people in our community who are familiar with the whole system of adoption and know all the tricks and shortcuts to obtain information from the various branches of government. They assist new members when they arrive in the Facebook groups looking for help. The Search Angels offer as much help as the survivor wants; sometimes just advice and addresses, right up to undertaking the entire trace for free, except for expenses such as the costs of bus tickets and birth certificates. Clodagh also does media work and had featured on an episode of *Adoption Stories*. We clicked instantly as campaigners and had a chance to talk at length after the event. She told me that one of the veteran activists had met her years before and within five minutes had declared that Clodagh was 'a typical adoptee'. However, since first meeting her, I have found her to be an extraordinary adoptee. Clodagh is a highly qualified counsellor and very active in the community. She runs an excellent group, offering practical advice on tracing as well as peer support. We were surrounded that day by other survivors who had turned out to support the Flowers for Magdalene commemoration and we saw the horrendous effects of the industrial schools and Magdalene Laundries at first hand. While almost all adoptees went to well-vetted, decent families, and had good lives, these people had suffered dreadfully and had their childhoods and adult years stolen from them. The detrimental effect that life in an institution had on many of them was painfully clear. Their suffering would be with them for life. The black shadow of the institutions will be in Ireland until the last survivor passes away. I truly hated the Catholic Church on that day.

RTÉ's flagship current affairs programme *Prime Time* continued to broadcast special programmes about our issues. In late 2011, the programme revealed a new and previously unknown, but officially authorised, fifth vaccine trial in Sean Ross Abbey in 1965. The second part of the programme made clear that the nuns in St. Patrick's Mother and Baby Home (Pelletstown), and its associated hospital St. Kevin's (now St. James's), had 'donated' 461 dead bodies of babies and children to various medical institutions for routine dissection.

In 2007, the community once again missed the publication of an important book, *Mother and Child. Maternity and Child Welfare in Dublin 1922–60* by Dr. Lindsey Earner-Byrne. This examines the worst practices of the Mother and Baby Homes in its last chapter, which is largely based on the *LGRs* of the 1920s and 1930s, which I was researching at the time. I felt I had struck gold because the book was so obscure.

While there was a gradual increase in interest in the media, the community itself continued to grow on Facebook. In time, groups formed for almost all the homes, at least four natural mother groups, a 24-hour news survivor/adoption-related links group and holding centre groups such as Stamullen. I founded or co-founded many of them. The newer groups were slowly finding their way and taking an interest in issues and historical facts that had long been neglected. The specific Mother and Baby Home groups focused their attention on their old homes and many followed the lead of Castlepollard regarding annual reunions and visits. Unfortunately, I discovered some resistance from veteran campaigners to any new tactics or strategies. They were attached to political lobbying and media work as an orthodoxy and would not consider new ideas or allow newcomers like myself to get involved. There was a two-tier membership in the biggest group, yet another artificial division that excluded ordinary survivors from the decision-making process.

With much help from non-activist adoptees, I gathered everything I could in terms of books, statistics and facts about the Mother and Baby Homes in Ireland. The results were pitiful. I had hoped to have a bank of information available from people who had been involved for up to twenty years, but the reality was that most could not answer even the most basic questions about Mother and Baby Homes. I needed to start from scratch and began by rereading the ten or so books on adoption that I already had, and also began ordering books online.

In May 2012 I was forced to put some order on my limited facts when I was asked to attend a meeting between the Archbishop of Dublin, Diarmuid Martin, and several survivors of institutions and childhood abuse. The Two Séans whom I had met at the Flowers for Magdalene's gathering at Glasnevin some months previously had been holding an ongoing weekly protest outside the Pro Cathedral every Sunday during the morning Masses. The protests had turned ugly, resulting in regular phone calls from priests in the Pro Cathedral to the local Gardaí at Store Street station. There was a series of arrests, and minor court cases followed. The Gardaí were fed up with the weekly complaints and keen to resolve the issue, so a meeting was arranged between Archbishop Martin, his press officer, a priest, a senior Garda and an independent witness, Michael Nugent from Atheist Ireland. 'Marie Kennedy' (not her real name), an adoptee I knew well, was in touch with some industrial school survivors on Facebook and because the Two Séans knew me, Marie and I were invited to the meeting.[3] I asked the veteran campaigners in our community if they wanted to come along or if I could say anything on their behalf, but they declined.

The meeting took place in the Parochial House beside the Pro Cathedral in a room with a portrait of Archbishop John Charles McQuaid on the wall glaring down at us. The other survivors demanded urgent action on various issues and received non-committal responses. Then it was our turn. Marie and I had agreed that I would write a statement, read it to the Archbishop and give him a copy. What saddened and frustrated me at the time was that, after the best part of a year devouring everything I could about the Mother and Baby Homes and the system of forced adoption, all I had was a 1,200-word statement to put forward the case for some 70,000 survivors from the homes. I read the statement about the Mother and Baby Homes and asked for a minute's silence for all the babies and children who had died. I estimated the total at 10,000 deaths above and beyond those who would have died if the *whole* system was included. Some 100,000 single mothers had given birth not just in Mother and Baby Homes but also the old workhouses and public and private maternity hospitals since 1922. I broke off at one point to ask the Garda if she had known that illegitimate people could not join the Garda Síochána until 1971. She had not. I pushed Archbishop Martin to take action, to call a press conference and join with us in demanding a public inquiry. 'Paul, they'd only laugh at me,' he said. I continued pushing, asking him what Jesus would have done, but he insisted over and over again that the media and politicians would just laugh at him. 'That's just not good enough, Archbishop,' I pointed out a couple of times, but he remained adamant. We left disappointed at how the meeting had gone but happy to have met each other.

A second meeting went much as the first. Sitting in the shadow of McQuaid's portrait, I pointed out to the Archbishop that it was like asking a delegation of Jews to sit in a room with a portrait of Hitler staring down at them. The meeting was a waste of time.

Marie and I had a third meeting about adoption-related matters. This time, when we arrived, we were shown into a different room, away from McQuaid's portrait. This meeting was about the Church holding baptism records with both original and adoptive names in their books but the vice chancellor, Rev. Fintan Gavin, had the Data Protection Act and adoption legislation as readymade excuses, so we got nowhere. I told the Archbishop that the truth about the Mother and Baby Homes would come out sooner rather than later and, as God was my witness, I would not rest until the truth was known. I felt I had affected him on a personal level but I knew he would never do anything that would damage his Church.

On 24 July, I got a phone call from a very excited Marie Kennedy screaming 'You did it Paul! You did it! You did it!' Archbishop Diarmuid Martin was all over the news. He had just addressed the McGill Summer School and part of his speech was about the Mother and Baby Homes. His Grace had called for 'new forms of research-based investigation into the quality of care in the homes and other institutions'.[4] It was a small victory of sorts.

Not long after the McGill Summer School speech I was on holidays with my family in Cork and bought a copy of the *Cork Examiner*. A letter I had written, complaining about the Archbishop, had been published under the heading 'Scandal of Mother and Baby Homes "care"'. It read:

I read Juno McEnroe's article on Archbishop Diarmuid's speech at the McGill summer school (Jul 25) and I am disgusted with the Archbishop's disingenuous reference to investigating the 'quality of care' in Mother and Baby Homes. These notorious hellholes were in many ways the worst of the Catholic institutions which scar Ireland's history. Mother and Baby Homes were maternity hospitals run by unqualified nuns without doctors or medical equipment, where scared, vulnerable girls (often the victims of rape and incest) were half-starved and terrified to the point that mortality rates consistently ran at two and three times the national average over generations. Between the three Sacred Heart Mother and Baby Homes, there are approx. 2,000 to 4,000 babies and children buried in unmarked graves without coffins, birth certs, death certs or even names. Archbishop Martin is well aware of these facts, having met with survivors on three occasions in the last few months, and he needs to apologise and demand an immediate public enquiry.[5]

I am embarrassed that there were clear errors in it, such as the fact that the babies were not buried without birth or death certs. However, I was pleased that my call for a public inquiry was now in the public domain. It had become my primary goal and I was hugely invested in ongoing research into the mortality rates and Angels' Plots in all of the homes. While other groups offered peer support and practical help with tracing and reuniting adoptees and their natural families, I was now one of a handful of individuals, both inside and outside the active community, researching the history of Mother and Baby Homes and adoption. We gradually connected over the next year or so.

My campaigning partner Marie Kennedy had written a blog piece on adoption under the title 'Adoption Rights Now' and, to support her, I set up a Facebook group with the same name not long after our final meeting with the Archbishop. It soon morphed into an activist group although I was uncomfortable with the name. Nonetheless it was a start and I was assigned to write the aims of the group. The first objective was straightforward:

> An immediate full Public Inquiry into the vicious treatment of mothers and babies, and the consequent high mortality rates, in government and Catholic and Protestant-run institutions in Ireland since the foundation of the state in 1922.

The 'Protestant' inclusion was inserted later at the request of a Bethany Home survivor, Colleen Anderson, who lives in Scotland. I set it up on my wedding anniversary so I would remember the date, 3 August 2012. The name Adoption Rights Now was a mistake I would not make again. We limited ourselves because our name and goal were at odds. At that point, I had very little interest in opening the sealed records because it was common knowledge that anyone who is adopted could simply go to the General Registry Office and find their original birth certificate and natural mother's name within a single day.

I organised another visit to Castlepollard in August. There were over twenty of us this time and it was a deeply moving experience. A public invitation to attend was posted in all the Irish groups but none of the veterans showed up. I later discovered that may have had something to do with the fact that nearly all of them were born outside the Mother and Baby Homes system and the visit was therefore beyond their personal field of interest. Nonetheless, I still feel strongly that if you claim to be 'leading' or 'representing' a community, everyone should be included, as should their issues and history.

I noticed immediately after the second Castlepollard visit that those of us who attended connected to one another in a very different way to everybody else online. We were no longer just 'Facebook friends' but real friends and we had also bonded as crib mates, among ourselves, and with our brothers and sisters in the Angels' Plot. More and more people began attending reunions, meetings, demonstrations and even just social drinks, and the personal contact became very important to everyone. I founded a Castlepollard group only a couple of weeks after Adoption Rights Now. It currently has almost 500 members and several others offline.

I wrote a very short *History of Castlepollard* at this time. It was only a few hundred words long but it was a start and, although I did not realise it then, it was only the third history of any of the nine Mother and Baby Homes, two years after Bethany and just after Catherine Corless's history of Tuam.[6] My interest, commitment and involvement grew at an exponential rate. I spent hours online every day, and made many friends who would do whatever they could to help, in their own countries and internationally. My interest extended from my own home, Castlepollard, to the Sacred Heart nuns themselves. I was digging into Pelletstown/St. Patrick's because I had been transferred there from Castlepollard when I was 13 days old.

After we established Adoption Rights Now, Marie Kennedy decided a petition was a good idea. I had made it clear to everyone involved that we were going to try new tactics and strategies and that there was plenty of room for fresh ideas. Anybody who wanted to get involved would be welcome. The rest of the year flew by as I pursued original research. One of the first things I discovered, after reading the original Adoption Act 1952, was that all adoptions had to be ratified and formalised by the courts and then published.

My research led me to the National Library where I located a full set of *Iris Oifigiúil* containing the list of all legal adoptions from 1953 to 1988. I applied for a reader's card. The copies of *Iris Oifigiúil* were held in binders, each containing a year's issues of just over a hundred copies. There was no index, so I had to painstakingly trawl through the first one I had ordered for the year 1959. I finally found several pages of names of adoptees and the names and addresses of their adoptive parents. I made photocopies. Over several visits to the library, I collected about 10,000 names – approximately one quarter of the total number of legally adopted people in Ireland. I offered to help a natural mother trace her child who had been lost to forced adoption. I believed I had found a new way of tracing adoptees for natural mothers and I was thrilled when I located this woman's child, and they reunited some months later. I still search occasionally and, while there are success stories, it is a difficult and time-consuming task that more often ends in heartbreak.

Luckily a good friend of mine, Liam Bodenham, put me in touch with his cousin, who was deputy editor of the *Mirror on Sunday*. She assigned Adelina Campos to the story. Adelina had won an award as Young Journalist of the Year in 2012 and I was eager to meet her. We arranged a meeting in town and I turned up with my boxes and bags of evidence. Adelina was repulsed by what had happened in the Mother and Baby Homes and was keen to run a major article in the *Mirror*. It appeared on 23 September 2012 and featured what information I could provide about the three Sacred Heart Homes. There were interviews with Greg Bayer from the Bessboro Home, who was banished to the United States and has since died, and Mary Creighton, a natural mother from Castlepollard. Mary told of her horrific experience at 16 years old in the 'screaming room' at Castlepollard where she had gone temporarily blind, although she recovered her sight a week later. To the best of my knowledge, this was the first media article to expose the hidden history of the homes and reveal some of the mortality rates. I remain honoured to be Mary Creighton's friend. Her testimony was an act of extreme bravery. As I continued researching and writing, I shared everything with the various groups and soon their files sections began to grow significantly.

Theresa Hiney Tinggal from the Adopted Illegally group, along with her friend Maria Keating Dumbell, had planned a series of events in Dublin during a trip home from Britain. They organised several meetings, and most importantly, a street protest. Adoption Rights Now did all we could to spread information on Theresa's petition for justice, at home and in the big international groups where it got huge support. Several hundred signed. Theresa and Maria handed it in to Minister Frances Fitzgerald where it was received with a polite 'Thank you!' but no action followed.

Adoption Rights Now officially supported the street protest and on Saturday, 6 October 2012 I joined my fellow protesters in front of the Central Bank in Dame Street. Unfortunately, the 'Occupy' group against economic inequality, social injustice and corporate greed was also campaigning that day and there were over 1,000 of them compared to about thirty of us. However, they were interested in our protest, signed our petitions and allowed us to use their PA system. It was my first time addressing a crowd as a campaigner. Around 1,000 people listened and applauded and I was deeply touched by the clear support.

As far as I am aware, this was the first protest about our wider cause, illegal adoptions, Mother and Baby Homes and the shocking infant mortality rates. I am proud to have been there and Theresa deserves enormous credit for her work. There is a picture of Maria Keating and myself holding either end of a banner Maria had made. I love that photo and regularly use it as my cover image on Facebook.

The rest of the year passed with reading and researching whenever I could find time. I continued to make new friends among the Irish and international communities and some of us formed an 'adoptees only' group that became very successful. My wife Siobhán was very supportive, as were my children, parents, and all my extended family and friends. I was now focused on a 'breakthrough' and felt I was on the right track.

CHAPTER 12

Campaigning: New Tactics, New Strategies, New Ideas

The year 2013 started well for us. On 10 January, TV3 broadcast a new series of *Adoption Stories*. Viewer numbers were up to a record 176,000 by the third episode. The series led to a steady rise in the membership of the Facebook-based adoption community and helped once again to bring our issues to the general public and media.

I had read a lot about the tactics and strategies of warfare over the years and I was keenly aware that the keys to victory are mobility and innovation. I resolved to start trying anything and everything to achieve our breakthrough. Marie Kennedy, Theresa Hiney Tinggal, Clodagh Malone and I, with a few others, began to work more closely together. We had no specific title or goal but we became a team and shared information. Many people were very kind in saying that my enthusiasm and workload encouraged them to become more involved but most of them were publicity-shy and I cannot name them but I sincerely wish I could. Thank you from the deepest part of my heart for all your help and encouragement.

I began by trying to lodge a criminal complaint over the high mortality rates in the homes. I went to Dublin for the official Magdalene apology in the Dáil following the release of the flawed McAleese Report and stood with the Magdalene women and their supporters outside the gates of the Dáil with my candle. Afterwards, I went to Store Street Garda station where I had an appointment with a mid-ranking Garda. She listened to me for three hours and went through all my notes and the references in the books I had brought. Unfortunately, while extremely patient and understanding, she diplomatically informed me that I could never lodge a complaint. I needed to find a witness to an actual act of negligence by a specific nun that directly caused the death of a baby. It was an impossible task. The Garda was decent enough to make inquiries at Garda Headquarters and, informally, with the Director of Public Prosecutions, but as expected, the legal system could do nothing. I was disappointed, although that genuine inability of the Gardaí to investigate or prosecute would later prove vital to our United Nations complaint.

The veterans had only one researcher and she had spent many years focusing on the names and details of public records. Over many years at the Genealogical Centre in London she had copied the names of tens of thousands of people born out of wedlock in Ireland from as early as the 1920s right up to the 1960s. She decided to retire from her project and since I was the only person interested in research, she chose to pass her considerable body of research to me. While the records were useful for searching and tracing, they contained nothing useful in terms of evidence, but they did give me an idea. I asked the researcher sending me the material if the online records of births, deaths and marriages in Ireland, that were in private hands, could be used to work out mortality rates in individual Mother and Baby Homes, and the answer was yes. It was a slog and myself and three others went to work, although I limited my role to double-checking the accuracy of the records. The method used was rather haphazard, so we probably missed some names, but I knew the ones we had found were accurate.

Our group managed to arrange a meeting with the then Minister for Children, Frances Fitzgerald, responsible for adoption and adoption legislation. I set to work over the space of several weeks to write up everything I knew in a report. The *Report into the History of Adoption in Ireland since 1922 and Sean Ross Abbey, Castlepollard and Bessboro Mother and Baby Homes, July 2013* turned out to be very important on several levels. It was 8,000 words long and a development of the statement to the Archbishop the previous year. I made a couple of questionable judgement calls and at least one clear mistake, but, while it brought considerable trouble to my door in the short term, the positives over the next year were huge and it proved crucial as the basis for the follow-up to the Tuam 800 story. It went on to inform dozens, if not hundreds, of articles and reports in the media. I still read newspaper pieces from time to time that repeat many of the facts and figures I assembled. It was only afterwards that I discovered it was the first report into the Mother and Baby Homes and the system of adoption in Ireland. It referenced sixteen books, and several films and documentaries as well as private research by a number of people. Most importantly, it served to bring together a team that I am still proud to be a part of – the 'Coalition of Mother and Baby home Survivors'.

I was careful to keep all estimates very conservative and clearly flagged them as such. A good example would be the total numbers for two of the homes. The Interdepartmental Report on Mother and Baby Homes released by the Department of Children and Youth Affairs in July 2014 was a preliminary 'scoping' exercise before the full inquiry began.[1] My figure for the total number of natural mothers who passed through Castlepollard was 'about 3,000' while the Interdepartmental Report gave the number of registered births at 3,763. As that figure does not include miscarriages and stillbirths, the total number for Castlepollard was likely to be about 4,000. The same applies to the estimate for Sean Ross Abbey which was given in my report as 'about 4,800'. This figure should be 'about 6,000'. I am unaware of a single estimate that I made that was later being shown to be an over-estimation and any precise figures that have emerged have always been higher than mine. Flawed though the report was, it spelled out the horror many tens of thousands of girls and women endured and the mere fact that it existed, and that I was not being sued by anybody, meant that there had to be some truth to it.

I created the phrase 'neglected to death' to describe what happened to the babies. As I was writing, I was sending updated drafts to several people for their approval and, as the meeting with the Minister approached, I made it clear to the others that while I was prepared to put my name to it, I did not expect anyone else to sign it, considering that we could be sued. Some people understandably shied away. Our community is not young and people have families, homes and responsibilities; no one should be asked to put them on the line for someone they have met on Facebook. However, Clodagh Malone and two other adoptees were willing to take the risk, although they both asked later for their names to be removed. I was one of three adoptees, including Clodagh, who went to the meeting with Minister Fitzgerald in the Dáil during July 2013. We were accompanied by Michael Nugent from Atheist Ireland, who attended as an independent witness.

As we waited in the Dáil lobby, the Cabinet was having their final meeting before its summer recess. Earlier that day we had found out that Derek Leinster of the Bethany Group and its secretary, Niall Meehan, had heavily lobbied the Deputy First Minister of Northern Ireland, Martin McGuinness. McGuinness had absolutely nothing to gain by supporting a group of elderly Protestants in the Republic but he had taken to heart their battle for justice and was willing to speak out publicly in support of the Bethany cause, and called on the Irish government to give the Bethany survivors justice. Alan Shatter, who was Minister for Justice at the time and who also supported the Bethany cause, brought the matter to the Cabinet to discuss the call for an immediate apology and redress. As we sat there, a man stormed across the lobby, shouting about injustice and discrimination. It was my first glimpse of the elusive Derek Leinster. The Cabinet had refused his demand for an apology and redress but, as a concession, had offered to fund a substantial monument for those who had died in the Bethany Home.

We were ushered in and seated around a table with three senior civil servants and the Minister. After we had said our piece, I personally put the report into the Minister's hand and said, 'Quite frankly, Minister, babies were murdered.' She promised to read the report that night and assured us that we would have a further meeting to go over it in detail.

I wanted to meet Archbishop Martin again after his McGill Summer School address when he had called for private research into the 'quality of care' at Mother and Baby Homes. The report he wanted was ready. However, the Archbishop was busy in Rio de Janeiro so the next day I sent him a copy by registered post after talking to his vice chancellor Rev. Fintan Gavin on the phone. If I marked the envelope 'personal', he assured me, then only the Archbishop would open it. I sent one to the vice chancellor too, by ordinary post but, apparently, his got lost. His Grace Diarmuid Martin also claimed in August 2015 that he had never received his copy either, although it was signed for at the Archbishop's Palace. Two weeks later, with no response from Church or State, I went ahead, with everyone's agreement, and sent the report to four media people and then published it online in all the groups. All hell broke loose. The positive benefits from the report would come in time but the negative reaction was immediate and vicious.

The Inner Circle

Within hours of posting my report in the various Facebook groups, I was attacked from all directions. Before I knew what was going on, numerous people were involved across several groups and it was a nightmare. I was on the verge of quitting after a week of infighting. I wanted to sort things out, but every time I tried, I was deliberately misinterpreted. It was extremely frustrating and detrimental to the community. Eventually, after a couple of weeks, the 'Facebook war' died, but then something more significant and downright weird happened. I received a call on my landline from a woman who refused to give her name. She claimed to represent a secret group of adoptees called the 'Adoption Apostles' who had been driven out of activism over the years by a particular cabal. I did not recognise her voice but she was articulate and well-spoken. The attack on me, she claimed, had been planned and well-orchestrated as a direct result of my report and while it had now gone quiet again, I would be undermined until I quit campaigning. I was a threat to the cabal, who were determined to get the credit for opening the adoption records and any related government action to do with our issues. From the start we were all being groomed as 'minions' by the cabal, which she called the 'Inner Circle'. I had become a problem for the inner circle. I had grown too big, too fast, and forming my own group within months of deciding to become an activist was a massive mistake. Now, she informed me, the honeymoon was over. I was a marked man.

I did not believe this particular conspiracy theory and declined her invitation to join the Adoption Apostles. I refused to believe that my fellow campaigners and friends would try to crush me in my efforts to get truth and justice for survivors. Nevertheless, I began to reluctantly research the history of the adoption community and spoke to many people who were not only willing but eager to talk. I discovered several people who had been serious activists over the years but had quit. I heard stories from them that made my blood run cold. A few weeks later I had lunch with a man who said it was amazing that I had got as far as I had, and that my report had caught the inner circle completely by surprise. They had no idea I had so much information and that our informal group could manage to meet Minister Fitzgerald, and then potentially alert the media. Seemingly, the inner circle felt that political lobbying and media work were their domain. A number of people informed me that there was at least one spy in my group and probably several. Around this time my wife received an anonymous call on our landline from a man threatening to come to the house and sort me out.

I was never sworn to secrecy when I received the Adoption Apostles' call but perhaps they were so sure I would join up that they forgot to ask me to remain silent about their group. I do know that all the caller's predictions came true. The Adoption Apostles warned me that many of my friends on Facebook would unfriend or block me over the next few months and that happened with depressing regularity. I began to take precautions by taking screen shots/captures of everything on Facebook that I thought was significant. I totalled over 2,000 pictures the last time I looked and that demoralised me. The person at the centre of the multiple smear campaigns lived abroad and publicly claimed to be broke and therefore could not be sued in a civil court case. She was careful to keep her behaviour just below the threshold for criminal charges. The inner circle operated in a grey area between civil and criminal law and those involved could harass someone online indefinitely and get away with it.

I learned a hard lesson and it left a bitter taste in my mouth. I was completely sucked in by experts at manipulation and reduced to petty infighting. We were children playing silly spy games but with horrifying consequences for the survivor community. I was disappointed in myself. I asked the person behind the attack to leave me alone and left it at that. I realise now that I was lost online when I first arrived, and I was naïve. I walked away and tried my best to ignore the relentless smear campaign for the next several months until it really exploded after the Tuam 800 story.

It is in the nature of all groups, regardless of their raison d'être, to become more fractious as they grow in size. Strong personalities, often with selfish motives or big egos, produce conflict and different 'wings' of the group develop on the extreme fringes. This is sadly true of all the institutional communities, including the Magdalenes and the industrial and reformatory school survivors. They are all split and torn apart by infighting. The activists across the entire network must learn, if we are to properly represent our communities, to keep the groups smaller and democratic, and to organise regular events beyond Facebook. Bitter and heartbreaking experience has taught me that democratic umbrella groups of campaigners are the best and only route forward, with non-political survivors left in peace.

Even though my report had brought wounding criticism, the positives far outweighed the negatives and continue to do so. The *Report into Adoption* grew a life of its own over the next few months. I organised a third annual Castlepollard trip and over forty people turned up. When we gathered in the Angels' Plot, I remembered what truly mattered to me.

The few media contacts I had were unable to feature my report for different reasons but once again Adelina Campos from the *Mirror on Sunday* believed that the story needed to be told and that it warranted a public inquiry. Her article appeared on 11 August 2013, a double-page spread. Adelina focused on Dr. Deeny, tracing his family and the report he had written about Bessboro. She also included the Sacred Heart nuns and their attempts to sell Sean Ross Abbey. Just as importantly, there was an editorial backing our call for a public inquiry. I also tried Journal.ie, an online newspaper, and got lucky. Paul Gallagher published an article on 10 August 2013. The headline and opening sentence called for a public inquiry and I was elated. Gallagher and Campos deserve full credit for publishing some of the first articles detailing the horror of the homes and their appalling mortality rates. I was momentarily convinced this was a potential breakthrough moment but once again that moment came and went.

One of the things I had noticed when Adelina was reading the report and asking for evidence was her sense of disbelief. She is French and told me that such a scandal could never have happened in France. She could recall no such institutions in that country and, if they did exist, they were relatively benign compared to the Irish homes I was describing. That made me think about how we deal with institutional injustice in Ireland, or to be more precise, how we do not deal with it unless our government is forced into action. The 2013 McAleese Report about the Magdalene Laundries had been ordered by the United Nations, following a complaint to the Committee Against Torture. I realised that I needed to look beyond Ireland.

I inquired about making a complaint on behalf of the Mother and Baby Homes to the United Nations. I sent my report to several groups, individuals and organisations and a legal adviser (solicitor) contacted me and offered to write a complaint. Once again, I found that luck was on our side. Before a complaint can be made to the UN, all domestic remedies must be exhausted. My complaint to the Garda in February, and the government's refusal to hold a public inquiry, meant that hurdle was already out of the way and we could proceed immediately. I was really hopeful and made a decision to try and do things better in our community. It was difficult to know whom to trust, but this was not just *my* cause and I wanted to include as many people as possible, despite the risks involved. Others with more media experience were happy to take on that role and I concentrated on research, histories and reports.

I contacted Derek Leinster in England and we spoke regularly on the phone. He was keen to be involved and immediately committed the Bethany group to the UN complaint. Dr. Niall Meehan, the Bethany group's secretary, was also eager to contribute, and Clodagh Malone was already on the team, as was Theresa Hiney Tinggal. It was a small group, but we were all involved for the right reasons and had the resources and the determination to finally realise our elusive breakthrough.

Theresa arranged another trip to Dublin and organised a very important meeting with Clare Daly, Independent TD. Over the years, I have come to know and respect Clare Daly and her assistant Rhona McCord. They work tirelessly for causes that are mostly unpopular and unfashionable and provide a vital safety net for the marginalised in our society.

Clare and Rhona met Theresa and me on 20 September 2013. Clare had booked a room in Buswells Hotel and organised a press conference. A handful of journalists were there and the event was quite informal but we got our main points across. I sent a copy of my report to Clare and Theresa and I began keeping them up to date on any developments. After the press conference I ended up chatting to one of the journalists, Alison O'Reilly, of the *Mail on Sunday*, one of a small number of reporters in Ireland with an interest in adoption. We exchanged phone numbers and promised to stay in touch.

The next day the press conference was reported in the papers. A quote from me had made it into *The Irish Times*, when Mary Carolan had cited my description of illegal adoptions as 'industrial-scale identity theft'. I was particularly pleased with another quote in the article by Eilish O'Regan in the *Irish Independent*: 'Of all of the Catholic institutions in this country, the Mother and Baby Homes are the last dirty little secret from Catholic Ireland – and in my opinion the worst.' Journal.ie also carried an article and it was fast becoming a solid news outlet for our cause. I was starting to get used to the media business and believed and hoped that the report and quotes were making a difference and getting our message across.

Theresa had also arranged a meeting with Minister Fitzgerald. There were four of us there – another adoptee, an illegally adopted man who was going through hell and wanted answers, and myself. Of all the ministers we have engaged with over the years, Minister Fitzgerald was the most open. She discussed the issues and problems, unlike others who simply sat there listening but not engaging in any way. I asked the Minister if she had had a chance to read my report and, if so, did she have any response. Her answer was impeccably polite and charming as always, but the end result was still the same. The meeting was unproductive. No public inquiry, no investigation.

A woman named Catherine Corless contacted me in late September after someone had forwarded her a copy of my report. She kindly described my report as 'breath-taking' and 'well-crafted with such meticulous detail'. I was flattered but, infinitely more importantly, Catherine told me that she had researched and written a history of the Tuam Mother and Baby Home, just as Niall Meehan and I had done for Bethany and Castlepollard respectively. I barely knew anything about Tuam and was shocked when she told me that she had discovered that 788 children had died in the Tuam Mother and Baby Home and she had the death certificates to prove it, with more on the way. Her research was a colossal leap forward, especially because she was so keen to continue studying Tuam and wanted to learn more about the other homes. Catherine wrote that she was part of a group of people trying to get a memorial for the Tuam Home babies and was currently raising funds. We exchanged research over several emails, including a scan of Catherine's article in the *Journal of the old Tuam Society*. We were delighted to have found each other and I felt that the UN complaint team, as we called ourselves, had found another kindred spirit. I cautiously asked if Catherine knew the total numbers who had gone through the Tuam Home because, if so, we would finally have a total infant mortality rate for one of the homes, but unfortunately she did not. I invited Catherine to join Facebook and meet the rest of the active community and she did. She also set up a community page for the Tuam memorial fund.

Shortly after the newspaper articles relating to the press conference Clare Daly had organised, a natural mother who had been searching for thirty years for her daughter wrote to Clare and asked for help in tracing her since she thought the adoption might have been illegal. With this woman's permission, her letter was forwarded to me and, as luck would have it, I found her daughter in the *Iris Oifigiúil* lists I had at home and contacted her immediately. Coincidentally, Clare and Rhona had a question scheduled on the issue in the Dáil that day. Clare mentioned the trace and how 'Paul' had managed to successfully find this woman's daughter when the official tracing service had been so unsuccessful. It was weird being mentioned in the Dáil. I was relieved that Clare had not mentioned my surname although she would in time, and more than once, but by then I was no longer the shy, retiring adoptee who had started out in 2011. Two years on, I had toughened up and was more determined than ever.

The report ultimately acted as a focus that brought the researchers in our community together. Within a year, our little group of amateur historians would find our research broadcast to the world, led by Catherine's Tuam 800 findings. There were several more positive outcomes and the report was seen by many people in Ireland and in the international groups. The Vance Twins and their large Facebook-based international group, Adoption Truth and Transparency, were very encouraging and invited Adoption Rights Now to join their international umbrella group, the Adoption Coalition Worldwide. This international coalition of over 10,000 adoptees and natural mothers also supported our umbrella group, the Coalition of Mother and Baby home Survivors (CMABS) when we formed, and added serious weight to our fight. I was asked by the Vance Twins to contribute part of the report, about the banished babies, to an anthology about international adoption called *Adoptionland* and I was happy to donate it as all profits were going towards our cause around the world. Meanwhile, a Romanian-American friend of mine had started an adoption blog and asked if she could put my report online. I was more than happy to help a friend and fellow activist. Little did I realise at the time that Georgiana Macavei's obscure blog about international adoption would play a key role in our fight for justice.

We expected more from the major box office success in Ireland of the film *Philomena* in November 2013. It was based on a semi-fictionalised book by Martin Sixsmith that told the story of Philomena Lee who lost her son to adoption in Sean Ross Abbey. He was sent to the United States as a banished baby. Many of us were deeply disappointed with the film because we hoped it would lift the lid on life in Sean Ross during the 1950s. The media debate it sparked in Ireland fizzled out quickly, and I felt that a golden opportunity to highlight our cause had passed us by.

Catherine Corless had effectively joined the team that was working to bring a complaint to the United Nations. She contributed her research – both the Tuam article and the 788 death certificates – as part of our proof of horrific injustice. Mary Lou McDonald came on board through our legal adviser and was a great support. Mary Lou and Sinn Féin, both north and south of the border, were already pushing the Bethany cause, much to the surprise and delight of the Protestant survivors. She asked many awkward questions in the Dáil and introduced us to yet another previously unknown researcher. Murry Kavanagh (not his real name) happened to be a Castlepollard crib mate of mine and, like Derek Leinster and Catherine Corless, he was eager to share his research and discuss the institutions. Murry had grown up between four different institutions, including a Mother and Baby Home, a county home and two industrial schools, one of which was the notorious Letterfrack. He told his story under a pseudonym on local radio and it was heartbreaking.

As Christmas of 2013 approached, I wondered just how many more researchers were beavering away unbeknown to us. I knew there had to be more of us out there. I resolved to mount a media and online campaign in the New Year to gather us all together. I believed that if we had sufficient detailed infant mortality rates from the Mother and Baby Homes, it would be more than enough to guarantee success for our UN complaint. As Christmas approached, I felt sure that our time was coming.

I remember the start of 2014 as a very happy time for me. I was keeping my head down in the Facebook groups and refusing to rise to any provocation. I wrote a submission to the Constitutional Convention, set up in 2012 to review the Irish Constitution, and asked them to consider the inhumanity of closed adoption. It was an attempt to get that particular issue onto the political and media agenda and to use it as a springboard to a public inquiry. My membership of the international communities helped, and people like the Vance Twins and several prominent Australian activists gave great support and advice: Lizzy Howard, Julia Freebourne, Jacqui Haycroft and Kate Mitchell were all amazing. The final submission was 5,500 words long. When I put it online in the groups and asked people to submit it to the Constitutional Convention, about twenty adoptees submitted a copy. I learned a very valuable lesson from the experience: the document was boring and too technical. After that, I pared back and heavily edited any submission or document I wrote and kept the focus on survivors and their suffering. It proved much more effective and yielded results.

While Derek Leinster was still furious with the Irish government for refusing to reopen the Redress Act 2002 and add the Bethany Home, he had accepted the money for a memorial. He had organised an ecumenical service and the unveiling of the memorial in Mount Jerome Cemetery on 2 April 2014. I was looking forward to finally meeting Derek in person. After the event we would have an opportunity to discuss the last details of putting together the UN complaint.

On the day, about a hundred people walked solemnly up the wide pathway to the right of the chapel to where the Bethany Home Memorial had been placed. It was chilling in its own way, particularly because we knew it was not complete. It represented the years 1921 to 1949 and the Bethany Home did not close until 1972. We looked at the list of 222 names and the ages, months, weeks, days, even hours, of those who had died. It was another stark reminder of what was important and what we were all fighting for. This was another Castlepollard, another Tuam, another home where hundreds of innocent babies and children had died.

Derek wanted it to go into all the papers the next day and he feared that none of the others would print it now because the *Irish Examiner* had got the scoop. He was correct. Apart from that, he was delighted with the turnout and the unveiling of the memorial. It was the largest gathering of Protestant and Bethany survivors together in one place and Derek now believes that everything changed for the better as a result. The memorial had not just brought Catholic and Protestant survivors together, it had united us as crib mates.

Our legal adviser arrived later and, when people had drifted off, the activists sat down in a quiet corner to discuss our complaint. Derek, Niall, Clodagh, our legal adviser and I had our first proper meeting. I missed Theresa Hiney Tinggal, Catherine Corless and Murry Kavanagh, but I knew it was difficult to get everybody together and that we had to seize the opportunity. We needed a name and had been discussing it online and now we needed to decide. I freely admit I was very pushy about this because I had come to believe that the specific use of language is crucial. I was not going to make the same mistake as I had made with the name Adoption Rights Now. Our name had to reflect as much of our community as possible, especially natural mothers, who had been sidelined up to that point. Our community were 'adoptees' and I knew we needed to rename, rebrand and redefine ourselves as 'survivors', a word that can be truthfully and accurately applied to anyone associated with the Mother and Baby Homes. It was a word that I believed would heal the artificial divisions in our community and bring us together. We had all attended commemorations at Angels' Plots and we were survivors. It was precise and descriptive and the subconscious connotations that come with that word applied to us naturally. Adoptees want open records but survivors want truth and justice.

The name of the type of institutions we were fighting to bring to public attention also had to be included, because it would hopefully enter the public domain. So our team became the 'Coalition of Mother and Baby home Survivors' (CMABS). The name turned out to be vital, completely redefining our community and our cause within two months.

Sealed and closed adoption was only a small part of the punishment for our natural mothers and and their babies. While the word 'adoptee' may be accurate and appropriate in other countries, it does not apply to the uniquely abusive mistreatment of natural mothers and their babies in the Mother and Baby Homes in Ireland. In a way, to label ourselves as 'adopted people' is to use the language of our oppressors and to victimise ourselves.

I am sure readers will have noticed that I have used very few names after I began to write about the adoption community in 1990. That is because the majority of the activists involved were decent and honourable people who made genuine mistakes that carried long-term disadvantages for our community. They are not to be blamed or named and shamed. It is also necessary to protect many of the people in our community who are still extremely private about their adoptions or the loss of a baby to adoption. Anybody who is named is a public figure or is named with their permission. Some activists in our community simply do not deserve to be mentioned because they actively blocked anyone pursuing other avenues of campaigning. Any semblance of systematic research was absent from our community for twenty years, except for the work done by Derek Leinster, but it was not the only thing missing. Memorials were postponed until after 'full restorative justice' (a meaningless phrase) was achieved. The only goal our community was pursuing was opening the sealed adoption records. Demonstrations were deemed ineffective when they were suggested and petitions were ridiculed. The only tactics considered acceptable were the same repetitive media releases and political lobbying, and individuals were demonised for trying new approaches.

I have no desire to reopen old wounds and become embroiled in another wasteful war of words. I simply want to be left alone to pursue the fight I started in Castlepollard six years ago. Ultimately, it is the thousands of survivors of Mother and Baby Homes who died during those lost years that I remember. It was time to prioritise living survivors and their needs and wants.

Our legal adviser recommended that we focus exclusively on the Mother and Baby Homes since they were a clear and easy way to get our complaint to the United Nations accepted. Our strategy was to force the door open with the homes and then fight for other rights, including opening the sealed records. We felt that we were on track for the first time and the CMABS team worked hard from late 2013 until 25 May 2014, when our world exploded.

PART 4

BREAKTHROUGH, 2014–2017

CHAPTER 13

From Tuam to Castlepollard via the Rest of the World

In the summer of 2013 I was at a social gathering of survivors and met a woman who was trying to trace two siblings who had died as infants in Tuam. I emailed her with some information that I thought was promising but I never heard back from her. However, she had heard about Catherine Corless's Tuam memorial and contacted her instead. Catherine had, of course, shared her research about the number of babies who were buried in the Tuam Angels' Plot and this woman had also contacted Alison O'Reilly of the *Mail on Sunday*, the journalist I had met at the press conference Clare Daly TD had organised in 2013.

Alison had contacted Catherine and I already knew that her research about Tuam was going to be published in the *Mail on Sunday* on 25 May 2014. On the day, I went to a shop on the South Circular Road in Dublin to buy the paper. I was initially taken aback as the banner headline screamed in block capitals: 'A MASS GRAVE OF 800 BABIES'. To see it like that in writing was shocking but, at the same time, I was glad to see our cause fill the entire front page, where it belonged.

The next day there was nothing in any of the other papers or news media, as far as I know, with the sole exception of Irish Central, an American-based, internet-only newspaper website. On Tuesday, the story was picked up by Journal.ie and it was also being discussed online in Politics.ie, one of Ireland's largest online discussion groups, but otherwise all the attention was coming from abroad. On Wednesday, the RTÉ Radio show *Liveline* was swamped with calls from survivors telling their stories. I have no doubt these heroic acts of bravery by former residents of Mother and Baby Homes, whether natural mothers or adoptees, were instrumental to what happened over the next three weeks.

The activists in the community could not understand why people around the world were picking up on the story while the Irish media seemed to be asleep. The three broadsheets, *The Irish Times, Irish Independent* and *Irish Examiner,* and the tabloid newspapers were silent until Thursday. The commentators on Politics.ie were talking about it and they had also remarked on the mainstream media silence. RTÉ News was also deathly quiet. We held our breaths and once again hoped for the best.

Then the mystery of why the story was spreading rapidly abroad was solved. A poster in one of our groups had checked out the *Mail* newspaper group on Wikipedia. It turned out that it was one of the biggest news websites in the world. The penny dropped. I looked it up and the *Mail* site was getting nearly ten million hits a day and nearly two hundred million unique hits a month. Alison O'Reilly had uploaded her Tuam 800 story and all it took was a tiny percentage of the *Mail* website readership to be outraged and begin blogging and suddenly tens of thousands were talking about Tuam. By midweek, the international attention was making its way back to Ireland. While Alison O'Reilly's original story had not mentioned the words 'septic tank', those words were now everywhere. In the eyes of the world, the 800 babies at Tuam had not only died, but had been 'dumped/thrown/tossed/flung' into a sewage tank. The Australian media reported the story and then the Associated Press. The story crossed all boundaries through blogs, mainstream media and websites and discussion pages. Hundreds of thousands of people abroad were reading and discussing the Tuam 800 story but in Ireland the initial publicity had already died down.

We could not believe our eyes. *The Boston Globe, The Washington Post*, French, German, Italian and Australian media all covered the story. Buzzfeed, an American internet media company based in New York City which focuses on digital media and feminism, posted the story and had over 6,000 views in just sixteen hours. Tuam 800 had gone viral by the end of the first week and only then did the story return to Ireland. By Friday, Newstalk 106 Radio and RTÉ News had caught up and the rest of the media were belatedly, and reluctantly, about to follow another media outlet's scoop. The question our community faced was how to build on the media attention and widen the focus to include the other homes and the mortality rates.

On the morning of Saturday 31 May, just six days after the Tuam 800 story, I drove to my local garage, my mind racing. Neil Michael, chief reporter for the *Daily Mail*, the sister paper of the *Mail on Sunday*, had promised me the previous evening that his article about the three Sacred Heart Mother and Baby Homes would be published today. Neil had phoned me on Thursday afternoon to ask if there were any more 'mass graves' like Tuam in Ireland. 'Yes,' I replied, 'there are several more and Tuam is only the fifth-biggest of the Mother and Baby Homes.' We spoke at length about the other homes and I made the decision to cooperate with him. The impetus for the story was from outside Ireland and we knew that the international dimension was what was needed for a possible breakthrough. The United Nations submission was ready to go. My report had focused on the three Sacred Heart Angels' Plots and the Tuam 800 story was about another such plot. It was a perfect fit.

The CMABS team was prepared. Derek Leinster had a list of the name and age of every baby who had died in Bethany. Clodagh Malone would do media work if it came our way, and I promised to stay with the *Mail* where the story had begun and give Neil Michael whatever help or support I could. Theresa Hiney Tinggal was ready to push the case of the illegally adopted and Catherine Corless was dealing with the Tuam 800 attention.

I sensed the bandwagon rolling and when the opportunity came, I jumped onboard wholeheartedly and enthusiastically. I felt we had nothing to lose and although I was wary of the media, there was something about Neil that made me take a leap of faith. I encountered some immediate criticism from some of the veterans for cooperating with the 'likes of the *Mail*!' but I remain unapologetic about that to this day. CMABS did what we felt was right and I certainly have no regrets. I consider Neil a genuine and brilliant reporter and we became good friends and remain so.

I sent Neil my report and some of the research relating to the UN complaint and we were in constant contact. With the international media now descending on Ireland in droves, driving past the other Mother and Baby Homes on their way to Tuam, we hoped against hope that Neil's story about the three Sacred Heart homes would widen the media's interest at home and abroad.

Two days later, Saturday 31 May, I drove to my local garage, eager and afraid at the same time. I literally froze when I saw the banner front-page headline in the *Daily Mail*: 'BABIES WERE STARVED TO DEATH IN NUNS' CARE'. I felt sick in the pit of my stomach and a sense of panic as I realised the full implications of what I had done. I had just accused an order of Catholic nuns of neglecting to death 2,500 infants and children and burying them in three mass graves. The reality of seeing it in print made my heart pound.

The moment passed and I realised that this was what I wanted and, more importantly, the accusations were true. If I was dragged into court and sued, I could prove every word that I had written in my report and in the *Daily Mail* article. I silently exhaled and thanked God and Neil Michael for this headline. I took a step closer. There was a quote underneath – 'State in denial about Irish "holocaust", says survivor'. Oh my God! That's me, I'm that survivor! After my initial shock, I felt a huge sense of relief. Relief that my obsession with the Angels' Plots and mortality rates at the homes was exactly the right research needed at the right time, in the right newspaper and going around the world. I felt a real sense of hope and bought three copies of the paper.

The next three weeks were a whirlwind of emotions, media attention and madness. Work took a back seat as I spent days and nights online and on the phone. I tried my best to answer all the emails, texts and Facebook private messages, and give some of the journalists the background information and hard facts off the record. I was totally swamped and sleeping very little but I knew I had to strike while the iron was hot. Dozens of people contacted the CMABS team, offering help, and we directed them to the radio phone-in shows. The *Mail* newspapers were at the heart of everything that was happening and I had enough research available to fill several more articles. Neil was phoning up to twenty times a day, going over all the details. He drove around the country following new aspects of the story and visiting and photographing the Mother and Baby Homes. I also put Neil in touch with the rest of the CMABS crew.

The media attention kept building and the community groups were posting comments and links to stories around the world. New members flooded in and it was hard to keep up. After years in the wilderness, we were the centre of attention both in Ireland and around the world. On Sunday 1 June, there was further media coverage as Philomena Lee joined hundreds of others for the first annual commemoration service for those mothers and babies who died in Sean Ross Abbey.

On Monday 2 June, the story finally appeared in *The Irish Times* and the *Irish Mirror* although both mentions of the Tuam 800 story were further down in articles that primarily reported Philomena Lee's visit to Sean Ross Abbey.[1],[2] The *Irish Independent* also reported on Lee's visit but never mentioned the Tuam 800 story. Meanwhile, the international media poured into Ireland, all looking for a unique angle. The story was now about all of the homes. While the national media responded to the global interest, it was the voices of living survivors on the radio stations, quietly recounting their personal experiences, that finally brought home the humanity and reality to the Irish public. Those brave souls from our community spoke out after decades of silence enforced by stigma and shame. Survivors found comfort in the media reports because they realised they were not alone. Adoptees who'd had no idea they were born in institutions where thousands of others had died told their stories. The nation shook its head in disbelief and wept.

The following day, our community was lifted by Colm Keaveney's intervention in the Dáil because he was a Galway TD and Tuam was in his constituency. He insisted on raising the Tuam 800 issue and when he refused to back down, he was ejected. As he said, 'In the process of trying to raise an issue that everyone in this country is talking about, apart from the Dáil, I was removed from the Dáil.'[3]

On Wednesday 4 June, Neil was back on the front page again, this time with fellow journalist Ferghal Blaney: 'MASS GRAVES, WE MUST HAVE A PUBLIC INQUIRY NOW.' The Irish media reacted to the call and were suddenly chasing the story flat out. On Thursday, *The Irish Times* reported on the front page that pressure was building for an inquiry into the Tuam Babies' scandal. The *Irish Examiner* carried a front-page lead story about the homes, although questions were asked about the reliability of the figures used. The *Irish Independent* also put the story on its front page, noting the Archbishop of Tuam's call for the nuns to cooperate with an 'examination' into how the 800 babies in Tuam had died. At this stage, I was exhausted and emotionally drained. One minute I was in tears over some new heartbreaking story on the radio and the next I was punching the air with joy that our battle was won. I knew it was not over by a long shot but, after Neil Michael's 'public inquiry' story, I wanted to believe that this genie was well and truly out of the bottle and neither the government nor the Churches could get it back in. Even President Higgins spoke out about his 'enormous sadness' upon learning of the deaths and how he was 'appalled'.

The previous year, Romanian-American activist Georgiana Macavei asked to include my report on her new blog. A month after the Tuam 800 story, I had seen figures from my report everywhere and wondered where they had come from. Georgiana got in touch to say her blog was registering 500 views a day and had gone from about 20 views to over 12,000 since the Tuam 800 story broke. Mystery solved and I was delighted and grateful. I spread my wings slightly and did a live interview with Newstalk 106.

On Thursday evening Neil Michael phoned and asked if I knew about the vaccine trials. He was starting a series of six reports beginning the following day. The Friday headline from the *Daily Mail*: 'THOUSANDS OF CHILDREN USED FOR VACCINE TRIALS WHILE IN NUNS' CARE' revealed previously unknown research by Michael Dwyer of University College Cork, which has been described in detail in Chapter 7. There was a further piece by Ferghal Blaney relating to a Dáil debate the previous day. The newly appointed Minister for Children Charles Flanagan announced an 'inter-departmental report' on the scale of the issues. The Taoiseach Enda Kenny had been questioned about it in San Francisco where he was on a trade mission.

Saturday's banner headline in *The Star* said that there were '7,000 DEAD BABIES' in the mass graves. The *Irish Mirror* was also banner front-page and I was delighted to see Adelina Campos's by-line. I was dealing almost exclusively with Neil Michael at this stage but did, however, speak to the *Irish Independent*. They mentioned my report, the fact that Minister Fitzgerald had received it and that I had attended three meetings with Archbishop Martin. I was hoping this would put pressure on the government and the Archbishop to respond favourably to the call for an inquiry after their previous inaction. It did.

The *Daily Mail* issued their fifth banner front page on Saturday: 'SO SISTERS, DID YOUR PR FIRM DEVISE THE IDEA OF AN APOLOGY?' by Kevin Keane. That weekend the Mother and Baby Homes were on the front of practically every single paper. From the *Irish Sun* to Britain's *Sunday Times* our lives and stories were everywhere. The *Mail on Sunday* headline read 'WE NEED TO DIG BABIES' GRAVES' but this time the by-line was by Alison O'Reilly and Neil Michael. There was also an editorial and a further eight pages inside, written by several reporters. It seemed like the entire *Mail* staff were on our side. The 'O'Reilly and Michael' by-line was pounced upon by our community and comparisons were made to the legendary 'Woodward and Bernstein' by-line of Watergate fame. After years in the wilderness, Neil and Alison were our heroes. The CMABS team made the decision to go public on the UN complaint and give the story to Neil.

That same Sunday something extraordinary happened. Helen Murphy, a woman unknown to our community, had called for a gathering at the gates of Bessboro and 300 adoptees, natural mothers and supporters arrived. They tied baby shoes, flowers and teddy bears to the front gates and railings. Helen was a Bessboro-born adoptee and had only recently founded a new Facebook group called 'Remembering Bessboro Babies'. It had hundreds of members within weeks. It was part of an outpouring from our community who had been denied the right to speak and act for generations. Now that the dam of silence was breached, the raw emotions poured out. The initial gathering that Helen had organised has since evolved into an annual commemoration in the Bessboro Angels' Plot. I was overjoyed. We were off our computers and out in the real world where we should have been for the past twenty-five years.

Catherine Corless's life was turned upside down after Tuam 800. The international media were camped outside her door and eventually made it inside because of Catherine's impeccable sense of Irish hospitality.

When I phoned Catherine one evening, she answered from her utility room where she was standing with her husband and daughter, eating fish and chips from bags resting on a washing machine. The media had taken over her kitchen and living room. We shared some laughs about the madness. I was still waiting every day for a solicitor's letter from the Sacred Heart nuns threatening court action, but it never arrived.

The *Mail* headlines continued and the national and international media were unearthing more and more details about the homes. On the third and final week of the media frenzy Neil Michael focused on the money. Neil had discovered that the Sacred Heart nuns had received in excess of €5 million over the previous few years, to provide services for 'vulnerable pregnant young women and teenagers in Bessboro'. His headline was 'NUNS GETTING MILLIONS FROM THE TAXPAYERS.' We were aghast.

That Monday was also the day I told Neil about the Coalition of Mother and Baby home Survivors. On Tuesday morning, the eighth *Mail* headline read 'HOW DARE THE NUNS DENY THIS SUFFERING'. The sub-headline read 'There was no forced adoption, say the sisters.' Neil kindly quoted me on the front page and the banner headline paraphrased a quote of mine that he had used in the article. I had finally overcome my reticence to cooperate with the media and found to my surprise that I was pretty chuffed. Clodagh Malone was quoted in the article and CMABS were well and truly on the map.

Between Catherine Corless, the CMABS crew, Neil Michael and Alison O'Reilly on the *Mail*, we accidentally formed a winning team, even though many of us had never met each other. All the ingredients were there; Catherine's irrefutable stack of death certs, the international dimension because of the *Mail* website, my report about the other homes, Georgiana's blog with 500 hits a day that journalists everywhere were using, the CMABS team and the UN complaint project. The voices of our community on the radios were the final and vital element of our breakthrough.

I made a point of going to the Adoption Rights Now and Castlepollard groups and explaining what CMABS was about. I called for a vote to decide if the groups would combine. The two groups voted to unite. I still believe our community desperately needs democracy built into our group constitutions as their very fabric. This community belongs to us all equally. Every survivor must be allowed to speak and contribute their unique experience, providing their voices do not drown out others.

But the backlash was picking up as well. While the original Tuam 800 story had not mentioned a septic tank, that detail had now entered the narrative. Then it was questioned. Rosita Boland, a journalist with *The Irish Times,* had gone to visit Catherine Corless and had written an article. Boland was well known to our community as one of the very few journalists who regularly covered adoption issues. She was also open about the fact that she was trying to adopt a child and wanted the adoption process streamlined to make international adoptions easier. As a rule, most well-read adoptees are against adoption, except in the most genuine or extreme circumstances and even then they will only support open adoption. While there are many who have no problem with adoption at all, a sizable minority are vehemently anti-adoption. Our entire community almost universally agrees that international adoption is a particularly nasty side of the process which involves the exploitation of poor and desperate families in developing countries with little or no adoption legislation, and often involves corrupt officials. What happened in our country not that long ago is currently happening in the poorest countries around the world.[4] Boland's article started a small but steady stream of people claiming the whole story was phony and the article became a focus for the deniers. They claimed the septic tank part of the story was false and therefore the whole story was bogus. They claimed that there was no hard evidence that any bodies were buried in Tuam and, if there were bodies, perhaps they were Famine bodies.

Our community pointed out the existence of the 800 death certificates that Catherine Corless had bought over many years. The deaths were registered by the nuns themselves. No one could ignore that evidence, although some tried.

The media and public controversy was relatively minor and focused on *where* the bodies were buried rather than denying their existence. The media editorials and opposition politicians were demanding an inquiry and, in a way, Boland accidently played into our hands. By questioning exactly who and what was buried at Tuam, she introduced an element of uncertainty which led to further calls for an inquiry to get at the truth. Even the Church was making the right noises as their professional public relations gurus went into action The Bon Secours nuns who had run Tuam hired Terry Prone to handle their public relations. When a documentary maker, named Saskia Weber, wrote to them asking for an interview, Prone replied:

Your letter was sent on to me by the Provincial of the Irish Bon Secours congregation with instructions that I should help you. I'm not sure how I can. Let me explain. When the 'O My God – mass grave in West of Ireland' broke in an English-owned paper (the *Mail*) it surprised the hell out of everybody, not least the Sisters of Bon Secours in Ireland, none of whom had ever worked in Tuam and most of whom had never heard of it. If you come here, you'll find no mass grave, no evidence that children were ever so buried, and a local police force casting their eyes to heaven and saying 'Yeah, a few bones were found – but this was an area where Famine victims were buried. So?' Several international TV stations have aborted their plans to make documentaries, because essentially all that can be said is 'Ireland in the first half of the twentieth century was a moralistic, inward-looking, anti-feminist country of exaggerated religiosity.' Which most of us knew already. The overwhelming majority of the surviving Sisters of Bon Secours in Ireland are over eighty. The handful (literally) still in active ministry are in their seventies. None of them is an historian or sociologist or theologian and so would not have the competence to be good on your programme.

If you'd like me to point you at a few reputable historians who might be good, I'll certainly do that.

Terry Prone (Ms)
Chairman
The Communications Clinic

After Neil revealed the existence of CMABS, requests for meetings flooded in and he put several senior politicians in touch with us. After a flurry of phone calls on Tuesday, several of us arranged to go to a number of meetings the next day. That day was extraordinary for all of us, the sort of day that stays with you for life; it shines brightly in your past and illuminates your future.

On Wednesday morning, 11 June, I put on my best jacket and headed off to town to meet the rest of the CMABS activists. We were now well into a third week of media frenzy and I was completely drained and in a daze from lack of sleep. I stopped along the way to buy the papers and the *Daily Mail's* front page was about Castlepollard. I just stood and stared.

The entire front page was a close-up picture taken by Neil of one of the nails in the Angels' Plot wall, in memory of the burial of a baby. Over the picture, there was a long headline in smaller writing down the left-hand side. It read: 'When a baby died in the Castlepollard Mother and Baby Home, a homemade nail banged into the wall was the only marker of burial. Yesterday, after *Mail* stories sparked worldwide outrage, a full State Inquiry was announced. And as yet unknown thousands of babies and mothers can find dignity at last.' And then in larger script and block capitals: 'SOON YOU WILL REST IN PEACE.'

I reached into my pocket and grasped the nail I had found on the ground during my first visit to Castlepollard almost three years before. I felt so many emotions in that minute, relief, sadness, regret, but also joy that the angels would never be forgotten again. I found myself crying silently. We had our breakthrough.

I bought all the papers and multiple copies of the *Mail* and marched back to my car. I decided I was not going to the meeting. I was going to the Angels' Plot in Castlepollard to leave a copy of the *Mail* there. I wanted them to know that ten million people around the world would read the *Mail* website that day and know the name of Castlepollard. I had made a promise to my crib mates lying forgotten in a silent, country cemetery in August 2011 and I felt I had kept my word. I wanted them to know they would never be forgotten again. From Tuam to Castlepollard in eighteen days via hundreds of millions of people around the rest of the world. Nobody would ever forget again.

The moment passed. The CMABS team were my friends and I could not let them down. I arrived first and went into Buswells Hotel across the road from the Dáil and sat at the bar and ordered tea. I laid the front page of the *Daily Mail* on the bar and took out my Castlepollard nail and placed it on the picture of the nail in the paper. I could not stop thinking about the Angels' Plot and where and how this had all started. Three weeks before, I could not have even imagined this.

I was glad to see Victor Stephenson from the Bethany and Westbank groups arrive first, off the early train from Belfast. I had huge respect for this shy, gentle and dignified man. He possessed an outstanding intellect and a deep commitment to our cause. We chatted for a while and stepped outside. Across at the gates of the Dáil we saw several journalists around the newly appointed Minister for Justice, Frances Fitzgerald. Amanda Maloney from Limerick and Robin Hilliard from Kerry had started an online petition and collected 30,000 signatures. Two little girls aged 7 handed the petition to the Minister and she accepted it outside the Dáil in front of the press. Victor and I crossed the road and stood nearby. We waited until they had finished posing for the press photographers before going over to thank the organisers of the petition. Minister Fitzgerald spotted me. I knew she had been questioned about my report and asked publicly why she had not acted. I did not imagine myself to be her favourite person at that moment. However, when the press was finished she walked straight over to me and held out her hand. I accepted the handshake and she smiled warmly, 'How are you Paul?' she asked. I replied that I was fine and introduced Victor. After some more small talk, the Minister said 'Well done', and politely took her leave. I was very surprised. That night I had nightmares about Frances Fitzgerald. I speculated to Victor afterwards, that perhaps the Minister was still worried about how it would look if my report received further attention and how she would explain doing nothing about it since I had handed it to her nearly a year ago. That thought would soon come back to haunt me.

Clodagh Malone and Dr. Niall Meehan from the Bethany group arrived, followed by others from our community. They were all there for a demonstration that was to take place around the other side of Leinster House in Merrion Square, organised by a solicitor named Gary Daly. Gary had no connection to our cause but he was moved by recent events and set up the protest to support us.

Once our unofficial legal adviser arrived to join us, we trooped into the Dáil. We started with a meeting with Mary Lou McDonald. When Gerry Adams unexpectedly appeared, we were all a bit stunned. It was initially somewhat surreal to be in the Dáil, in a meeting with Sinn Féin, discussing a public inquiry into the Mother and Baby Homes. We chatted for about an hour and while I knew Mary Lou was very familiar with our issues, Gerry surprised us with his in-depth grasp of the details. We went over what Sinn Féin was doing that evening in the Dáil and their Private Members Bill calling for an immediate judicial inquiry. By the time we left, a room had been booked in Buswells Hotel and a press statement prepared for immediate release announcing a CMABS press conference in Buswells in a couple of hours' time. I stuck my neck out and asked if Clare Daly could join us. Mary Lou and Gerry were very generous in welcoming her. It was important to me that no one who had supported us when we needed it was left out. Mary Lou was reluctant as she felt it was our day and her presence might distract from our central message. I insisted that she join us and she finally agreed.

The five of us sat down in Fianna Fáil's meeting room. Across from us on the wall above were large photographs of all the party leaders. Sitting underneath the photographs of Irish Taoisigh and directly opposite us was the current leader of Fianna Fáil, Micheál Martin. He was flanked by Colm Keaveney who was the local TD in Tuam and was personally outraged by the Tuam 800 story, and Robert Troy, front bench Spokesperson for Children. Robert remained a key supporter and our liaison with Fianna Fáil while he was Opposition Spokesperson for Children. He was always a gentleman who took a keen interest in our cause. However, at the time, all I was thinking of was the Fianna Fáil representative who had contacted me to arrange the meeting. He had mentioned that Micheál Martin had read my report into adoption and wanted to discuss it with us. As I sat there I was suddenly very conscious of the last line in that report – 'De Valera was a bastard.'

The meeting was positive and we got our issues across well. We returned to Buswells for the press conference and I grabbed the chance to return several missed calls from Neil. He was going after Frances Fitzgerald, determined to hold the Minister to account for ignoring my report. I had no time to think about the implications. We were being thrown in at the deep end. We sat down and grabbed another cup of tea while we went over exactly what to demand in the press conference. We already had a fair idea and finished up quickly, thanks to Niall's professionalism. I felt a bit melancholy in the quiet moments and I regretted the absence of Derek Leinster and Theresa Hiney Tinggal, and Catherine Corless to whom we all owed a huge debt. Her labour of love in collecting 798 death certificates over many years had started all this.

None of us wanted to 'chair' the conference but I was pushed into it as I was the historian among us and could answer any questions thrown by the assembled journalists. I sat at the centre of our team at the top table, flanked by Mary Lou McDonald and Clare Daly at either end. I took a deep breath and said my piece. I made it a priority to thank everyone who had supported us when we needed it and listed the demands. I was glad Niall had raised the idea. We hoped to set the agenda for the forthcoming Inquiry with our information. Our focus was on speedy justice for the most elderly survivors in our community, including an acknowledgement, apology, redress and full inclusion for all survivors.

I introduced each of the CMABS team, and Clare Daly and Mary Lou McDonald, and each spoke movingly. Victor spoke softly and from the heart and stole the show. The natural mother who had arrived late surprised us by shouting out her piece from the floor. We were all very emotional afterwards and relieved that nobody had frozen or stumbled. Our priority was to call for an inquiry that would be all-inclusive, modular and act quickly, given the number of aging survivors. We had referred to the mortality rates and the vaccine trials. We had asked for survivors to be consulted and involved every step of the way and requested immediate funding for memorials, in line with the Bethany Survivors Memorial. Victor and Niall had made sure that Westbank and Ovoca (sometimes Avoca) House in Wicklow were put on the agenda, as well as the Bethany Home itself. I made a point of singling out Clare and Mary Lou as the only two politicians who had helped us. We called for an international judicial figure to head the Inquiry. Clodagh and her husband Paul came up with an apt quote: 'As a society we may think we are done with Ireland's past, but the past is certainly not done with us.'

We sat there together, men and women, Catholic and Protestant, legally and illegally adopted, natural mothers and adopted people. The State and Church had tried for generations to separate us but here we were, united. We issued a collective statement later, outlining the basic agenda for future demands from the survivor and adoption communities, and our meetings helped to set that agenda. We were not going to let the government off the hook again.

We made our way to Merrion Square to the demonstration and candle-lit vigil. The Dáil railings were covered in a poignant display of baby booties, candles and flowers. I wandered off to be by myself and read some of the personal messages, expressions of sadness, pain and love written by natural mothers, adoptees and ordinary people who had no personal involvement but cared enough to join and support us. I felt humbled by the attention but I also felt a great sense of relief. It still had not quite sunk in that we'd had our breakthrough. That same day there was also a similar vigil in Eyre Square in Galway and hundreds had attended. Mary Joyce from the Castlepollard group showed reporter Ciaran Mullooly and an RTÉ crew around our Angels' Plot and it featured on the main RTÉ News that night.[5]

My wife Siobhán and our two children, Molly and Gavin, had come in to town to attend the vigil and the Dáil. The CMABS team returned to the Dáil visitors' gallery to watch the debate on Sinn Féin's Bill.

The media and public pressure for an inquiry had been building. Mary Lou McDonald and Sinn Féin introduced the aforementioned Private Members Bill for a comprehensive inquiry into the Mother and Baby Homes and related issues. Everyone knew the Bill would be rejected but the real purpose was to force the government's hand. Several TDs spoke on the issue, including McDonald, Gerry Adams and Caoimhghín Ó Caoláin of Sinn Féin. Richard Boyd Barrett let it be known that he himself was born in a Mother and Baby Home and adopted. Anne Ferris, Labour TD, who is also adopted and a natural mother, gave a moving speech. The public gallery was full of adoption activists and campaigners and we all breached protocol and applauded each of the three Sinn Féin speeches. Many of the TDs, including Clare Daly and Robert Troy, mentioned my report several times and paid tribute to the various groups that made up CMABS.

The Taoiseach had been forced to respond to Sinn Féin's Bill by announcing earlier that day that there would be an inquiry. Incredibly, we had won. We had made history.

After that remarkable day, although our lives returned to normality over the following weeks, we were never quite the same. We had all been changed by the experience. Our community often refers to the series of *Mail* headlines as the 'Mail 9'. It has become a shorthand code for our breakthrough and those three manic weeks.

Taoiseach Enda Kenny stated, in relation to the Commission of Inquiry, that 'if this is not handled properly then Ireland's soul in many ways will, like the babies of so many of these mothers, lie in an unmarked grave'.[6] Like so many political promises, it was unfulfilled. The Taoiseach also confirmed that Bethany would be included in the Inquiry and Derek Leinster was ecstatic.

The following day I had cause for grave concern. Ireland was in the throes of a recession and needed a stable government. A controversy only five or six weeks beforehand had ended with the previous Minister for Justice, Alan Shatter, resigning. Frances Fitzgerald had been promoted to replace him. Neil had phoned me during the round of meetings the day before, determined to hold Minister Fitzgerald to account for ignoring my report. I was keenly aware that the last thing the country needed was to lose a second Minister for Justice in such a short space of time. In the heated atmosphere of the Mother and Baby Homes uproar, anything could gain traction. I worried about it and that night I dreamed that all the TDs we had met in the Dáil stood up and screamed and shrieked at Minister Fitzgerald but without sound. I woke in a sweat convinced I was responsible for her resignation and the government falling and the whole country was blaming me. I woke again next morning with the nightmare still replaying in my mind. For the first time, I was reluctant to go out and buy the day's papers. I dreaded seeing the *Mail* but mercifully there was nothing on the front page. However, on page 4, there was a powerful story headlined 'SPEECHLESS' and the sub-headline was 'Adoption rights campaigners' stunned reaction after Frances Fitzgerald defends her failure to respond over babies' scandal'. It was all there, a large extract from my report with my name all over the article. Worst of all, I read that Minister

Fitzgerald had been challenged by Séan O'Rourke about my report on the RTÉ News the night before. I had not seen the news but thankfully the story faded and died. I was quietly relieved.

I had thanked Clare and Mary Lou for helping when no other politicians would, and I was glad to see that quoted in *The Irish Times*. The *Irish Independent* strangely did not mention the press conference but Martina Devlin wrote a column that suggested that the sealed adoption records should not be opened, to protect natural mothers. The piece was in reaction to Enda Kenny saying that he would love to open the adoption records but it was complex and a legal minefield because of the I. O'T Supreme Court judgement. However, Kenny had surprisingly suggested that we might need to hold a referendum to get around the Supreme Court ruling. This was excellent news. We could not lose with the public so outraged by current events and one of the biggest scandals to rock the country.

A few days later the new Minister for Children, Charles Flanagan, invited submissions from interested parties regarding the Inquiry into the Mother and Baby Homes and approximately 160 submissions were received over the summer. A front-page article by Pamela Duncan in *The Irish Times*, with a follow-up inside, revealed that 'More than 660 children died in Dublin residential home in seven-year period.' Duncan's article was the result of original research and it was based on the 'Unmarried Mothers' section in one of the *LGRs*. It was the first article to go into detail about St. Patrick's Home on the Navan Road, even though it was the oldest and biggest of the homes.

A couple of weeks later, I got into my car with the intention of going to work but without thinking about it I ended up on the road to Castlepollard. I had kept a copy of the *Mail* headline with the Angels' Plot picture tucked away in the boot.

Regrettably at this time, the trouble with some of the veterans flared up again. I was convinced that there would be a change of attitude from them when CMABS had collectively done so much to expand on the original breakthrough and put all the Mother and Baby Homes on the international and domestic political agenda. Despite being warned not to post by several of the CMABS crew, I had put up a post in all of the groups the night before Neil's article about CMABS had appeared.

Regardless of anything else, the community had to come first. This was an opportunity for all of us to unite and go forward together. My first post, politely inviting all the groups to join together in a single umbrella group, had not gone down too well. It was deleted in the veterans' main group and then some other groups. A second repeat post was deleted too, but at least I had tried.

However, the reaction soon moved well beyond deletion and censorship. A couple of days later, I received an extraordinary email from one of the veterans informing me that a previously unknown and unheard of 'steering committee' had decided that there was too much confusion over group names and I was being expelled from their group. I wrote back, practically begging them not to go down this road of splitting the community when we were so close to victory. I suggested independent mediation and asked them to consider the best interests of the community, but it was all to no avail. I was systematically removed from several groups. A predictable smear campaign began and it was insinuated that I had been 'paid for my stories by the *Mail*': a complete lie. I never received a cent or payment of any kind whatsoever. People felt intimidated. Dozens of people were contacted, including politicians and journalists, and many decent and genuine activists were removed from groups without notice or explanation. Some people left our community altogether and that saddened me most of all.

After several weeks of harassment, I went to my solicitor and learned the hard way that I was now classed as a 'public figure' because I had been in the media so much and therefore I was fair game for this sort of behaviour. My solicitor became another in a long line of people who advised me to 'toughen up and fight back'.

The predictable result in the groups was an almighty row and about twenty people stormed out of the veteran groups after angry and bitter fights. It was heartbreaking for me to see my community torn apart at the very moment we should have been uniting, but I did toughen up and knew what I had to do. I sat up for three nights and wrote a massive 6,000-word diatribe against the worst of the veterans and I named them. I included the email booting me out of the groups with a clearly phony reason from a never or since heard of 'steering committee'. I criticised their bad attitude, lack of support and years of incompetence. I publicly invited them to sue if it was not true. The row in the groups increased. More people walked out and, to my great surprise, several senior members of the community verbally attacked the administrators who had kicked the whole thing off by expelling me. It was then I knew that the Adoption Apostles were real and I figured out who most of them were. Once again, I waited for a solicitor's letter threatening court action if I did not withdraw my exposé but it never came. As my own solicitor had said to me, 'If you're not sued in six months you can forget it, although you may be allowed to take action up to a year afterwards if you apply to the courts and can show there were exceptional circumstances that prevented you taking action within the time limit.' Over three years have now passed. The veterans never came after me again.

CHAPTER 14

The Inquiry into Mother and Baby Homes

I realised that we were about to become political advocates more than activists and it would undoubtedly get dirty. However, one of the advantages of having an umbrella group like CMABS is that we can make in individual as well as joint submissions. As CMABS, we had a tense meeting with Minister for Children Charles Flanagan on 10 July 2014. He was replaced the next day by Dr. James Reilly.

A couple of weeks later, Minister Reilly announced that Judge Yvonne Murphy had agreed to chair the Commission of Inquiry into Mother and Baby Homes. *The Interdepartmental Report on the Commission of Investigation into the Mother and Baby Homes*, which outlined the size and scale of the Mother and Baby Homes issue, was released and discussed in the Dáil.[1] The high-powered team of senior civil servants who compiled it had ignored our offers of help. As a result, the Interdepartmental Report contained a huge number of flaws. The most obvious was the inclusion of Stamullen holding centre and the omission of its far larger counterpart in Temple Hill. However, the report was still useful in many ways to researchers and contained numerous hard facts and figures that were new to us. I sat up the night it was released and wrote a 3,000-word critique which Clare Daly TD used in the Dáil the following day to challenge the government.[2]

I was organising the meetings and doing some press work and was determined to be as inclusive as possible and make decisions by consensus. There is a saying in our community that I have come to hold as a core belief: 'Every survivor must be allowed to speak with their own voice.' There is normally a limit of three people allowed to attend meetings with ministers, but I began to fight for five people to be included. From that point, CMABS rotated different people to attend our meetings. Everyone who wanted to speak was included where possible and people surprised me and the ministers with their quiet dignity as they recounted the horrors inflicted on them. Natural mothers, adoptees, men, women, a solicitor, a professor, Catholics and Protestants were all given the opportunity to say their piece. My Castlepollard crib mate and noted author, Anne Biggs, flew over from America to present her group's issues. I believe it was the first and only time a banished baby has been at a meeting with a minister. Around this time, we also connected with Rosemary Adaser of the Association of Mixed Race Irish, a group comprised of people who had suffered in Ireland's various institutions. They are mainly based in Britain and, though small, were very well organised and we began including their issues in our submissions.

Before I knew it, the annual Castlepollard reunion was approaching. I was contacted by a BBC producer named Ian O'Reilly who asked if they could film us during our visit. The journalist involved was Sue Lloyd Roberts, an award-winning reporter who was well known for the high quality of her work. I put the proposition from Sue and Ian to the group and I was surprised when they voted overwhelmingly in favour. The footage was featured in a short mini documentary about the Mother and Baby Homes and Magdalene Laundries in Ireland. It was broadcast in September 2014 and went out on the BBC News Channel, which had an average viewership of over 200 million people at the time.[3] Over sixty people turned up to our annual reunion, including people from Britain, America and Spain. Sue and Ian were discreet and respectful. Jenny, a natural mother from Wexford, was interviewed and revealed that she had seen two nuns carrying a shoebox down to the Angels' Plot containing the body of a baby. The *Our World* documentary can still be found on YouTube.

Sinn Féin had become increasingly involved in our cause since Tuam and invited about thirty-five activists, across all the groups, to Brussels on a sponsored trip to present our case to the European Parliament. We packed our bags for the overnight trip on 8 September 2014. I spoke before the two committees we attended. It was far more casual than I had expected. I focused on the bigger picture, trying to get across the sheer scale of the numbers of living survivors and the pain they were living with every day and spoke about how 'illegitimate babies' were described in the *LGRs* as 'handicapped'. Being in Brussels was an experience from which we all benefitted.

Meanwhile in the media, Conall Ó Fátharta in the *Irish Examiner* published a front-page headline article featuring original research.[4] The year Dr. Deeny had turned up at Bessboro's door without warning, the situation was actually worse than even Deeny realised at the time. Conall disclosed that the correct mortality rate for 1944 was 68%. It was the start of a series of gut-wrenching articles from Conall.

CMABS was well and truly on the map by now and our goal of uniting the groups was shared by Mary Lou McDonald. There were constant rumours in the Dáil and our community that the long-awaited Terms of Reference for the Inquiry were about to be announced. Mary Lou brought the leaders of about fourteen groups together. We agreed on a joint press statement timed to squeeze every possible concession out of the government. Unfortunately, two of the veteran groups pulled out at the last minute. Sinn Féin reluctantly also pulled out and, although CMABS tried to rescue the initiative, it was too late. However, the remaining eleven groups went ahead on 12 December. Even the Irish Women's Survivors Support Network in London joined in, as well as the Association of Mixed Race Irish, the new Remembering Bessboro Babies group and a private Natural Mothers group. That press release remains the largest collective statement from our community.

Meanwhile I rushed to put out a standard reference guide to all the homes in the form of an ebook, in the hope of influencing the terms of reference. Many volunteers helped transcribe some 30,000 words of *LGRs* from photocopies I had made. One volunteer from Cork did Trojan work in memory of her great-aunt, Esther Harrington, who had spent a staggering seventy years in a Magdalene Laundry, and the ebook was dedicated to Esther.

The formal announcement of the Inquiry finally came in January. We were invited to a presentation by the Department of Children in

Government Buildings. Minister James Reilly gave us a synopsis of how the Inquiry would work and what exactly it would investigate. Minister Reilly seemed genuine enough to us and one of his political appointees, a specialist on our issues, was very supportive. Catherine Corless attended the meeting and I finally met her and thanked her for the work she had done for our community. Clodagh Malone was there and Victor Stephenson from Belfast represented the Bethany and Westbank Homes, while Theresa Hiney Tinggal had flown in from Britain to speak on behalf of the illegally adopted, and Margaret McGuckin, from the Survivors and Victims of Institutional Abuse group, based in Northern Ireland, was also there for moral support.

The terms were initially excellent. All of the nine Mother and Baby Homes would be investigated including, at last, the Bethany Home. The county homes were there, although only some would be fully investigated using a 'sampling' technique. The Regina Coeli hostel and the flatlets in Dublin 4 were also included. Everything from the list we had submitted was included: the vaccine trials, 'donation' of dead bodies to science, treatment of mixed-race Irish, missing babies with special needs, 'entry and exit pathways' (routes to/from Mother and Baby Homes), banished babies, infant mortality rates and burial practices. In total, over two-thirds of our community were included, but there was bad news too.

Anyone not born in a Mother and Baby Home, county home or other named institution was excluded. The legally and illegally adopted people who were born in private nursing homes and in maternity hospitals or at home were not included. For Theresa Hiney Tinggal and the illegally adopted, it was a huge disappointment. Our campaign from that point became a battle for 'full inclusion' and focused on the illegally adopted.

While we did not get the modular approach we had requested, the Inquiry was limited to three years. For some in our aging survivor community, this would be too long. Victor Stephenson was another person who was deeply disappointed that day because Westbank, Avoca and Breamar House were excluded. Victor has since died and never saw justice for his cause.

We received some more good news when Minister Reilly announced a 'back door' in the terms of reference. The Inquiry itself could recommend to the government that the terms be widened in the 'public interest'. I was delighted after this last announcement. I always knew that we would not get everything we wanted, but this was very close. The homes and the county homes were fully included and we had the 'the freedom to achieve freedom' and a clear route to full inclusion. At the end of the meeting I asked about memorials and Minister Reilly said he had forgotten to mention it in his briefing, but yes, there would be money for memorials for all the homes. I breathed a personal sigh of relief for Castlepollard.

After the meeting, we met the press outside. I spoke first and welcomed the terms and said the Inquiry was long overdue. Then Terri Harrison, a natural mother, spoke from the heart about her son and one of the television crews ended up filming a longer piece with her. Others spoke too and everyone got their chance. We went to a nearby hotel to discuss the next step. We all agreed we needed to prepare a submission and arrange a meeting with the Inquiry so that we could begin to apply pressure immediately. We had a new battle ahead, one that involved making a legal and moral case to the Inquiry, a judge and two professors. At the time we felt we were finally close to victory. However, we are still fighting for full inclusion and no progress has been made.

In his speech that day Minster Reilly said:

> Thanks for individuals and groups in assisting formulation of terms of reference. For those who gave me individual accounts of their experiences, I found these compelling … and I greatly appreciate the willingness and courage of those most centrally affected in sharing their experiences with me. On my own behalf, and that of the government, I want to thank them for taking the time to meet with me. Other advocacy groups, public bodies and political colleagues across the spectrum also provided me with a wide range of views. These have assisted me greatly in focusing the terms of reference in what was an extensive scoping process, given the complexity and sensitivity of the issues.

In the Frequently Asked Questions section on the department's website, number five was: 'Has the minister consulted with interested parties and those most centrally involved in these matters?' The answer given is:

Given the level of public interest in these matters, the Minister for Children and Youth Affairs, and his predecessor, consulted widely with a view to achieving the widest possible consensus on the scope and format of this important investigation. The Minister also met with Ms Catherine Corless, to discuss her research into the Tuam Home, work which has contributed greatly to bringing these sensitive matters to public prominence. Minister Reilly and his predecessor Minister Flanagan met opposition deputies on a number of occasions, in addition to meeting a broad range of interested parties, including the Coalition of Mother and Baby Home Survivors, Adoption Loss – Natural Parents Network of Ireland, Mixed Race Irish, Irish First Mothers, Justice for the Magdalenes, Adoption Rights Alliance, Archbishops Diarmuid Martin and Michael Jackson, Bethany Survivors Campaign, Survivors of Protestant children's institutions, the Council of Adoption Agencies, Cúnamh, Irish Women Survivors Support Network, and the Irish Human Rights Commission. The willingness and courage of those most centrally involved to share their experiences has contributed significantly to this process.

We were top of that list for a reason and I firmly believe it was not because we had emerged as the largest representative group. CMABS always rotated in a couple of non-political survivors who simply told their stories. I watched across the table and, regardless of what anybody says about politicians, they are human and mostly in politics for genuine reasons. They and their civil servants were clearly affected by the tearful accounts and dignified testimonies from CMABS people. I had formal written submissions and moral and legal arguments but I personally believe it was the voices of survivors that made the difference, just as the survivors who testified on the radio phone-in shows had made the real difference. It was neither planned nor cynical. Sometimes, doing the right thing can be more than its own reward.

Minister Reilly bought himself a lot of goodwill through the terms of reference and the way he singled CMABS out after the announcement and again on the Department's website. He was a man we believed we could work with and we were getting on well with him in person.

The Dáil debate on the Inquiry took place over several days in January 2015. We attended the debates and it was an emotional time for us all. I released the ebook just in time and Billy Kelleher, Fianna Fáil TD, described it as a 'harrowing read'. Clare Daly, Colm Keaveney, Sinn Féin, Fianna Fáil and many others were very supportive. After Labour TD Anne Ferris gave an emotional speech on widowed and separated mothers who had lost their babies to adoption, Minister Reilly included them in the Inquiry. There were no other changes, despite the best efforts of the opposition and independents like Clare Daly, but it was nonetheless another step towards justice.

We requested an appointment with Judge Murphy and the Inquiry as soon as possible but it would turn out to be a long wait.

My Story, Part VI

My father went into hospital in April 2015 and passed away in June. I still miss him every day. My parents had been very encouraging ever since I took up activism and shortly before he died I called in one Sunday afternoon with a copy of that day's Sunday Times *Magazine and showed him an article written by London journalist Tanya Gold. She had flown over in 2014 and we had driven to Castlepollard with Clodagh to see the home and the Angels' Plot. One thing I had never done was to go into any detail about my personal life or attempts to trace my natural mother in the media. I was asked numerous times and even live on air, but I always fobbed it off with a couple of brief sentences and moved on. I am an activist, not a human-interest story. I have nothing but admiration for the courage and bravery of survivors who tell their personal stories and expose themselves live on air or in the papers to thousands of strangers, but it is not for me. Tanya, however, eventually persuaded me to tell my personal story and wrote a special feature in the* Sunday Times *Magazine to mark the first anniversary of the Tuam 800 story.[5] It was this report that I showed my Dad and my Mum during a visit to St. Michael's Hospital in Dún Laoghaire. I was in a feature that was several pages long and shared with Catherine Corless and Clodagh Malone. My parents were touched*

at what I had said about them: '[Redmond] loves his adoptive parents'
and 'They have been and still are amazing.' My father asked how many
people read the paper. 'Tanya said about seven million,' I answered. We
all shook our heads and smiled. Dad raised his eyes to heaven. I will
always treasure that moment.

The second annual Bethany Commemoration in Mount Jerome in July
2015 gave us the opportunity to meet up again. The turnout was far
bigger than the previous year and included the Lord Mayor of Dublin,
Críona Ní Dhálaigh. Derek Leinster made a moving, passionate
speech and I spoke about how united we had become as a community.
Afterwards, in the pub, we felt certain we could convince the Inquiry to
recommend including every survivor.

The community was becoming stronger and it was heartening
to see the increase in annual gatherings in the groups. The Bessboro
protest organised the previous year by Helen Murphy had now become
an annual event attended by hundreds, jointly organised by the two
Bessboro groups.

CHAPTER 15

Opening the Adoption Records

At the start of 2015, three Senators, Averil Power, who was adopted from a Mother and Baby Home, Fidelma Healy Eames, who is an adoptive mother, and Jillian van Turnhout, a leading children's rights activist, had produced a Private Members Bill to open the adoption records. The problem of the I. O'T Supreme Court ruling, granting the right of privacy to natural mothers, could be solved by sending a letter of notice to the natural mother when an adoptee applied to get his or her records. I had my doubts about whether the 'letter' solution would pass in the Dáil or survive a court challenge if it was passed but what was important was that the notion of an open records Bill was forcing the government into action.

In July, a bombshell was dropped on our community in the form of the main headline in *The Irish Times*: 'Adopted get right to know birth parents in new Bill' it read. My first thought was to wonder what sort of compromise had been included which would get around the I O'T Supreme Court ruling. The story was clearly an 'official unofficial' leak. The details were sparse but the article said that 'adopted people would be required to sign a statutory declaration obliging them to respect the wishes of birth parents in cases where they do not wish to be contacted'. We were concerned and needed to know if there would be consequences such as fines and jail sentences for adoptees who breached the 'no contact' veto as the previous open records Bill had proposed almost fifteen years before.

A few days later we were invited to another presentation where Minister Reilly announced the details. There was a veto in the new Bill and it was a strictly no-contact veto. Most importantly, there would be no penalties for breaching the no-contact veto, no jail sentences, no fines. This veto was the bare minimum that was required to get around the I. O'T Supreme Court ruling.

Although the difference may seem subtle to an outsider, it is important to understand that, to the adoption community, there is a world of difference between a 'no-information veto' and a 'no-contact veto'. The first is called a 'mummy dearest' veto because it means a natural mother must be asked if she will consent to releasing her identity to her son or daughter when they apply for their original birth certificate. A 'no-contact veto' means that an adopted person can have his or her birth cert and file but cannot contact his or her natural mother directly, unless she gives her permission. The new Bill would not have a 'no-information veto' for natural mothers, unless they could prove in court that there would be a real and substantial danger to them by releasing the information.

Some of the veteran groups focused on the 'no-contact veto' and denounced it as discrimination. Their approach mirrored the philosophy of an extremist, single-issue group in the United States called Bastard Nation. It was like watching people trying to bash a square peg into a round hole. The veterans chose to ignore the I. O'T case in their media statements. I spoke to dozens of non-political adoptees on and offline and they were universally of the same opinion: if there are no penalties, then the 'no-contact veto' is not an issue. The wider community also strongly believed that an adopted person cannot, and should not, force a mother to have a relationship with him or her, no matter how much the adopted person wants it.

The veterans had justifiably mounted a campaign against the previous open records Bill, because it criminalised adoptees, but this was different. I was not going to stand idly by and let them wreak havoc on this Bill, when the criminal punishments had been completely removed. I began by writing an opinion piece and sent it to Journal.ie and anyone else who would listen. It was published on 31 July 2015, within days of the new proposals.

Should adopted children have the right to contact their natural mother?
Not if it endangers vulnerable women

Having been born in a Mother and Baby Home, I am among perhaps a few hundred members of the active adoption community. But there are also about 50,000 silent adoptees in Ireland today, mostly aged 45 and upwards. At present, natural mothers are 'protected' by the constitutional right to privacy. Many do not want it, but some need it. I know one elderly lady who is married to an abusive drunken husband. For over forty-five years, she has dreaded him finding out she gave birth to a baby in her teens. She dreads the post, the phone ringing, the unexpected knock at the door.

Currently one in twenty natural mothers, who have registered with the voluntary national contact preference register, have indicated they do not want contact with their own sons and daughters. Minister James Reilly published a new Adoption Bill that will give adopted children the right to access their birth records. The legislation is important and rightly signals the end of an era where adopted people were treated as second-class citizens.

But what about the constitutional right to privacy of the natural mothers, many of whom live in fear of being found out? Well, the final compromise between adoptees' right to know their mothers and the Supreme Court's precise definition of 'privacy' is to require adopted adults to sign a 'no-contact veto'. We would be required to sign a piece of paper stating that if our natural mother wants no contact, we will respect their wishes. There are no sanctions or penalties attached to breaching the veto.

At present, the campaigners within the community number about fifty involved to varying degrees from 'keyboard warriors' to those of us who turn up at everything. And we are having a frank exchange of views, as they say. Now, I'm the bad guy to a few of the real campaigners and the armchair activists, because I agree with the no-contact veto. Between the legal quagmire and the moral issues, I can see no other way forward. Although I know that while our natural mothers are losing their anonymity (wanted or not), many of them will still want their privacy. I respect that.

My natural mother wants nothing to do with me and I leave her and my whole natural family in peace, however painful it is to do so. She is not registered as wanting no contact, as she is not registered at all.

The adoption community agrees that no one can or should force contact onto a person who does not want it. But who speaks for those who cannot speak out because of fear? Because of the horror they went through in Mother and Baby Homes like Tuam, where 800 of our crib mates ended up in one of several mass graves around the country.

Who speaks for those who may have caught reports in the newspapers or seen the TV news reports on Monday evening? Or heard gossip locally?

I speak only for myself but I refuse point blank to fight the no-contact veto. If it gives even one frightened, elderly woman, a full and equal member of our community, active or silent a scrap of peace, then that's the least I can do.

Are we as a community so self-obsessed that even after winning open birth certs, most information from our files and medical records and 90% of everything we fought for, we cannot find the generosity of spirit to leave something to those of our own mothers who live in dread?

Do we really need it all? Every scrap of the rights going? Must we strip natural mothers bare? Where there are two parties to any issue of civil and human rights, there must be some sort of balance. Where there are rights, there are also responsibilities.

At a time like this, we need to think of our whole community, including the most vulnerable and the substantial number of natural mothers silenced by dread.

The irony of this whole debate is that there is a legal way to get your birth cert right this minute that all the activists have used, and no one must sign this veto. It is voluntary as well as carrying no sanctions, and it gets us around the legal quagmire. But that's still not enough for some people.

There are several issues in the bill that I'm deeply unhappy about, including the one-year lead-in. How many of our community will die between now and 2017 when it comes into effect? For those hundred and possibly thousands who desperately wish to reunite, that lead-in will be a death sentence.

I know where some of my battles lie ahead. I also regret that one huge matter has been overlooked in all this controversy. After this bill is passed, illegally, *de facto* and informally adopted people will finally be treated equally alongside legally adopted people.

No one has the right to force contact onto another person, regardless of whether or not their birth children have been adopted.[1]

All the media headlines noted a 'mixed reaction' to the Bill while the veterans demanded the entire Bill be scrapped. One of them, Susan Lohan, and I went head to head, along with Senator Averil Power, on *The Last Word* radio show presented by Matt Cooper on Today FM. I gave as good as I got. I was stunned at the level of support I got privately, and it strengthened my determination to see this Bill passed. I was not going to allow the records to be sealed for another fifteen years after the last catastrophic activist campaign. I heard from a reliable source in the Dáil that Minister Reilly had argued with the Attorney General's office for several months over the precise wording of the 'no-contact veto' and had worked proactively to get it right since Christmas 2014. The landmark Bill contained a wealth of positives for our community. These were overshadowed by the focus on one minor point that was turned into a manufactured controversy. Minister Reilly lost his seat in the general election of 2016: a huge disappointment for us, but we were lucky to get him for the short time we did.

The annual Castlepollard visit took place in August and sixty of us met up. This year was slightly different, as we had built up a solid working relationship with the local HSE. The buildings had finally been vacated after eighty years and I was handed the keys and we were given the run of the place. We filmed and photographed and peered into every corner. Although it poured rain all day and we were nearly washed out of the Angels' Plot, it was a very special day for all of us there.

However, a week later, a two-page spread appeared in the *Mail on Sunday* about an individual at the gathering, previously unknown to our group, who claimed to have found over 1,600 HSE files wrapped in plastic. He said in the article that he had seen them, through the heavy downpour, on the driveway in Castlepollard when he was leaving. It transpired, through an internal HSE inquiry, that those same files had been left in our old Mother and Baby Home and were stolen during our visit by a person or persons unknown. The files were supposed to be disposed of by a specialist firm. They were the files of patients in St. Peter's from its time as a residential centre for people with severe intellectual problems, and sheets of work schedules from its time as a Mother and Baby Home. According to the article, the Gardaí were investigating as were the HSE and the Data Protection Office. The criminal investigation is still active and over two years later still causing me problems regarding our visits to Castlepollard.

Ashling O'Brien, from Atheist Ireland, had contacted me about a woman named Milana Kearns, who was trying to singlehandedly change the Step-Parent Adoption process.

In Step-Parent Adoption, Milana the biological mother would become the *adoptive mother* of her own child. The process requires a natural mother to legally relinquish her child before the child can then be legally jointly adopted by her and her new partner. Milana Kearns refused to sign over her daughter on a point of principle and her new family was in legal limbo. Milana was fighting to change the law.

An opportunity to influence the government on the new Adoption Bill came quickly in October 2015. Minister Reilly was pushing the Bill through at breakneck speed. Around twenty-five groups and individuals were invited to testify over three sessions at the Joint Oireachtas Committee on Health and Children, chaired by Jerry Buttimer TD. We were invited to give a verbal testimony lasting about five minutes to the committee and submit a written document with our ideas for changes to the Bill. I wrote a short, four-page submission that doubled as our verbal testimony. We took a neutral stance on the 'no-contact veto' and outlined clearly the effect it would have.

Some groups at the session were highly critical of the Bill and others strongly supported the veto.

Politicians rarely have the time to read long documents, so less is more. They are also more likely to listen to suggestions and solutions that are cost neutral. Below is part of our submission:

Submission to the

Oireachtas Joint Committee on Health and Children

Adoption bill 2015

From

The Coalition of Mother and Baby Home Survivors (CMABS)

An umbrella group consisting of:

Adoption Rights Now, The Bethany Home Survivors, Beyond Adoption Ireland,

Adopted Illegally Ireland, The Castlepollard Mother and Baby Home Group;

and supported by

The Association of Mixed Race Irish

The Adoption Coalition Worldwide

One Year 'Lead-in'

1. The one-year lead-in to the activation of the bill is a major problem. This is an unrealistic provision for a bill primarily dealing with an ageing community of adoptees and natural mothers. Approximately half of all people adopted since 1922 under various names (fostered, boarded out) have already passed away and since the natural mothers involved would be on average twenty years older, it is clear that far fewer than half of them are still alive. To delay this bill for one year will undoubtedly lead to many of the survivors of forced adoption

and Mother and Baby Homes missing any potential reunions. This is grossly unfair and goes against any sense of natural justice. It is immoral and unethical and further amounts to age discrimination in the worst possible meaning of that phrase. There is no question that because of, and during that one-year lead-in, both adoptees and natural parents will end up reuniting with headstones in cold and lonely graveyards.

2. Solution:

    Reduce the lead-in to the bare minimum and reassign the resources to be used over a year to a more intensive information campaign ideally over thirty to sixty days at the very most.

    (Unenumerated) Forced Relinquishment in modern Ireland

3. Although it is not mentioned in this bill at all, there is one major outstanding matter in contemporary adoption in Ireland that needs to be addressed and included in this bill. At present, we have a outdated provision in current adoption law known as the 'Step-Parent Adoption process'. This provision forces a parent who wishes to legally unite their family, usually after a marriage, to legally relinquish their own child so they can be readopted by the relinquishing parent along with their new spouse. Legally, a natural mother must become an adoptive mother. In other words, we still have an odious form of forced relinquishment in Ireland which demands a natural parent sign away their child and transform themselves into an adoptive parent. There are no plans to change this bizarre provision. Clearly this new bill is the ideal opportunity to shelve this degrading anomaly. This is a simple enough matter to include in the new bill and would also certainly be cost neutral if not actually saving the State money and the valuable time of both social workers and gardaí from vetting and paperwork. Appended to this submission is a link to a public petition initiated by Milana Kearns, a dedicated and loving mother unwilling to sign away her children for anyone or anything. Milana is caught between wanting to unite her family and her principled stand against signing away her own child. CMABS fully supports Milana's fight for a fair and just system to be put in place. If you take the time to read the petition, it will spell out the heart-breaking issues involved in

Milana's own words. The public comments also clearly record the anger of a selection of those members of the public who have been caught in this legal anomaly and their desire for a fair and just reworking of the system to recognise the reality of the many new and loving families in Ireland who simply want their reality legally recognised and accommodated. It is abundantly clear that there are many families caught in this legal quandary. There has been a lot of talk and discussion in Ireland over the last year about Equality, especially regarding family life and Equality is desperately needed in this situation. I urge the Committee to go to the petition and read Milana's summary which is concise, clear and a heartfelt plea from a loving mother caught in a legal minefield.

4. Solution:

A couple of short paragraphs in the new Adoption bill would sort this problem instantly. Natural parents would not have to relinquish and readopt their own children and the General Registry Office would produce a new template certificate for use in such situations headed 'Birth and Adoption Certificate' listing the natural and new adoptive parent.

To my continuing surprise, the Committee's final report recommended that the 'no-contact veto' be dropped and possibly replaced by a mandatory preparatory session. During this session, issues concerning respect and privacy would be discussed. This was unexpected considering the number of groups that strongly supported the veto, including the Adoptive Parents Association, Treior, the National Federation of Services for Unmarried Parents and their Children. Tusla, the Child and Family Agency, recommended that the 'no contact veto' be not only retained, but be extended to allow adoptees to refuse contact with their natural mothers.

We made significant progress on the specific issues we had chosen. In the case of illegal adoptions, the Committee affirmed our submission and recommended our suggestion to provide a 'dedicated unit to actively investigate those cases'. The Committee also agreed that illegal adoptees would be 'discretely approached and informed of same'. It was telling that the committee reused our specific language.

The one-year lead-in was recommended to be reduced to six months. On the issue of the Step-Parent Adoption process, it turned out that Dr Conor O'Mahony, a law lecturer from University College Cork, had also addressed this issue. Although it was not part of the proposed Bill, there was an entire section (12) relating to the Step-Parent Adoption process. The Committee noted that, although it was outside its scope, it should 'merit further consideration by the Minister for Children and Youth Affairs'. The Know my Own survivor representative group based in Cork were namechecked many times after their excellent submission. CMABS were also quoted and mentioned multiple times in the 'Issues considered after they had been raised by stakeholders' section. Some of the veterans had submitted fifty pages of dry, legalistic technical arguments with footnotes and they were ignored. Representing our community with a strategy that consistently achieves nothing over fifteen years needs to be urgently addressed by many of the leaders in our community.

The same day I testified to the Committee, CMABS had a meeting with Minister James Reilly. Milana joined us and presented a strong case. The meeting went well, and we reiterated all our issues regarding the Adoption Bill. Milana was informed that they were already looking at reforming the Step-Parent Adoption process. Not long after, 'Milana's Law' was passed as part of the Adoption (Amendment) Act and I was delighted. Thousands of people and children will benefit from Milana's Law in the future and her principled and courageous battle should be widely acknowledged. The meeting with the Minister went well, although I criticised the lack of consultation and warning about the new Bill. He took my criticism with a smile and engaged with us as no minister had ever done before. Before we left, we all firmly believed that Minister Reilly would have the Bill through the Dáil, complete with recommendations from the Committee, by early 2016. Unfortunately, this did not happen. The Bill has been stalled since the election of 2016 when Katherine Zappone took over as Minister for Children.

The Children's Referendum that had been passed in 2012 was, despite what the name suggests, not in the best interests of children. The referendum was almost entirely about extending all aspects of adoption in modern Ireland for the benefit of the State. Up to that point, only illegitimate children could be adopted in Ireland, with a few exceptions to do with in-family adoption. After the referendum all children could be adopted, legitimate or illegitimate. The adoption community was appalled because the referendum granted the courts the power to dispense with parental consent in future adoption cases. In other words, the State could now remove children, both legitimate and illegitimate, from their home or residence, and adopt them out into a closed adoption system. No Irish child will ever be truly safe again. Five years later, on 17 October 2017, the legislation giving effect to the Children's Referendum was signed into law and the Adoption (Amendment) Act commenced.

The reasoning behind this move was to allow children in State care to be adopted by their foster parents into 'forever homes', giving them the security they needed. It is worth noting that the thousands of children in State care are costing millions of euro a year.[2] If they are adopted out, the State saves a fortune and frees up hundreds of social workers.

The only other country in Europe that has anything resembling this system is Britain and it is an unmitigated disaster. The drive to increase adoptions began under Tony Blair's government in an attempt to reduce the numbers of children in long-term care. It has, in many cases, broken up families unnecessarily. The stories are heartbreaking and frightening. There have been cases involving children with medical conditions, whose parents were wrongly accused of abuse. The majority of cases are women caught in domestic poverty and abuse who are deemed unsuitable to bring up a child. There are horrendous stories from Britain where parents have fought for years to prove their innocence and recover their children. In some cases, they have won their court battles and received apologies, but did not get their child or children back. The court ruled that the child was already settled in with their new family and it would be 'in the best interests of the child' to remain adopted. These situations will be no doubt be mirrored in Ireland and that is deeply depressing.

I fought against the Children's Referendum and proposed other options such as permanent legal guardianship and open adoption.

Neither involves 'identity theft', the child's name need not be changed and his or her natural parents and siblings would have the right to contact. I failed and the de facto forced adoption in Ireland's past has now been legalised and enshrined in Ireland's Constitution, courtesy of Frances Fitzgerald and Katherine Zappone. I firmly believe that the electorate was not fully aware of the implications of the referendum.

CHAPTER 16

Fighting for Full Inclusion

We did as much as we could with the Adoption Bill to open the records and fight for the inclusion of all survivors in the Inquiry. We finally got an appointment with the Inquiry in January 2016, almost a full year after it was set up. It was a very formal meeting with Judge Murphy, two professors, a solicitor and a Senior Counsel. Our team was composed of a natural mother, three adoptees and a survivor from Tuam, on the request of Catherine Corless. We had to swear an oath and were cautioned not to discuss the meeting in detail until the Inquiry was over. We presented our submission and asked for full inclusion using every moral and legal argument we could. Survivors were given the opportunity to tell their personal stories.

Derek Leinster of the Bethany group had also been to see the Inquiry. For many years Derek maintained that the easiest and most effective way to deal with the living survivors was to reopen the 2002 Redress Act, which was passed primarily for industrial school survivors. This would then serve to include all survivors from Bethany and the other Mother and Baby Homes in the list of approved institutions for redress. Derek firmly believed that inquiries and memorials could come later. In his twenty-three years of campaigning, Derek had lost many friends and crib mates. His philosophy was simple – living survivors must take priority.

We wanted to keep the Inquiry under continuous pressure until the halftime 'Interim Report' required under the terms of reference and due on 18 August 2015. One of the unusual aspects of the terms was that not all county homes would be investigated. There were too many of them and only a few would be examined in detail in a process called 'sampling'.

After the meeting, we lodged a formal document with the Inquiry about 'sampling'. We wanted to widen the scope of the 'sampling' and the document outlined a simple and cost-effective way of sampling each of the institutions and situations that were excluded. I chose five places and one situation (a home birth) that could be 'sampled' in a few short months and, therefore, would include all survivors of the forced separation of single mothers and their children in the Inquiry. I specifically selected institutions where partial investigations were already underway as they were 'entry' or 'exit' 'pathways' to and from the named Mother and Baby Homes.

When the Inquiry announced that they were to sample four county homes, we were fuming. CMABS lodged a formal complaint in June, stating that they should have selected one or perhaps two county homes, with the rest of the resources used to sample our suggested institutions, and thereby include all survivors. As the deadline for the interim report approached, we made one last-ditch attempt to influence it and called a street protest outside the Inquiry's office on Baggot Street, Dublin. About thirty people turned up on one of the hottest days of the year, including Joe Little from RTÉ News, and we appeared on the main evening news. There was other media coverage too and it was all sympathetic.

Afterwards we all went home and held our collective breath. Meanwhile Clare Daly TD continued to ask awkward questions in the Dáil and kept our issues on the political agenda.

The release of the Interim Report was a non-event. Minister Zappone gave us barely a few hours' notice that an announcement was imminent. We were starting to suspect that perhaps she was not on our side at all. Her announcement was a huge anti-climax and the Inquiry had simply asked for more time. The Inquiry also wanted more time to conduct 'confidential' meetings with survivors as it was overwhelmed by the numbers. It had already seen 150 people but another 350 had applied to testify. Minister Zappone brought the requests to the Cabinet and they approved the multiple delays. During an interview, she unilaterally ruled out including illegal adoptees in the Inquiry. There was no explanation or reason given. Because of the government's refusal to include illegal adoptees, thousands will be denied justice.

Victor Stephenson, who died in May 2016, would never have seen justice for Westbank in Greystonesin Wicklow or Braemar House in Cork. He was one of so many who have been denied justice.

I had contacted the Department of Children and Youth Affairs on 6 May 2016, the day Katherine Zappone was announced as the new Minister, to arrange a meeting with her. We were finally granted a meeting in September.

The meeting was difficult, to put it mildly. Professor Lundy's confirmation that she was engaged in bringing the matter to the United Nations was ignored. Theresa Hiney Tinggal asked the minister to bring the issue of illegal adopted people to the Cabinet and she just sat and stared at her. Theresa asked if she was going to answer and Minister Zappone said she already had. 'No, you did not!' Theresa said, clearly exasperated. When pressed, the Minister refused to bring the matter to Cabinet and Theresa told her to 'grow yourself a pair of balls, Minister'. It got worse. Minister Zappone turned to me and asked, 'Have I to listen to her the whole time?' 'Yes,' I replied, 'until you answer her.'

I raised the issue of the memorials and why there was such a delay. Minister Zappone's team stared blankly at me. 'Memorials? What memorials?' they asked. 'The ones we were promised by Minister Reilly and noted in our agenda for this meeting, the agenda you asked for weeks ago,' I replied. One of the civil servants asked, 'Do you have any proof of this?' It was unbelievable. It seemed like we were being accused of lying. They had not even read our agenda, despite the fact that they had asked for it. I pushed and insisted on a timeframe for a reply. Minister Zappone promised that if I presented our proposals for the memorials, we would get a response in two weeks. We are still waiting. My request for a follow-up meeting was refused.

After the meeting we spoke to the press and Anne Biggs said: 'I think that it is important for Minister Zappone and her people to have a better and deeper understanding of the reality of the lives of survivors.' Clodagh Malone added: 'We hardly scratched the surface of our issues. Surely over 60,000 survivors are worth more than an hour, after a wait of several months for an appointment!' Professor Patricia Lundy said that 'the minister needs to listen to survivors'. Theresa Hiney Tinggal said:

'Because of the exclusion of the illegally adopted, Ireland and Minister Zappone are effectively supporting and condoning child trafficking and covering up crimes.' I added the Minister's promise of a response about the memorials and sent a copy of the press release to her office.

As we were making no progress, CMABS contacted the Taoiseach's office. Years later, we are still waiting for anything beyond an automated reply. Theresa was fuming and headed straight to the media; there was a major article in the *Mirror on Sunday* a few weeks later. She declared that she would go to the United Nations in response to the Minister's point-blank refusal to include the illegally adopted and give a reason why they were excluded.

The Inquiry had sent the full interim report to Minister Zappone in advance of our meeting with her in September and it was parked with the Attorney General for 'legal advice', we were informed. It would be released as soon as they got it back. So we waited, and waited. Christmas came and went. We believed that there was bad news for the government in the report and, as the months slipped by, we convinced ourselves it was huge.

In October, a team of specialists appointed by the Inquiry had carried out a test dig at the Angels' Plot in Tuam. A twelve- to fifteen-foot hoarding had gone up and the parallels with the 'High Walls' of the old days were obvious. We expected the results to be released with the final report, but the Inquiry released them on 3 March 2017. It was a Friday and many activists had plans for the weekend – a classic political trick. The results were exactly as we expected. There were numerous bodies found, ranging from 35 foetal weeks to 3 years old, and there was a septic tank in the ground. The media exploded, and the public was outraged. It was like the Tuam 800 and Mail 9 uproar all over again but the Inquiry and Minister Zappone had a slick press campaign ready this time.

We missed the opportunity to respond on Friday, so we desperately needed to send out a press release before the newspaper deadlines for Saturday and hopefully set some of the agenda. I fired out a hastily written press release, which thankfully the media picked up on straightaway.

While Catherine Corless and her research were the main focus, and rightly so, I was determined that the spotlight on Tuam would once again widen to all the homes. 'Tuam was the tip of the iceberg' and 'the worst is yet to come' we said in our release and thankfully those two phrases were on the front pages of two of the three broadsheets the next day. Our old friends in the *Mail* went banner front-page and it brought memories flooding back for us. Alison O'Reilly was on the front page and there was a very generous piece about me inside. Tuam was also banner front-page in *The Sun* and the *Mirror*. The debate had been widened and the media covered all the homes, thanks to those two simple phrases. The international media returned and suddenly we were back in the thick of it.

We did everything we could to keep up the pressure and over the following weekend we were all over the papers, radio and television again, both at home and abroad. Many of the Sunday papers ran large, in-depth articles. Catherine was invited to write a column by the *Mail* and her piece was front-page. On Monday, we took another step up the media ladder when we were invited onto the *Claire Byrne Show* on RTÉ Radio 1. I sat with Clodagh Malone and Dr. Niall Meehan from the Bethany Home and we spoke about the other homes besides Tuam. Our segment ended with the full list of the Tuam 800 names scrolling down the screen. It was deeply moving for us and there were plenty of tears in the audience, including my own.

There was a third *Mail* banner headline on Monday and a fourth on Tuesday. Alison O'Reilly was writing daily articles. Conall Ó Fátharta was also publishing well-informed and insightful articles almost every day in the *Irish Examiner*. I began skipping work again and resumed my daily trips to the garage to buy the papers. Survivors once again poured out their hearts on the radio shows and the media focus stayed on us far longer than it might have otherwise, thanks to their bravery. More survivors joined our groups and our community experienced another growth spurt.

Within days of the announcement, Taoiseach Enda Kenny was in the Dáil declaring that the Angels' Plot in Tuam was a 'chamber of horrors', but also that 'No nuns broke into our homes to kidnap our children.' Minister Zappone went to Tuam to meet Catherine Corless and said all the right things about listening to survivors and wanting to meet us to discuss ways to move forward. But in the end no progress emerged.

There were several reports that the government was considering expanding the terms of the Inquiry, but once again it seemed that was said to deflect attention as the result was inaction.[1]

Minister Zappone was back a week later in the Dáil where she proposed a 'Truth Commission', as was used in post-apartheid South Africa from 1996, or the notion of Museums of Memory in places such as Argentina and Chile, to record our stories. The comparisons seemed bizarre to us. We never asked for it and never wanted it.

The Castlepollard group had been researching the names of all the babies buried in the Angels' Plot in Castlepollard. One member of the group did an extraordinary amount of work and refused to take any credit. The entire group of almost 500 survivors remains deeply appreciative of her harrowing work. We released the figures after discussion and a democratic vote. There were 200 names and the ledger totals that the group had obtained listed a further 77 stillbirths over two-thirds of the lifetime of the home. Over 300 babies and children lie in the Castlepollard Angels' Plot. The details were reported in several papers including the *Irish Independent* and the *Mirror* among others. The local *Westmeath Examiner* published a banner front-page story and included the list of those who died.[2] More importantly, local radio stations around the country picked up on the release and it was broadcast in many bulletins and included interviews with members of the group.

As quickly as it had started, the media coverage ended. A couple of weeks later, Minister Zappone suddenly released the full interim report on 11 April and it was a bombshell for reasons that completely threw us. The instant I read it I just grinned and said, 'Derek bloody Leinster!' His submission to the Inquiry was the reason for the delay. The Inquiry had strongly recommended Derek's fifteen-year-long demand to reopen the Redress Act 2002 and include the Bethany survivors. Judge Murphy had gone even further and recommended that all survivors who had been *unaccompanied* in any of the homes should receive immediate redress. It emerged, however, that the Cabinet had rejected the recommendation because of its cost, up to a staggering one billion euro according to some reports.[3] As campaigners, we had always known that the greatest single obstacle to getting justice and truth would be the financial cost to the government. That was now proven true. The civil servants had worked out that over 14,000 survivors were eligible, although how they came up with that figure remains a mystery.

I called Minister Zappone's refusal 'immoral, repulsive and cold hearted' at the time. I was deeply angry on behalf of Derek Leinster and the Bethany survivors. They had fought for over twenty years and watched their friends die one by one. Derek went on the attack: he called Zappone's refusal to implement the recommendation of the Inquiry 'shameful and immoral' and stated that 'She has betrayed the trust of survivors who put their faith in the Commission [of Inquiry].'[4] Bill Donohue is the President of the powerful Catholic League of America and well paid for his role as the Catholic Church's attack dog. Donohue is in receipt of a salary of over $500,000 a year to do what the Holy See is unable to do publicly – attack its enemies. The Catholic League is a deeply conservative collection of old-fashioned Catholics who wish that Vatican II had never happened. On 12 April 2017, Donohue released a press statement claiming the Interim Report fizzled out and proved nothing. He used it as an opportunity to get in another dig against Catherine Corless and myself. Catherine was described as 'a local typist from Galway' while I was ridiculed as 'the poster boy for victims', among other low blows.[5] Catherine said I got away lightly. You know you are making progress when Bill Donohue attacks you.

There were other disappointments in the interim report. Theresa Hiney Tinggal's proposals for the survivors of illegal adoptions were ruled out. Judge Murphy said it would be difficult to do anything at all for the illegally adopted and that a DNA database would not help everyone. The Inquiry had proposed an amnesty for the baby traffickers and child abductors in the hope that they would provide much needed information on their illegal adoptions. The government ignored this recommendation, but Minister Zappone promised that she would meet survivors to discuss how exactly to go about listening to them. CMABS put in for a meeting immediately after the announcement but once again we waited in vain. She never got in touch and the deadline passed, causing more pain to our community.

Minster Zappone had clearly prepared for the backlash and used the 'Truth Commission' to try and distract us. She set up meetings in

Dublin and Cork, where survivors could tell their stories over lunch, paid for by the Department. I was away on holiday in Brittany when they were held but I would not have gone anyway. CMABS and all the main activist groups also stayed away.

The survivors who had been invited were already included in the Inquiry and no one who attended was demanding what the wider survivor community really wanted: full inclusion. Minister Zappone had stalled real action with a talking shop and sadly, it worked. It was a carbon copy of the political tactics used after the debacle of the 2001 Adoption Bill.

The long-anticipated interim report contained nothing that we had campaigned for and the delay had also cost the activist community several months. We resolved to look around for new opportunities to bring pressure to bear and to focus on legal challenges, but the clock was counting down to the end of the Inquiry.

Clodagh Malone and I had discussed a Pelletstown/St. Patrick's reunion on many occasions, but the problem was that the building has been demolished and there was no place to visit. Clodagh finally decided to organise it in Glasnevin Cemetery and it went ahead in August 2017 and was a success. Alison O'Reilly was back in the *Daily Mail* to support the reunion on the Monday beforehand. In her article, the banner front page announced: 'NUNS: WE DID OUR BEST IN MOTHER AND BABY HOME'. Unlike the media-savvy Sacred Heart nuns, the Daughters of Charity had responded to Alison's inquiries and ended up looking like amateurs and deniers. The seventh Castlepollard reunion was attended by over 130 people and Derek Leinster organised a late Bethany commemoration to finish what has become an annual round of events where the community continues to connect and bond.

The debate over the future of the Angel Plots continues in our community with strong opinions on both sides. Galway County Council has opened a consultation process regarding the future of the Tuam Angels' Plot. The options range from leaving it alone to a full excavation followed by DNA testing of all the remains in the plot and then reinterring them afterwards in a separate place.

On 5 December 2017, all the activists received an email at 10.47 a.m. informing us that Minister Zappone was bringing a third interim report from the Inquiry to the Cabinet that afternoon. Later that day, we learned in the media that the final report of the Inquiry was to be delayed by a year until February 2019, because the volume of paperwork to be scanned and analysed was proving overwhelming. We were furious. I issued a press statement which was widely reported and included the observation that 'This is yet another delaying tactic by the government to deny survivors truth and justice. The current inquiry is already too limited and excludes many survivors and this delay will now ensure that thousands more survivors are denied justice by death.'

In early 2018, Derek Leinster announced that he and another researcher, John Thompson, had found more names of the babies and children who died in the Bethany Home and even some related Protestant children's homes in south Dublin. Leinster has announced plans for another commemoration on 29 June 2018 in Mount Jerome Cemetery in Dublin, where a new memorial will be unveiled with more names, bringing the total to 344, although this figure may increase before then.

These days the active survivor/adoption community in Ireland is almost entirely based on Facebook. Thankfully, the groups are very safe spaces as a rule. If you join Facebook, just type 'Adoption Ireland' into your Facebook search box and, you will find a 'signpost' page with a list of most of the active groups.

CHAPTER 17

Reflections

There are still so many questions left unanswered, most significantly, how the nuns and the Church got away with it all for so long. From 1922 to around 1950, the inhuman mortality rates in the homes were a matter of public record. They were well known to politicians, the Church hierarchy and, to a lesser extent, the general population. The figures were published by the government and they were not secret in any way. However, the strongly held view that illegitimate babies were weak and therefore more prone to death was largely unquestioned. People accepted the unusually high death rates. The *LGRs* dropped the annual reviews of the homes after 1945 and the network began to disappear from public and political consciousness.

While the National Inspectors for Children, Litster and Fitzgerald-Kenney (and later Fidelma Clandillon, who replaced Fitzgerald-Kenney), and Dr. James Deeny, did their best at the time, the power of Catholic Ireland was unassailable. The fact that the mortality rate in Bessboro shot up to over 80% after Deeny challenged the Sacred Heart nuns says all that needs to be said about Ireland during that era. The continuing deaths of hundreds of babies through wilful neglect was the definitive declaration of their absolute power by the Sacred Heart nuns and the Catholic Church. Archbishop McQuaid ordered a media blackout about the banished babies in the early 1950s and that ban extended to the entire Mother and Baby Home network.

In Britain, the press was largely respectful towards the establishment until 1963 and the Profumo scandal, involving prominent politicians, sex, spies and salacious details. After that, the gloves were off, and the media became ever more intrusive and sensationalist. As the distrust between the media and the establishment in Britain grew, politicians learned to either behave or to be discreet.

In Ireland, there was no such break between politicians and the media. The old boys' network and the 'gentlemen's agreement' to turn a blind eye to certain issues still exists, to a large extent. Corruption thrived in Ireland in the 1970s and 1980s. Many reporters are desperate to dig deep into all aspects of Irish public life but cannot find any media organisation that will give them the resources and time to carry out in-depth investigations. I know several of them and they are frustrated by the lack of will in the media organisations to support them.

When the Tuam 800 story broke in May 2014, why was there such an instant response of shock and horror abroad and so little interest at home? There is no single or simple answer.

Part of the answer is obvious. While there are many mass burials in the world, it is the fact that it was exclusively babies and children in the Tuam plot that caused the initial outrage. There is an axiom in the media that a great headline should sum up a story but make you curious enough to make you want to know more. The initial headline did that. 'A mass grave of 800 babies' is in many ways the ultimate narrative hook. Our human nature demands more, and we start reading. The questions keep flooding in as we struggle to understand. Why did a home for unmarried mothers exist? How did the babies die and why were they buried in such a casual and cruel manner? Such a horror is unique to Ireland and that is why it caught the world's attention. It took longer to spark the outrage in Ireland because in some strange, uniquely Irish way, we have been numbed to such revelations because of the endless Church scandals of the 1990s and beyond.

The Irish media slept through the first few days of the international fury and two sad facts are now clear. Firstly, all media groups hate picking up another organisation's scoop. It is simply professional rivalry; morality and ethics have nothing to do with it. It is an all too human flaw that severely limits the media and probably always will. Secondly, ignoring horror is the Irish way. During several hundred years of colonisation, it was drilled into us to keep our heads down and mind our own business. We have a natural distrust and instinctual fear of the establishment. Even after 1922, people were well aware there were 'dreadful places' in Ireland but they were so afraid of ending up in them that they preferred not to think or speak about them.

The break during the late 1980s and throughout the 1990s between the Irish people and the Catholic Church is comparable to a messy divorce. The deepest love can very quickly turn to the deepest hatred when the stench of betrayal is in the air, and Ireland was utterly betrayed by the Church. Many people wanted to believe that the full horrors of child sex abuse, the Church's cover-ups and its facilitation, and the revelations of the institutional abuse, were over and done with. They were not. Many people during the Tuam 800 revelations said they were ashamed to be Irish.

From 1922, successive governments either turned a blind eye to or actively cooperated with the Catholic Church, while the Protestant Churches were officially ignored as the Local Government Reports show. The hunger within the Catholic Church for money and complete control of their institutions was taken for granted by all concerned. There was no one to challenge the Church, although the State did mitigate some of the worst excesses that McQuaid would have inflicted, had he been left completely unchecked.

The sectarian race to save souls was far more intense in Ireland compared to Britain, in the decades after 1922 because of the different demographics. Britain was moving towards a more enlightened future and Catholicism was a minority religion. In Ireland the opposite was true. Ireland was regressing and the Protestant Churches in Ireland were the minority and under siege after independence. Certain Protestants simply aped the Catholic Church's attitude to the treatment of single mothers and illegitimate children and the rest is history, as the Bethany memorial in Harold's Cross Cemetery, with 227 names of babies, clearly shows. While the national media did respond to the global interest, it was the voices and stories of living survivors on the radio stations that finally brought the humanity and reality home to the Irish public. It was a painstakingly slow process from our perspective, but finally we were being heard and treated with a long overdue sensitivity and understanding.

The future for many in our community is one of disappointment. Many will not live to hear an apology and acknowledgement in the Dáil. Those who have been excluded will fight on and I will fight with them. We are dying, but we are not going gently into that dark night. There are a few more protests in the old bastards yet. Thankfully, the Tuam 800 story, the Mail 9 headlines and the Inquiry into Mother and Baby Homes mean that no future Irish history book will exist without mention of what happened to us.

Sooner or later, someone in the government with a heart will hand over the funds for our memorials in the homes. They too will be a testament to our existence and to the innocents who will no longer be nameless or forgotten. The fact that we fought for our fallen crib mates and will erect memorials for them also says a great deal about us as a community. Personally, I will be at the Angels' Plot in Castlepollard every year for the rest of my life. I hope the voices of survivors on the radio will be preserved and heard by generations to come. They are my heroes and their testimonies healed wounds, touched hearts and won the day.

Many of us at annual reunions talk about how our children will gather every year in the Angels' Plots around the country when we are gone. I truly hope so.

CHAPTER 18

Talking with Shadows

My Story, Part VII

After I became involved with the adoption and survivor communities in 2011 I got up to speed pretty quickly on many aspects of tracing and reunion. I often gave people advice on how to proceed and encouraged them to take a chance with a letter. I believed that whatever the truth, it is better than the black hole of not knowing that adoptees feel and carry throughout their lives. I felt that having my own flesh and blood had filled an emptiness in me but the feeling of 'not knowing' still lingered.

I decided on a plan of action and forced myself to follow it through to arrive at some sort of final resolution. I wrote a gentle letter to Adeline acknowledging the fact that she wanted nothing to do with me. I asked if she could please give me my natural father's details, as maybe he might want contact. I thanked her for giving me life. I also wanted to see if her other children, my two half-brothers, wanted anything to do with me. I waited months and received no reply. Those times when a letter has been sent will be familiar to both adoptees and natural mothers. They are horrible and depressing times. Endless waiting, waking up every morning hoping for a letter and feeling a little more disheartened every day. It is a form of torture. I gave up and sent out Facebook friend requests to my entire extended natural family over a period of months. Everyone got a chance to come back to me and respond to the fact that I was one of the family. Finally, I had a break, when an uncle was thrilled that I had 'found my way back' to the family after nearly fifty years. We emailed and then chatted on the phone. My reappearance after so long caused upheaval in the wider family but he persuaded Adeline to take a call from me.

I remember that phone call as though it were five minutes ago. To my surprise, I ended up answering question after question and going through my life. My family, my education, my children and wife were all covered. I asked the odd question as gently as I could, but I got very little information. I think that the reason Adeline asked so many questions was to deflect me from asking her any. She spoke reluctantly and only briefly about anything related to my birth. I realised very quickly that she had a full memory blackout, from the time of my birth to the time her father collected her at St. Patrick's on the Navan Road, thirteen days later. She was adamant that the Sacred Heart nuns had whipped me out of the delivery room as soon as I was born and that she never saw me. Adeline was also certain that she had been put on a train to Dublin the same day I was born and that her father had coincidently collected her outside a 'place like the one I'd been in'. There were two weeks of her life missing. She has no memory of us being brought to St. Patrick's together by Mr. Murray, the local taxi driver and part-time janitor, and separated in the hall. No memory of Sister Agnes phoning her father and arranging for her to be collected. Our conversation was clearly very difficult for her. She repeated several times during the conversation 'I prayed for you. I prayed so hard for you.' My heart went out to Adeline and I genuinely felt sorry for her and ended up trying to comfort her. She was clearly still traumatised by her experiences. She had named me Jude after the patron saint of lost causes and hopeless cases. My life, that name and her prayers were all Adeline could give me.

And that was it. It was over. I was told more by a sound she made than words never to call again. She simply could not handle it. I was gutted, but at least I still had some of the extended family to cushion the blow. In the days and weeks afterwards, however, I was made aware that the people who had welcomed me back to the family were being given the cold shoulder by other family members. A feud and serious split was brewing and so I decided to cease contact with all of them for the sake of peace. It was very difficult after their welcome and help, particularly my uncle. I still miss chatting to him and sending him the occasional email. I have stayed away now for four years and I continue to honour Adeline's wish that I have no contact with the rest of my natural family.

I am one of those people who connect songs to events in their lives. For over thirty years my adoption song was Paul Simon's 'Mother and Child Reunion'. For the last few years, it has been Pink Floyd's 'Comfortably Numb'. It sums up exactly how I feel. I am now close to being completely indifferent to my former shadow. She no longer hides behind me like a ghostly Banshee, calling me softly and vanishing from the edge of my vision when I turn. Yet I confess that in the deepest part of my heart, that tiny glimmer of hope still exists and will always be there until either Adeline or I pass away. If there was one single thing I could change about my life, I wish more than anything that Jack and Neita Redmond were my natural parents. They are the best people I know.

I know that DNA tracing has become huge in our community over the last few years, both at home and abroad. The possibility is there in the back of my mind to find my natural father, but once again I'm drifting and in limbo. I honestly don't know when, or if, I will take that course of action, but I suspect that one day I will. DNA tests are getting cheaper all the time and the cost can be as low as €69. Results can be uploaded to the giant international DNA databases and dozens of fourth- and fifth-generation cousins are usually identified immediately. Sometimes, even a father or sibling is instantly located. It is a straightforward process and there are dozens of adoptees online who have done it and are happy to guide and assist newcomers. I may ask for help myself one of these days, but for now, my children's love is still healing me day by day and part of me is truly comfortably numb towards my past. Who knows what the future will bring? Right now, I'm happy to drift like a leaf in the wind. Comfortably numb ...

And remember this:

An ugly truth is better than a beautiful lie.

Paul Jude Redmond

March 2018

APPENDIX

Tracing Guide for Natural Mothers and Adoptees

A ll adoptions in Ireland are 'closed'. This means that the records are sealed and secret and neither adopted people nor natural (birth) mothers have the right to information about the other party, except for 'non-identifying' information. This has been the traditional method of dealing with so called 'illegitimate' babies since the foundation of the State in 1922. The Adoption Act 1952 formalised the practice.

While the Adoption Authority of Ireland is exempt from Freedom of Information requests, the Adoption Agencies are not.[1] Applying for personal information is straightforward, clear-cut and free. Freedom of Information Officers are employed fulltime to deal with requests from the public. An adopted person or a natural mother is legally entitled to have what is known as 'non-identifying' information. In practice, this means you will get a portion of your file, but any information that may identify either an adopted person or a natural mother to the other party is withheld or blacked out. Any documents in an adoption file that are solely related to the other party will be withheld. For example, a Relinquishment form signed by a natural mother will be withheld from an adoptee, and equally any forms with details of an adoptee's whereabouts, adoptive name, baptism certificate, etc., will be withheld from a natural mother. The way forward, therefore, is to obtain whatever information you can from the Adoption Authority, and then, when you know the adoption agency/society involved, submit a Freedom of Information request. The information you will receive is more than enough to find an original birth certificate or adoption certificate.

Here is a simple guide to making a request for both adoptees and natural mothers. You can find all the details online at the Adoption Authority of Ireland, www.aai.gov.ie, or email them: tracing@aai.gov.ie.

If you do not have access to a computer, you can write to the organisation. The address is:

Adoption Authority of Ireland

Shelbourne House,

Shelbourne Road

Dublin 4

DO4 H6F6

Ireland

Anyone with a connection to a particular person can also apply but, depending on the circumstances, you may receive no information. There are no hard and fast rules for relatives applying and it all depends on the individual situation. There is nothing to lose by making a request. Write a straightforward, polite letter, handwritten or typed, to the Adoption Authority of Ireland at the address given above. Simply state that you are adopted, or a natural mother, or a relation of one or the other. Explain that you are looking for any and all information that is available. Include all the details you have to assist them in finding your file. There is no need for forms or legal language. You will get some basic information back in a couple of weeks that will include the name of the adoption agency/society who handled the adoption.

Once you know the agency/society involved you can make a Freedom of Information request to them. Just state clearly at the beginning of your letter that 'I am applying under the Freedom of Information Acts 1997 and 2003 for information.' Politely request 'as much as possible of your file and all other information held in all formats'. Include all the information you have, such as:

Adoptive name/natural mother's name

Address at time of residence before or after adoption

Your date of birth or your child's date of birth

Where you were born or where your child was born

Adoption date

Adoption order number

Do not worry if you are missing any of the information. Some people barely have a name and a rough date when they start. The Authority will generally find your file if there was a legal adoption (after 1 January 1953). If you were 'pre-1953' you should still get some information, but you may be referred to another department, which may have more information.

Some Vital Hints and Tips

Register all your letters (this is not necessary, but I strongly recommend it). You must include a photocopy of Photo ID such as your driving licence or passport as proof of identity. It is now standard practice to accept photocopies.

They must respond within twenty-eight days maximum, as provided for in the Freedom of Information Act. Requests for personal information are free of charge.

You can apply by email with a scanned copy of your passport/ driver licence but it is best if your first letter is an old-fashioned hard copy and contains a photocopy ID enclosure. You can include your email address and choose that further communication can be by email if you prefer. Ask the person who will be handling your request to acknowledge your letter with an email so you will have their name and email address.

You will receive a hard copy of your information by post. If, however, you have any extra questions or need further clarification, email will be a lot faster than regular post.

I strongly recommend that you keep a copy of everything in writing, either as a hard copy or email, and begin a file, or keep everything in a single large envelope.

You can include your phone number if you wish. However, please note that anything said in a phone call can be later denied, as has been my experience on several occasions, although I was making very big requests in relation to sensitive matters involving ledgers and file details, and not personal requests. I still recommend avoiding phone calls and keeping everything in writing.

There is an official guide available online or in hard copy from the HSE and Tusla on your rights to information and making a Freedom of Information request with official forms. However, this simple guide will yield an identical result.

Appeals Process

If you are not happy with the result, you can and should appeal. There is one internal appeal allowed under the Freedom of Information Act within Tusla. The address for appeals will be included in the reply you receive.

IMPORTANT: You must appeal within four weeks of receiving your result.

Second Independent Appeal

If you are still not happy with what you have received, then you can make an appeal to the independent agency listed below:

The Information Commissioner

Lower Leeson Street,

Dublin 2

D02 HE97

In my experience, it is worth appealing at least once. You will sometimes get a page or two with more information. If you receive copies of any material and the photocopies are unclear, request new copies. You are entitled to them.

Tracing your Natural Mother or your Son or Daughter

If you wish to initiate a formal search for your natural mother/son/daughter, you must apply to Tusla at your local social services office, also known as Intreo Centre, either in person or in writing. The best advice here is to be patient, as there are waiting lists of several months or even several years in extreme cases where the files are being transferred to Tusla from an adoption agency that has closed. The tracing services are part of social services and are suffering the effects of years of austerity, recession and cutbacks. Do not be afraid to keep inquiring and applying polite pressure.

Please also be aware that many attempts at reunion fail for various reasons and it can be difficult and 'triggering' to cope with bad news. Talk it over with a friend or loved one first and seek counselling if you need it or online peer support in the various Facebook groups.

If you wish to trace for yourself, it is important to remember that Irish birth, death and marriage certificates are public documents, and anyone can use them to search for themselves.[2] You can order the President's or Taoiseach's birth certificates online right this minute, and have it in your door within three or four days. It is your legal right and absolutely 100% legal to trace for yourself and there are guides on the internet explaining how to do this. It takes no more than a day in the General Registry Office in Dublin to get a name. Google the phrase 'adoption rights in Ireland', trawl through the various adoption groups and you will find a self-help guide in less than five or ten minutes. Do not worry if you cannot find or access anything online as you can still just go to the General Registry Office and find out more in about twenty minutes with the help of the staff. They are very helpful and not remotely interested in why you want to search.

The National Contact Register

The Adoption Authority maintains a 'contact register' for people who are adopted, natural mothers and relatives of adoptees. Thousands have registered but the 'hit' rate is tiny. Like anything involving tracing in 'Adoptionland', it is definitely worth a try. When you are first contacting the Adoption Authority for information, request a form for the Contact Register, fill it out and hopefully you will get a positive result. Unfortunately, if a match is made, the Authority sends both parties back to their original adoption agency. The adoption agency will arrange the actual contact and potential reunion, but this process is slow.

I wish anyone who begins a search the best of luck. Take your time and double-check everything. Have a friend or loved one clued in so they can give you emotional support. It is important to realise that you may not find your son, daughter or mother but you may find brothers and sisters, grandchildren, aunts, uncles and other relatives. Never give up.

ENDNOTES

Chapter 1

1   See Ruth McClure, *Coram's Children* (Yale University 1981), which used the primary source Jonas Hanway, *A Candid Historical Account of the Hospital* (1758).
2   Gillian Pugh, *London's Forgotten Children* (History Press: 2007), p. 33.
3   Ibid. p. 98. Robert Dingley was one of the governors of the Foundling Hospital and co-founded the first Magdalene Laundry.
4   Francis Finnegan, *Do Penance or Perish* (Oxford University Press: 2004), p. 8.
5   Sister Rosemary Clerkin, *A Heart for Others* (privately written and published history of the Sacred Heart congregation, Chigwell, in 1982 to commemorate the death of their founder Fr. Braun in 1882), p. 51.
6   Excerpts from her annual Report by Aneenee FitzGerald-Kenney in Local Government Report, 31 March 1915; Appendix B: page 12.

Chapter 2

1   See *The Story of the Rotunda Hospital* by former Master Alan Browne (Rotunda Hospital, 1970s, undated booklet).
2   Extract from the 'Annual Report of the Rotunda Girls' Aid Society, 1887–8' as reproduced in Maria Luddy, *Women in Ireland. A Documentary History* (Cork University Press: 1995), p. 70.
3   'Excavating the past: Mother and Baby Homes in the Republic of Ireland' by Paul Michael Garrett from NUIG's school of Political Science and Sociology: *British Journal of Social Work* 17 December 2015, pp. 358–74.
4   Lindsey Earner-Byrne, *Letters of the Catholic Poor* (Cambridge University Press: 2016), pp. 115, 237, 238.
5   Conall Ó Fátharta, 'Excluded agency 'aware of illegal birth registrations', *Irish Examiner*, 13 April 2015. https://www.irishexaminer.com/ireland/excluded-agency-aware-of-illegal-birth-registrations-323568.html.

Chapter 3

1   *Local Government Report 1933–1934*, p. 146.
2   *Ireland's Hospitals 1930–1955* by The Hospitals' Trust (1940) Ltd. P. 51, Appendix 1, lists all the recipients of grants between 1930 and 1955 although Bethany is missing from the list.

3 'Clare's Baby Shame', Joe O'Muircheartaigh, *Clare People*, 10 June 2014.

4 *Clare Tribune*, 15 October 1927.

5 *Local Government Report 1928–1929*, p. 113.

6 Lindsey Earner-Byrne, *Letters of the Catholic Poor* (Cambridge University Press: 2016)

7 *The Clare Champion* 2014. 'Kilrush Mother and Baby home part of Inquiry', Peter O'Connell, *The Clare Champion*, 2014. http://clarechampion.ie/kilrush-mother-and-baby-home-part-of-inquiry/.

8 See *Local Government Report* 1932, p. 290 as noted by Aneenee Fitzgerald-Kenney in her report that year.

9 Sacred Heart Nuns internal newsletter, 2009.

10 Rosemary Clerkin, *A Heart for Others* (privately written and published history of the Sacred Heart congregation), Chigwell, 1982, p. 68.

11 *Evening Echo*, 13 August 2009.

12 *Ireland's Hospitals 1930–1955*, p. 60.

13 'The Home', historical essay by Catherine Corless, *Journal of the Old Tuam Society*, 2012.

14 Rosemary Clerkin, *A Heart for Others* (privately written and published history of the Sacred Heart congregation, Chigwell 1982), p. 86.

15 *Ireland's Hospitals 1930–1955*, pp. 61 and 71.

Chapter 4

1 Mike Milotte, *Banished Babies* (New Island: 1997 and 2011). First edition p. 112 and second edition p. 126.

2 Mavis Arnold and Heather Lankey, *Children of the Poor Clares* (Appletree Press: 1985).

3 *Report of the Inter-Departmental Group on Mother and Baby Homes* (Department of Children and Youth Affairs, July 2014), p. 14.

4 *Westmeath Topic*, 11 June 2014: based on Danny Dunne, *The Town at the Crossroads*.

5 See the *Our World* BBC documentary first broadcast 27 September 2014 for an eyewitness account of two nuns carrying a shoebox down the laneway to the Angels' Plot in Castlepollard.

6 Extracts from *Local Government Reports*, 1935/1936, p. 162, 1936/1937, p. 146, 1937/1938, p. 97, 1938/1939, p. 71, 1939/1940, p. 74, 1940/41, p. 81.

7 See *Local Government Reports*, 1935/1936, p. 162, 1936/1937, p. 146, 1937/1938, p. 97, 1938/1939, p. 71, 1939/1940, p.74, 1940/41, p. 81 with extracts as per chart

8 *Report of the Inter-Departmental Group on Mother and Baby Homes*, p. 14.

9 Clerkin, *A Heart for Others*, p. 99.

10 Ibid. p. 104.

Chapter 5

1   June Goulding, *Light in the Window* (Poolbeg Press: 1998), p. 121, and several eyewitness accounts and interviews with author.

2   Adelina Campos, 'Revolting. Nuns sold us off as babies', *Sunday Mirror*, 23 September 2012.

3   *Local Government Report 1927*, Appendix XXXIII, p. 196, distinguishes between the homes and lists all those approved for the reception of single pregnant girls and women. The list was added to year on year as new ones were approved by the various Ministers for Local Government.

4   Goulding, *Light in the Window*, p. 36.

5   *Ireland's Hospitals 1930–1955*, p. 60.

6   See *Local Government Reports 1930* through to 1942 for details of Capitation Grants and comparisons by various people but especially by Aneenee Fitzgerald-Kenney in her annual reports to be found in the Appendices. See *Local Government Report* 1927/1928, p. 90.

7   Goulding, 'Light in the Window', p. 193.

8   Mike Milotte, article in the *Sunday Business Post* magazine, 2 September 2012.

9   Mike Milotte, *Banished Babies*, p. 203: from a total of 1,933 babies although this is not the full amount, but it is a reasonably accurate guide to the overall totals although no official figures are available for the early years of the trade.

10 *Irish Daily Mail*, 9 June 2014. Article about the Sacred Heart finances by Neil Michael.

11 Neil Michael, 'Nuns getting millions from the taxpayers', *Daily Mail* (Irish edition), 9 June 2014, front page and pp. 4–5.

12 Freedom of Information request; appeal TA15/001/17 February 2015.

13 The four '*Admissions Books*' are all heavy-duty ledgers and labelled '*Castlepollard Mother and Baby Home – Admission Book*'. It was believed that the Sacred Heart Nuns had these '*Admission Books*' custom printed for their three Homes but recent information has cast doubt on this assumption. Book number 4 has an identical label to numbers 1, 2 and 3, except it also has '*Private Patients*' appended. '*Admission Books*' number 3 and 4 contain mostly overlapping information but photocopies of number 3 show it to be a generic ledger bought 'off-the-shelf' and hand-customised by the nuns for their own requirements as it includes specific spaces for both 'House Names' and 'Dates of Baptism'. Book number 4 was different and it was custom-printed to specifically comply with the requirements of the Registration of Maternity Homes Act, 1934. These custom ledgers were almost certainly printed by the Department of Local Government and sent out to the nuns, as they contain no spaces for House Names or Baptisms. Private patients were dual recorded in both '*Admission Books*' number 3 and number 4 from July 1961 onwards.

14 The antenatal notes from 1939 to 1966 are in the form of old-style school copybooks. The notes were kept in pencil and have faded badly.

15   The antenatal card index system that was introduced in September 1966 uses index-type cards and were kept in 1960s-style plastic boxes with flip-up lids hinged at the centre of the boxes.

16   The six Maternity Books all have two labels. The first says *'Registration of Maternity Homes Act 1934. Records and particulars Book of Maternity Home (or hospital) – known as St. Peter's Maternity Hospital Castlepollard'* and *'St. Peter's Maternity Hospital Castlepollard Co. Westmeath. Records & Particulars Book of Maternity hospital'*.

17   There is no explanation for the four-year gap between Maternity Books numbers 19 and 20 (from 13 August 1947 to 10 June 1951), nor is there any detail as to whether Maternity Books were started in 1943 or the ones from 1935 to 1943 are missing?

18   The Wasserman (also Wassermann) Test is a blood test for the sexually transmitted disease Syphilis.

19   Part of author's personal entry from Freedom of Information request 14/023/12– May 2014.

Chapter 6

1   Lindsey Earner-Byrne, *Mother and Child* (Manchester Press: 2007), p. 195, and the *Interdepartmental Report* 2014, p. 8.

2   James Deeny, *To Cure and to Care* (Greendale: 1989), p. 85.

3   Conall Ó Fátharta, '68% of babies in Bessboro home died', *Irish Examiner*, 25 August 2014.

4   Deeny, *To Cure and to Care*, p. 96.

5   RTÉ *Prime Time*, 20 June 1996.

6   Milotte, *Banished Babies*.

7   John Cooney, *John Charles McQuaid. Ruler of Catholic Ireland* (O'Brien Press: 1999), p. 246, and for further elaboration see Milotte, *Banished Babies*, p. 35.

8   Goulding, *Light in the Window*.

9   Mary Raftery and Eoin O'Sullivan, *Suffer the Little Children* (New Island: 1999), p. 154.

10 *Sinners*, a BBC 1 film directed by Aisling Walsh in 2002. Unfortunately, the BBC mixed up two separate types of institutions in the film: Mother and Baby Homes, and Magdalene Laundries. Ignore the references to 'Magdalene Laundries' in the film as these references are completely wrong.

11 See Mavis Arnold and Heather Laskey, *Children of the Poor Clares* (Appletree Press: 1985) for an in-depth exposé.

12 LMFM News 7.3.2017.

13 Freedom of information request; appeal TA15/001/17 February 2015.

Chapter 7

1   See Marion Dante, *Dropping the Habit* (Poolbeg Press: 2007).

2   Arnold and Laskey, *Children of the Poor Clares*, p. 107.

3   Milotte, *Banished Babies* pp. 174–9.

4   For a general lay person's introduction to this difficult and complex subject, see: *Primal Wound* by Nancy Verrier (Verrier Publishing: 1993). Often called the *Adoptees Bible*, it goes through the problems faced by natural mothers and adoptees over the course of their lives. See also Ann Fessler, *The Girls Who Went Away* (Penguin: 2006). Although this book is about Americans it is highly accessible and the parallels in terms of how women were affected in later life is almost identical although the horror of Irish Mother and Baby Homes magnified the post-traumatic stress disorder in the Irish context.

5   See Ruth J.A. Kelly, *Motherhood Silenced* (Liffey Press: 2005) for detailed and accredited research into the experiences of Irish natural mothers, including some in unnamed Mother and Baby Homes. For further information see the 'Origins Canada' Website, which specialises in this subject and includes a substantial list of academic reports and personal testimonies. Thanks to Origins Canada and Valeria Andrews for kind permission to recommend this invaluable resource.

6   Dáil Joint Committee on Health and Children debate. 'Discussion with Council of Irish Adoption Agencies', 8 December 2009, p. 7 of 9.

7   Verrier, *Primal Wound*.

8   Michael Dwyer, 'Vaccine trials: Dark chapter that needs answers', *Irish Examiner*, 1 December 2014.

9   Conall Ó Fátharta, 'Vaccine trials', *Irish Examiner*, 17 November 2016.

10 Cooney, John Charles McQuaid, p. 349 and Tim Pat Coogan, *Ireland in the Twentieth Century* (Hutchinson: 2003), p. 732.

Chapter 8

1   Rosemary Clerkin, *A Heart for Others* (Poor Clares: 1983), p. 118.

2   Ibid.

3   Ibid.

4   Finola Kennedy, *Frank Duff. A Life Story* (Continuum 2011), p. 97.

5   Dáil Eireann, 26 November 1987, Question 64, vol. 375, No. 9, p. 53.

Chapter 9

1   Dáil Eireann, 9 April 1997, vol. 477, No. 3, p. 24 of 135.

Chapter 10

1 Department of Health, Press Release, 24 May 2001.
2 Eoin Burke Kennedy, 'New bill to allow adopted people to see birth certs', *The Irish Times*, 24 May 2001.
3 Eilish O'Regan, 'Adoptees in state homes to be given their birth details', *Irish Independent*, 24 May 2001.
4 Conall Ó Fátharta, 'Groundhog Day delays to adoption procedures', *Irish Examiner*, 26 September 2014.

Chapter 11

1 Conall Ó Fátharta, 'In search of a long-lost boy', *Irish Examiner*, 19 April 2010.
2 Fiachra Ó Cionnaith 'Examiner journalist scoops top award', *Irish Examiner* 3 June 2011.
3 Not her real name.
4 Juno McEnroe, 'Archbishop calls for fresh inquiry into laundries', *Irish Examiner*, 25 July 2012.
5 Paul Redmond, 'Scandal of mother and baby homes care', *Irish Examiner*, 28 July 2012.
6 Catherine Corless, 'The Home', *Annual Journal of the old Tuam Society 2012*.

Chapter 12

1 See the Department of Children's website for the full document. https://www.dcya.gov.ie/documents/publications/20140716InterdepartReportMothBabyHomes.pdf.

Chapter 13

1 Aine Hegarty, 'Mass grave of 800 babies found at Galway children's home is a stain on the nation', *Irish Mirror*, 2 June 2014.
2 Ronan McGreevy, 'Philomena Lee visits Roscrea home where son was taken from her', *The Irish Times*, 2 June 2014.
3 James Ward, 'Gagged: TD booted out of the Dáil for trying to discuss the baby grave scandal', *Irish Mirror*, 4 June 2014.
4 See Kathryn Joyce 'The Child Catchers' (Public Affairs 2013).
5 RTÉ news special report about Mother and Baby Homes, 11 June 2014.
6 Marie O'Halloran, 'Babies scandal "an abomination" says Kenny', *The Irish Times*, 11 June 2014.

Chapter 14

1 Still available in full on the Department of Children and Youth Affairs website: https://www.dcya.gov.ie/documents/publications/20140716InterdepartReportMo thBabyHomes.pdf.
2 Clare Daly's Dáil contribution is available on *YouTube* or the Oireachtas website: http://oireachtasdebates.oireachtas.ie/debates%20authoring/debateswebpack.nsf/ takes/dail2014071700030?opendocument.
3 Sue Lloyd Roberts and Ian Reilly, 'Our World', BBC World News Channel, 27 September 2014.
4 Conall Ó Fátharta, '68% of babies in Bessborough home died', *Irish Examiner*, 25 August 2014.
5 *Sunday Times Magazine*, 24 May 2015.

Chapter 15

1 Journal.ie, 31 July 2015.
2 Carl O'Brien 'Reforms may make 2,000 children eligible for adoption', *The Irish Times*, 27 November 2014.

Chapter 16

1 Fiach Kelly and Kitty Holland with Lorna Siggins, 'Mother and Baby Home Inquiry may be greatly expanded', *The Irish Times*, 7 March 2017.
2 *Westmeath Examiner*, 16 March 2017, including the full list of names of those who died.
3 Fiach Kelly, 'Cabinet will not extend redress scheme due to €1bn cost', *The Irish Times*, 12 April 2017.
4 Adam Shaw, 'No redress for homes' survivors', *Irish World*, 17 April 2017.
5 Catholic League Press Release by Bill Donohue, 12 April 2017.

Appendix

1 Adoption Authority of Ireland, Shelbourne Road, Dublin 4. https://www.aai. gov.ie/.
2 See HSE website and search for 'Save time buying certificates online'. You can order any birth, marriage, death or adoption certificate online for about €20 and it will be posted to you in a few days.

BIBLIOGRAPHY

Secondary Sources

Altrama, Erin, *Candle in the Mirror* (Donohue Publications: 2013).

Arnold, Bruce, *The Irish Gulag* (Gill & McMillan Ltd.: 2009).

Arnold, Mavis and Laskey, Heather, *Children of the Poor Clares* (Appletree Press: 1985).

Barnardos, *Information leaflet about Castlepollard Mother & Baby Home* (Barnardos: undated: approximately early to mid 1990s).

Barrett, Monsignor Cecil J., *Adoption: The Parent, The Child, The Home* (Clonmore & Reynolds Ltd.: 1952).

Browne, Alan, *The Story of the Rotunda Hospital* (Rotunda Hospital, undated: 1970s).

Buckley, Sarah-Anne, *The Cruelty Man* (Manchester University Press: 2013).

Collins, Pauline, *Letter to Louise* (Bantam Press: 1992).

Costello, Nancy, Legg, Kathleen, Croghan, Diane, Slattery, Marie, Gambold, Marina and O'Riordan, Steven (eds), *Whispering Hope* (Orion: 2015).

Clerkin, Sister Rosemary, *A Heart for Others* (Self-published by the Sacred Heart nuns.

Printed by the Sisters of the Poor Clares: 1982).

Corless, Damien, *The Greatest Bleeding Hearts Racket in the World* (Gill & Macmillan: 2010).

Coogan, Tim Pat, *Ireland in the twentieth century* (Arrow: 2004).

—, *De Valera, Long Fellow, Long Shadow* (Arrow: 1995).

Cooney, John, *John Charles McQuaid* (O'Brien Press: 1999).

Coppinger, Maureen, *Annie's Girl* (Mainstream 2009).

Dante, Marion, Dropping the habit (Poolbeg Press Ltd.: 2007).

Deeny, Doctor James, *To Cure and to Care* (Glendale: 1989).

Doyle, Fiona, *Too Many Tears* (Penguin: 2013).

Doyle, Paddy, *The God Squad* (Raven Arts Press: 1988).

Dunphy, Shane, *Hush, Little Baby* (Gill & McMillian: 2008).

Earner-Byrne, Lynsey, *Mother and Child. Maternity and Child Welfare in Dublin 1922-1960* (Manchester University Press: reprint edition 2013).

—, *Letters of the Catholic Poor* (Cambridge University Press: 2016).

Fagan, Kieran, *The Framing of Harry Gleeson* (Collins Press: 2015).

Fahy, Bernadette, *Freedom of Angels* (O'Brien Press Ltd.: 1999).

Ferriter, Diarmaid, *Occasions of Sin* (Profile Books: 2009).

—, *The Transformation of Ireland, 1900-2000* (Profile Books: 2004).

—, *A Nation of Extremes: The Pioneers in Twentieth-Century Ireland* (Irish Academic Press: 1998).

Fessler, Ann, *The Girls Who Went Away* (Penguin: 2006).

Finnegan, Frances, *Do Penance or Perish* (Oxford University Press: 2004 edition).

Galvin, Patrick, *The Raggy Boy* trilogy (New Island: 2002).

Goulding, June, *The Light in the Window* (Poolbeg Press: 1998).

Hamilton, Phyllis, *Secret Love* (Mainstream Publishing: 1995).

Hawkins, Margaret, *Restless spirit* (Bushel Press, 2013, second edition).

Hogan, Sean, *In Harm's Way* (Arrow Books: 2008).

Holloway, Sarah (ed.), *Family wanted* (Granta: 2005).

The Hospitals' Trust (1940) Ltd., *Ireland's Hospitals 1930–1955*).

Houghton, Rosie, *Abandoned Love* (Matador: 2012).

Jones, Maggie, *Everything You Need to Know About Adoption* (Sheldon Press: 1987).

Joyce, Kathryn, *The Child Catchers* (Public Affairs: 2013).

Kelly, Herman, *Kathy's Real Story* (Perfect Press: 2007).

Kelly, Irene, *Sins of the Mother* (Pan Books: 2015).

Kelly, Ruth J.A., *Motherhood Silenced* (Liffey Press: 2005).

Kennedy, Finola, *Frank Duff. A Life Story* (Continuum 2011).

Kershaw, Roger and Sacks, Janet, *New Lives for Old* (UK National Archives: 2008).

Kierans, John, *Stop the Press!* (Merlin Press: 2009).

Kunzel, Regina G., *Fallen Women, Problem Girls* (Yale University Press: 1993).

Lawless, Sharon, *Adoption Stories* (Carnegie Hill Publishing: 2016).

Leinster, Derek, *Hannah's Shame* (Self-published: 2005).

—, *Destiny Unknown* (Self-published: 2008).

Lewis, Gordon and Crofts, Andrew, *Secret Child* (HarperElement: 2015).

Luddy, Maria, *Women in Ireland 1800–1918* (Cork University Press: 1995).

Malone, David, *The Boy in the Attic* (Mainstream: 2011).

McCafferty, Nell, *A Woman to Blame: The Kerry Babies Case* (Attic: 1985).

McClure, Ruth, *Coram's Children* (Yale University: 1981).

McKay, Susan, *Sophia's Story* (Gill & McMillian: 1998).

Milotte, Mike, *Banished Babies* (New Island: 2011, second edition).

Myung Ja, Janine, Potter, Michael Allen and Vance, Alan L. (eds), *Adoptionland; From*

Orphans to Activists (Against Child Trafficking: 2014).

O'Beirne, Kathy, *Kathy's Story* (Mainstream: 2005).

O'Brien, Lily, *The Girl Nobody Wants* (Matador: 2012).

O'Connor, Alison, *A Message from Heaven* (Brandon Press: 2000).

O'Connor, John, *The Workhouses of Ireland* (Children's Press: 1994).

O'Halloran, Barry, *Lost Innocence* (Raytown Press: 1985).

O'Malley, Kathleen, *Childhood Interrupted* (Virago: 2005).

Owen, Cynthia, *Living with Evil* (Headline Review: 2010).

Patrick, Angela, *The Baby Laundry for Unmarried Mothers* (Simon & Schuster: 2012).

Pugh, Gillian, *London's Forgotten Children* (History Press: 2007).

Raftery, Mary and O'Sullivan, Eoin, *Suffer the Little Children* (New Island: 1999).

Reilly, Francis, *Suffer the Little Children*. Orion: 2008).

Robinson, Jane, *In the Family Way* (Viking/Penguin: 2015).

Rossini, Gill, *A History of Adoption in England and Wales 1850–1961* (Pen & Sword 2014).

Sixsmith, Martin, *The Lost Child of Philomena Lee* (Macmillan: 2009).

Smith, James, *Ireland's Magdalene Laundries* (Manchester University Press: 2008).

Shideler, Martha, *Coming Together, An Adoptee's Story* (TigerEye Publications: 2011).

Tofield, Shelia, *The Unmarried Mother* (Penguin: 2013).

Touher, Patrick, *Fear of the Collar* (O'Brien Press: 1991).

—, *Scars That Run Deep* (Ebury: 1994).

Tyrell, Peter, *Founded on Fear* (Irish Academic Press: 2006).

Verrier, Nancy, *Primal Wound* (Gateway Press Inc.: 1993).

Yallop, David, *Beyond Belief* (Constable & Robinson Ltd.: 2008).

Wilson, Tom and Crofts, Andrew, *Tears at Bedtime* (Arrow Books: 2007).

Films and Documentaries

Adoption Stories. Directed, written and produced by Sharon Lawless & Flawless Films.

Prime Time. A long-running investigative series on Ireland's national television station, RTÉ 1, which has exposed various aspects of the Mother and Baby homes including specials on the banished babies, the vaccine trials, the Bethany home and more.

Sex in a Cold Climate. Directed by Steve Humphries. Channel 4: 1998.

Song for a Raggy Boy. Directed by Aisling Walsh. XV: 2002.

Sinners. Directed by Aisling Walsh. BBC Northern Ireland: 2002.

Suffer the Little Children. Directed, produced and written by Mary Raftery: 1999. Three-part documentary series about Ireland's industrial and reformatory schools.

The Magdalene Sisters. Directed by Peter Mullen: 2002.

The Forgotten Maggies. Directed by Steven O'Riordan: 2009.

INDEX